THE SEARCH FOR THE
DUROTRIGES

THE SEARCH FOR THE
DUROTRIGES

Dorset and the West Country in the Late Iron Age

MARTIN PAPWORTH

First published 2011

Reprinted 2012

The History Press
The Mill, Brimscombe Port
Stroud, Gloucestershire, GL5 2QG
www.thehistorypress.co.uk

British Library Cataloguing in Publication Data.
A catalogue record for this book is available from the British Library.

ISBN 978 0 7524 5737 6

Typesetting and origination by The History Press
Printed in Great Britain

CONTENTS

ABSTRACT

This book considers the evidence for the Durotriges, one of the groups of people listed by the Greek geographer Ptolemy in the second century AD. Traditionally it has been believed that the Durotrigans formed a tribe whose territory included Dorset and parts of neighbouring Somerset, Wiltshire and Hampshire. More recent commentators identify significant differences between the communities living within this Durotrigan area. This survey of the region brings together the evidence gathered by archaeologists working across the Durotrigan zone and combines it with new fieldwork and excavation.

East Dorset was the principal study area, and the original research was concentrated here. The whole area of the Dorset environs was considered, but seven 10km by 8km study boxes were looked at in detail and compared. It is proposed that the Durotrigan people resulted from a gradual linking of disparate groups between c.200 BC and AD 40. This may have been no more than a fragile alliance forming a convenient economic and military association. The high tide of its influence was reached with the inclusion of the communities of south Somerset shortly before the Roman Conquest.

ACKNOWLEDGEMENTS

This survey would not have been possible without the help and advice of many people. Particular thanks to my supervisors at Reading University, Professor Michael Fulford, Professor Richard Bradley and Dr John Creighton for their help and advice and for suggesting that I shift the focus of the research from the Badbury environs to the Durotriges.

Many thanks to Peter and Ann Woodward for introducing me to a range of published and unpublished sources, and for access to the ceramic assemblages held at Dorset County Museum, Dorchester. Thanks also to local authority archaeologists for providing information from the various sites and monuments records, Claire Pinder at Dorchester, Chris Webster at Taunton and Lesley Freak at Trowbridge. Many thanks to the following archaeologists for information on sites before publication: Keith Jarvis, Poole Museum archaeologist, for access to the Lake Farm legionary fortress archive; Peter Bellamy for information on the excavations at Maiden Castle School and Hamworthy; Ian Barnes for information on the Battlesbury Bowl and Beach's Barn sites; and Peter Cox for information on the Heron Grove, East Knoyle settlements and Shillingstone villa. Particular thanks to Richard Tabor of the South Cadbury Environs Project for discussing his research with me and providing copies of the field reports. Thanks to Martin Green for information on his latest research on Cranborne Chase, and to Mark Corney for his guidance on the sites of south Wiltshire and for directing me to published and unpublished research. Thanks also to Andy Payne of English Heritage who provided information on the Castle Ditches geophysical survey before publication of the Wessex Hillforts Project, and to Barry Cunliffe for editorial advice.

My thanks to Ann Garvey for her excellent analysis of the pottery from the Iron Age sites around Badbury, and to Lorraine Mepham of Wessex Archaeology for co-ordinating the specialist reports from the various excavations in east Dorset. Many thanks also for the generous help provided by Melinda Mays and Philip de Jersey for answering my questions about Iron Age coins and providing access to unpublished information. Thanks also to Lisa Brown of Oxford Archaeology for her advice on Poole Harbour pottery. I must also thank Jim Gunter for allowing me to include work from his thesis on the Wylye valley. Francesca Radcliffe has been very kind in allowing me to include some of her amazing aerial photographs of the Dorset hillforts.

Many thanks to David Thackray, Head of Archaeology, and to David Bett, previously Wessex Regional Director, at the National Trust for their support and encouragement. Thanks also to my colleague Nancy Grace, for her careful and friendly guidance of the many volunteers who kindly helped with the excavation and post-excavation work on the project.

My special thanks to John and Della Day for their leadership of the East Dorset Antiquarian Society, and to the many members who have assisted us over the years. Thanks to Dave Stewart for his wonderful geophysical surveys of Hod Hill, Norden Iron Age temple and Shapwick. He kindly brought together these and other surveys to create some of the excellent geophysical images for this book.

I must particularly acknowledge Geoff Brown's help and support of the past 10 years. His geophysical surveys of Bradford Down, Sweetbriar Drove, Badbury hillfort, Badbury temple and particularly the Crab Farm settlement at Shapwick have achieved excellent results and are the product of an enormous investment of time.

Lastly, I must thank my wife Janet for her love, patience and support; and our children Kate, Emma and Simon whom I have neglected for too long while conducting this research.

INTRODUCTION

Late Iron Age Britain has been divided into tribal areas using the names of the communities recorded by the second-century geographer Ptolemy, but these labels may be misleading. The classical authors who wrote about the British were alien to the societies they were describing. Therefore, the tribal names may only have been convenient Roman administrative divisions that masked many sub-groups, and not the names the British people personally identified with. Bearing this in mind this book will critically examine the evidence for the existence of one of Ptolemy's 'tribes' – its name now an icon used to found the narrative of an English county.

Dorset is small and beautiful, geologically diverse and composed of stunning landscapes. It is famous for its large Iron Age hillforts and for some, these massive earthworks are evidence that 2000 years ago there was once a 'Greater Dorset' linked to a people known as the Durotriges.

The land attributed to this Durotrigan nation is the whole of Dorset and the bordering edges of its neighbours, Devon, Somerset, Wiltshire and Hampshire. The evidence for a cultural cohesion amongst the communities living here consists of distinctive Iron Age coins and pottery found on archaeological sites across this area.

However, there seem to be clusters of archaeological evidence which indicate differences between groups. This has led archaeologists to refer to the Durotriges as a confederacy (Cunliffe 1991, 159; Salway 1993, 39; Brown 1997, 40) although they have not attempted to describe in detail what this consisted of.

It has been supposed that the many hillforts in this area were occupied as local political units influencing the surrounding farmsteads and settlements. The effort and manpower required to create the hillforts indicates that considerable power and authority influenced their construction. During the Iron Age certain hillforts may have acted as focal points, places that were used for a variety of key functions, but archaeologists disagree over the exact ways in which hillforts may originally have been used.

To demonstrate the similarities and differences of the Durotrigan zone, seven 10km by 8km study areas were created. The areas were chosen where extensive previous fieldwork had taken place. The work of previous archaeologists was reviewed and, where possible, additional fieldwork was commissioned or carried out by the author. The Badbury landscape, in east Dorset, became the principal study area because this is where I have carried out much new survey and excavation work. The origin of this book lies within this undulating chalk landscape which seems to lie at a crossroads between Iron Age communities (1).

The survey of the Durotrigan zone was a considerable undertaking but I have the advantage of having lived, worked and trained as an archaeologist in Dorset for over 30 years.

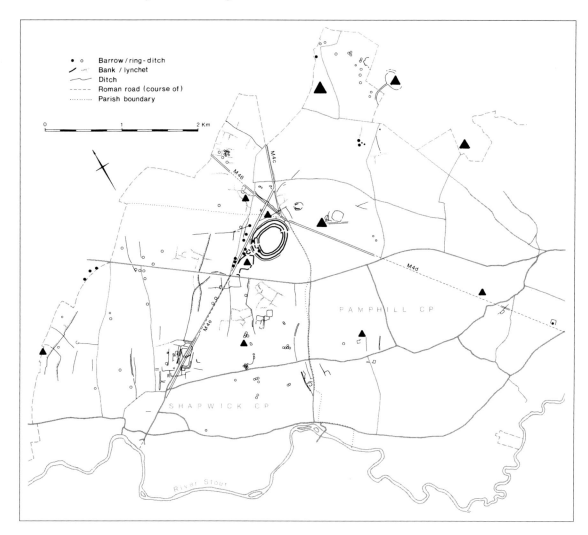

1 Kingston Lacy Estate plot of aerial photograph sites (RCHM 1992). *Crown Copyright*

I arrived at Weymouth College during the hot summer of 1976, just as many new archaeological sites were being revealed as parch marks in the Dorset countryside. I eventually
became the National Trust's Regional Archaeologist in Wessex, employed to create archaeological survey reports for National Trust properties. These include the Kingston Lacy Estate,
centred on Badbury Rings, and the Corfe Castle Estate, which covers many of Purbeck's
Iron Age industrial sites. The Trust also manages Hod Hill and Turnworth in central Dorset,
the Golden Cap Estate in west Dorset and the hillforts of Pilsdon, Eggardon, Lambert's
Castle and Coney's Castle spaced around the northern rim of the Marshwood Vale. The
advantage of access to these and other properties in Somerset and Wiltshire, together with
the help of many Wessex archaeologists, has enabled the research to progress. Each year
there have been new discoveries and this in turn has led to new ways of looking at the
combined evidence.

This book broadly covers the 1500 years from the Late Bronze Age through to the end of the Roman Empire in Britain, although the research is particularly focused on the 200 years from 100 BC to AD 100. This period is at the brink of British history, when the expanding Roman world was increasingly influencing the lives of British people. During this time, the communities of the Durotrigan zone were producing distinctive material evidence.

The first four chapters of this book give context to the survey of the Iron Age 'Greater Dorset'. In Chapter One, British Iron Age research is reviewed, demonstrating how ideas have developed and changed over time. In Chapter Two, the sparse historical sources that depict southern British society are examined. Having explored the written evidence for the Durotriges, Chapter Three considers the Iron Age archaeology of the Dorset environs. This is a history of past research, demonstrating the way the Durotrigan tag has been attached to the various pre-Roman sites across the region. In Chapter Four, the individual material elements attributed to a Durotrigan 'culture' are analysed. Then each of Chapters Five to Eleven consider a study area in detail: Purbeck, Maiden Castle, Pilsdon Pen, South Cadbury, Hod Hill, Cranborne Chase and Badbury. Chapter Twelve is the conclusion and this summarises the evidence for distinct communities within the Dorset environs and questions whether there ever was a tribe known as the Durotriges.

I

IRON AGE STUDIES –
CURRENT DEBATES AND THEMES

DIFFICULTIES IN UNDERSTANDING IRON AGE COMMUNITIES

A difficulty in writing about the Iron Age from the modern perspective is that ours is an alien society that has no real appreciation of the life and death struggle of subsistence farming. A twenty-first century urban Englishman's dependence on agriculture is so distant from his day-to-day cycle of life that he barely recognises the need to produce food to live.

An archaeologist will adopt the attitudes of his time just as a film director presents history to an audience from a contemporary perspective. For instance, whether intentional or not, films of the Second World War are clearly dated and the truth of the society they portray deteriorates over time. The social reality and propaganda of the 1942 film *In Which We Serve* can be contrasted with the heroic 1963 film *633 Squadron* or the glamorous 2001 film *Pearl Harbor*. The costumes, locations and storylines try to reflect the period but the historic perspective on the war becomes increasingly faded and the attitudes and beliefs of the actors are clearly of the decade the film was produced.

With the Iron Age, it is even more difficult to place our stories about people and places in a context approaching reality. Although there are a few written records for the very end of the British Iron Age, the Middle and Early Iron Age societies were probably very different from those of the Late Iron Age. The written sources demonstrate the British contact with the Roman world and this contact would have caused dramatic social and economic change. John Creighton (2000, 4-21) has argued that the influence of Roman politics and trade on the peoples of southern Britain was profound from before the Gallic Wars (58-50 BC) until the Roman Conquest (AD 43-44). This influence is reflected in the changing designs on coinage, in a time when exotic agencies such as Roman objects, ideas and people gradually infiltrated Late Iron Age society.

Historians and archaeologists have recorded examples of similar dramatic social change resulting from alien contact. One of these would be the way the Plains Indians became increasingly dependent on horses after the Spanish Conquistadors introduced these animals to North America. Another would be the transformation of Maori warfare after the British traded muskets to certain communities. These weapons changed battles from skirmishes to massacres, and gun pits were dug as an additional defence within New Zealand hillforts. The pits were used first to protect defenders against attack from other Maori communities and later to serve as a defence against British soldiers.

The surviving Roman documents record only a few British leaders, places, events and tribal names but as these documents are Roman they are written from the perspective of superiority and conquest not from the perspective of the people themselves. Many Late Iron Age beliefs, ways of working and attitudes may have been preserved from earlier generations but it is difficult to distil these from the snapshots of Iron Age society depicted by classical writers such as Julius Caesar (*Gallic War*) and Tacitus (*Agricola & Germania*). It is useful to acknowledge these difficulties before attempting to understand the evolution of change amongst Iron Age peoples.

ATTITUDES TO CHANGE IN IRON AGE STUDIES

Barry Cunliffe (1991, 1-20) provided a summary of the history of Iron Age studies in Britain and he drew attention to views on invasion as the explanation for change. In 1886, Sir Arthur Evans identified the Belgic cemetery at Aylesford by comparing its grave goods with those from cemeteries in northern France. He concluded that the 'Aylesford Culture' was evidence to support the writings of Julius Caesar who stated that the southern parts of Britain had been settled by Belgic invaders.

In the early twentieth century Late Iron Age archaeological evidence was fitted to the historical sources and Early and Middle Iron Age changes were also linked to waves of invasion. The climax of this way of thinking was the division of the Iron Age into A, B and C (Hawkes 1931, 60-97). Cunliffe suggested that this early twentieth-century perception that the principal catalyst for Iron Age change resulted from invasion sprang from the imperialist culture of the time.

At the beginning of the twenty-first century, post-imperialist Britain produces archaeologists who consider that egalitarian individual households may once have formed the fundamental building blocks of Iron Age society. This type of society, although absorbing outside influences, evolved its own way of doing things without the need for invasion to explain change (Hill 2001, 95-116).

Some academics challenge the whole concept of invasion in an Iron Age context, as the idea of political tribal territories is considered to be a modern interpretation of the evidence. Britain was not a nation in the Iron Age but a disparate group of communities with overlapping zones of interest. For example, boundaries were not defined during the archaeological landscape study of Cranborne Chase as the communities there were considered to be permeable entities. The local systems of social reproduction within the area were not closed but part of a wider geographical system. According to this way of thinking the assessment of 'indigenous' and 'foreign' elements within the Iron Age were considered to be obsolete (Barrett, Bradley & Green 1991, 227).

John Collis reviewed past approaches to the Iron Age and considered the ways society was transformed over this period. He created a list of catalysts for change. He noted the difficulty of identifying invasions and migrations as the reason for any change in material culture. On his list are commercial trade, that is items bartered for mutual gain, but also social trade, when objects are exchanged to forge alliances, as gifts between friends or as a bride price. The movement of specialist craftsmen or indigenous invention or imitation might also have caused change.

However, British history records the effects of migrations and invasions (the forcible occupation of territory by one group at the expense of another) and it would be difficult to declare that such events could not take place during the prehistoric Iron Age. Burnt gateways and the distribution of sling stones within hillforts, such as Danebury in Hampshire and Hod Hill in Dorset, indicate the likelihood of warfare between groups. Clusters of distinctive artefacts and new types of settlement may indicate the movement of alien communities into new areas. The Early Iron Age burials found in Yorkshire, known as the Arras culture, can be linked to similar burials in France. These were thought to represent evidence for invasion or migration, just as the burials from the Aylsford/Swayling area indicate a similar folk movement from France to south-east England in the Late Iron Age (Haselgrove *et al.* 2001, 3, 13-14).

Archaeologists' ideas of the way Iron Age society worked have varied over the last century. However, it is likely that many of the explanations for change were true during this 800-year-long period. These were not static communities.

Bronze Age to Iron Age

Barry Cunliffe (2000, 149-196) described the pattern that he saw in the archaeological record from 1500 BC-AD 100 using his research on the monuments of the Danebury environs. The social change over time is discussed using the evidence of the most common site types and these are as plentiful within the landscape surrounding the Durotrigan study areas as they are at Danebury.

To summarise: the Early Bronze Age (2200-1500 BC) landscape of round barrows, field systems and scattered open farmsteads and settlements gradually gave way to the Late Bronze Age (1500-800 BC) landscape. This was characterised by long linear boundaries that sometimes incorporated and sometimes cut across earlier field systems. During this period, increasing numbers of farms and settlements became enclosed and burial monuments gradually ceased to be used. This ordered division of the landscape is suggestive of social groups defining and protecting their interests, either through negotiation and mutual agreement or as an imposition from a higher authority on the affected individual farming units.

In the Early Iron Age (800-300 BC), hilltop enclosures were transformed into univallate hillforts. In the Middle Iron Age (300-100 BC) some smaller hillforts were abandoned and others were enlarged with better, more elaborate defences. Field systems are rarely dated to this period. Settlements around Danebury became depopulated and the round houses within the hillfort increased in number.

In the Late Iron Age (100 BC-AD 100) hillforts became depopulated and new types of enclosed settlements of various sizes and types expanded from existing sites or reoccupied abandoned places. Large enclosed settlements tended to be located beside rivers and these were usually constructed on new sites. They are termed *oppida* in southern England but generally are not thought to have been as developed or intensely occupied as the *oppida* of France.

In the Late Iron Age, field systems were re-established in the landscape, and following the Roman Conquest, farmsteads and settlements continued to occupy the same sites. As the

Roman influence took hold in southern England, rectangular buildings replaced circular buildings and timber and daub constructions tended to be replaced by buildings of mortar and stone.

Barry Cunliffe concluded that the basic motivator for change was the growing importance of land and its productivity. He highlighted two particularly significant changes during the period: the ending of burial mound construction and the decline of hillforts. Round barrows, he argued, symbolised a claim over a broad territory, and enclosures symbolised a claim over a precise location. The greater agricultural productivity of the Iron Age enabled a greater population density. The division of the landscape by boundary and enclosure enabled each group of people to know what they were entitled to and determine when a trespass had been committed. This interpretation of enclosures and linear banks and ditches contrasts with the fluid social structure proposed for Cranborne Chase as outlined above (Barrett, Bradley & Green 1991, 227).

Another change from the Bronze Age was the disappearance from the archaeological record of materials such as gold, amber and faience. These precious materials, sometimes found adorning burials within round barrows, indicate that these individuals were wealthy people of high status. The lack of golden objects or other prestige items in the British Early and Middle Iron Age suggests that either there were no wealthy members of society or that wealth and prestige were measured in another way. The decline of overseas trade and exchange of durable prestige objects took place between 800-500 BC and this apparent isolation from the continent continued until second century BC, when gold objects were found once again on settlement sites in southern England. Mortimer Wheeler (1943, 382) noted that even bronze was rarely found in the Early Iron Age levels at Maiden Castle. He concluded that the local farmers were self-sufficient with no significant surplus and had nothing to trade for exotic materials such as copper, tin and gold.

In the Iron Age there seems to have been a shift from fighting or hunting with bows and arrows to the adoption of the sling. Finely worked flint arrowheads disappear from the archaeological record and heaps of pebbles are found instead. Domestic animal bone assemblages seem to have the remains of few wild animals within them. If the archaeological record is reliable, hunting and fishing cannot be claimed as high priorities within Iron Age societies.

From the Early Iron Age, there is evidence of storage of agricultural surpluses within settlement enclosures. This is in the form of pits cut into the bedrock and arrangements of four, five or six posts-holes that are interpreted as supporting buildings raised on stilts. Both of these types of Iron Age feature are generally considered to be for storing grain. The pits are thought to have been for seed corn to enable the grain to germinate more quickly, while the post-hole structures indicate the foundations for granaries for storing agricultural surplus for consumption or exchange. If the post-holes supported granaries, then the stilts would have prevented infestation of the stored grain by rodents in the same way that staddle stones supported granaries on farms in the post-medieval period. This concentration within the archaeological record of features devoted to grain production and storage suggests a devotion to agriculture that is not as conspicuous in the Bronze Age.

The 'treatment' of human remains in the Iron Age contrasts significantly with the funerary activity of the Early Bronze Age with its apparent pre-occupation with the veneration of the individual within burial mounds. From the Late Bronze Age until the Late Iron Age, human remains, if they are found at all, tend to be concentrated in pits and ditches as though they had been discarded as rubbish. However, there is probably a religious explanation for this disposal. Burials, found as complete skeletons or skeletal fragments, are sometimes included in structured pit fillings suggesting that human bones were precious commodities. It is assumed that above-ground funerary rites were the norm and, therefore, most human remains were disposed of in a way that cannot be interpreted from the archaeological remains. In an attempt to explain this gap in our understanding it has been suggested that some of the four-post structures that are often found on Iron Age sites may have been used as platforms to expose dead bodies.

The structured filling of some Iron Age grain storage pits included special deposits. These might be human and animal burials, quantities of grain, quern stones and other objects. It has been thought that these were symbols of propitiation to the deities to ensure fertility and good harvests (Cunliffe 1992, 69-83). The ideas that link burial, belief and agriculture arise from the careful analysis of the contents of grain storage pits, one of the key sources of artifactual evidence that survives from the British Iron Age (Hill 1995a). Although there are few objects of high status found on Early and Middle Iron Age sites, there is considerable evidence for storage of agricultural surplus. At Danebury, 2400 storage pits were excavated and an additional 2000 unexcavated examples probably lie within the hillfort (Cunliffe 1993, 87). Aerial photography and excavation have demonstrated that this concentrated storage capacity was normal within the Iron Age farmstead and settlement enclosures across Wessex, including the settlements of the Durotrigan zone. This great storage capacity implies that status, particularly in the Early Iron Age, was measured by agricultural surplus rather than precious objects.

This link between agricultural production, storage, ritual and funerary practice can be seen in other cultures. The example of the New Zealand Maori and their division of all tasks into sacred and profane may provide explanations for the British Iron Age evidence. Even during a siege, the Maori would not collect water from the roof of a hut for drinking because the roof was sacred (*tapu*). The bones of the dead were also *tapu* and those of revered chiefs were brought to the fields during planting to enable a good crop. It is likely that similar belief systems affected British Iron Age behaviour. Julius Caesar indicated this division between sacred and profane. He noted that the British thought it unlawful to eat hares, fowl and geese although they would rear them 'for pleasure and amusement' (*The Conquest of Gaul*, V.12).

The archaeological record has to depend on the interpretation of the material remains. Therefore, it is the evidence from the archaeological features and artefacts that will indicate the shifts in the way certain tasks were achieved over time. The evidence suggests that the attitudes and belief structures of Middle Bronze Age farmers were fundamentally different from those of the Middle Iron Age. This revolution is summarised as the shift from a situation where funerary and ritual monuments dominate to a time where settlements are conspicuous and burials rare. This process has been described as a change from 'the dead and the living' to the 'living and the dead' (Barrett, Bradley & Green, 1991). People continued to live in round houses but increasingly settlements and farmsteads were surrounded by enclosures.

ENCLOSURES TO HILLFORTS AND THE CENTRAL PLACE DEBATE

In certain favoured locations, enclosures were developed and became multivallate hillforts. Places like Badbury Rings, Maiden Castle and Hambledon Hill are prominent earthworks and seem to enclose the most significant settlements within their locale. Were these central places and what would be the functions of an Iron Age central place? Did these differ significantly from the functions of other contemporary settlements in their vicinity? These questions are not easily resolved and have led to disagreement between Iron Age specialists, particularly as many Iron Age communities did not seem to need hillforts in their locality.

The concept of hillforts as central places has been considered by Barry Cunliffe from his work at Danebury (1984, 559-562; 1995, 91-94). Cunliffe's ideas have been vigorously challenged by J.D. Hill (2001, 101) who has questioned the traditional view that hillforts were social pivotal centres and suggested that they represented just another type of settlement enclosure, distinctive, separate, but not necessarily superior to other site types.

Central place theory was developed in 1933 by the German geographer Walter Christaller to describe the central goods and services provided by settlements to serve or be served by regional communities (Haggett 1979, 362-371). His basic hierarchy of settlements was defined as hexagonal zones of influence spread out over an ideal level landscape where all other factors, such as soil fertility, water sources and accessibility, were equal. This model enabled a simplified understanding of the distribution of levels of settlement function. He then went on to consider traffic optimising, market optimising and administration optimising situations. His ideal hexagonal distribution of places could be rearranged to demonstrate:

- The hierarchy of roads between ordinary and principal places.
- The hierarchy of competition between different villages, towns and cities providing different types of specialised goods and services.
- The hierarchy of administration which can be used to illustrate a network of political and religious power.

In the Iron Age, one assumes that communities operated as groups of households that were mutually supportive, gaining most of their staple resources from the local environment. They would have had some contact with neighbouring communities and rare contact with larger more distant places. Roads and transport were poorly developed and travel over distance was difficult and, therefore, less likely to be undertaken by ordinary farmers unless there was good reason to do so. Rivers and the sea acted as corridors for easier distant contact. Undoubtedly communities did migrate, but usually they did not and, therefore, the theory of a Christaller-style network of principal places surrounded by lesser places every 10-15km is attractive.

Various assumptions might be put forward at this stage:

- A household occupying a farmstead would co-operate with households in neighbouring farmsteads and worship at the local shrine.

- At certain days of the year they would go to a larger place where there was a bigger shrine or a community gathering where many households would come together perhaps to trade and barter their produce.
- They would dominate or be dominated; as in all societies there is a pecking order.
- The greater the population density the greater the need for social organisation.
- This would be controlled from the centres of power, which tend to be concentrated in the larger settlements.
- Local and regional centres of power compete and shift over time.

The above assumptions for Iron Age Dorset would not meet with universal approval but in surveying the Iron Age archaeology of the Dorset environs it has become clear that many areas were densely occupied. From common experience, in areas of high population it is difficult for people to co-exist without a hierarchical social structure.

Geographical analysis will assume significance from site and artefact distribution maps. Ian Hodder (1977, 8-16) highlighted the need to understand the mechanisms that dictate distribution before drawing tentative conclusions. For example, he questioned whether prehistoric pottery distributions are the result of goods marketed from production centres, such as the Iron Age kilns on the Isle of Purbeck, or derive from more primitive exchange networks that highlight the positions of social groupings.

Across any landscape there will be social and physical corridors and barriers that affect exchange and distribution. Within an area there may be a single production centre which manufactured objects with a distinctive style. Alternatively each community within the same area may produce the same object in the same style because it demonstrates part of the common inheritance and identity of the area.

While the ordinary everyday objects may be used and produced locally, items that are made of non-local materials may be produced using techniques unknown to the locality and imported from outside the community. Goods may be transferred from a higher ranking place within a settlement hierarchy, to which skilled craftsmen gravitated, or from a similar but more distant community with a geological advantage (e.g. in Dorset, shale objects from Purbeck, Greensand querns from the Shaftesbury area).

Ian Hodder listed different kinds of mechanism for distribution within primitive societies that are outside the modern understanding of a market economy. He divided primitive communities into centralised and non-centralised societies.

In the centralised society there is a ranking of individuals. This may operate as English medieval society operated. The commoner may owe goods and services to the chief. The chief may store the goods in granaries and storehouses and redistribute them to his people. In this sort of society a prominent settlement may be a status symbol and residence for the head of the hierarchy and his retinue.

Although distribution patterns would gravitate towards and radiate out from such centres, there would still be other levels of exchange including that between local farmsteads and between one centre and another.

In the non-centralised society there is no central point to which goods flow. All the various spatial segments of society are equal and equidistant. None is more important than any other, and goods do not flow by redistribution but by reciprocity. Reciprocity involves the exchange of gifts between socially defined partners. These will be partnerships forged by kinship groups, formed by marriage alliances, enabling the flow of goods between families.

In this sort of society a hillfort may be one of many types of settlement in an area. Hill (2001, 112) would support this view and maintain that most hillforts were communal centres for specific activities that served to link disparate individual households.

Each community in the British Iron Age would have been slightly different and may have leaned more towards the centralised or non-centralised system at different times. Therefore, we must ask how can the archaeologist determine what can be interpreted from distribution patterns? Hodder suggested that settlement type and size should be a good indicator, such as a large hillfort surrounded by smaller settlements and farmsteads. The impressive earthwork defences indicated the seat of authority for a hierarchical system. This was supported by an accumulation of high-status objects at such a place to indicate the presence of occupants of high rank. J.D. Hill uses the lack of evidence for accumulations of high-status objects within Middle Iron Age hillforts as evidence of a non-centralised society at this time. However, this interpretation assumes that we know what the symbols of power were within Middle Iron Age societies and that they survive within the archaeological record to be recognised. If wealth and prestige were measured in the size of a herd or the number of granaries then certain hillforts provide evidence for the concentration of these riches.

Archaeological evidence can be used in different ways to form opposing ideas. There are no set answers or firm conclusions that all British Iron Age specialists subscribe to. Each enquirer is left to consider the composite body of data and commentary and write their own Iron Age.

J.D. Hill used the archaeological evidence to dismantle each of the claimed central place functions of Danebury. However, at the end of this exercise there is a hierarchical void that is not easy to fill using known historical and ethnographic examples of political and social organisation. Using a historically attested example, Maori communities were often ruled by a chief who occupied the largest hillfort within a locale. Were massive built structures like Hod Hill and Maiden Castle created, developed and maintained by co-operation amongst equals? Hill admits that there cannot be a general model to cover all hillforts and cites the Dorset area as a special case (Hill 2001, 113). The evidence for large nucleated hillfort communities, particularly at Maiden Castle, implies a dominant class able to restrict occupation to the confines of the hillfort (see Chapter Six). This process might be compared with Saxon lords who brought together local populations to create nucleated villages and open field systems, for example Shapwick, Somerset (Aston & Costen 1994, 68).

Barry Cunliffe (Payne, Corney & Cunliffe 2006, 151-162) has looked again at the functions of hillforts and has questioned whether they should all be placed within the same settlement category. Some hillforts show signs of significant habitation, others are sparsely settled and others appear empty. Some developed hillforts will have had many functions, others would have had one short-term function, or may never have been completed or occupied. This variety of function, status and length of use can be seen in the New Zealand hillforts (*pā*). Some are documented as being used as places for temporary refuge and others as defended permanent settlements.

John Creighton (2000, 21) noted that the more hillforts are interpreted as communal monuments rather than as the focal points of warlike elites, the greater the gap that needs to be filled. The leap of change from Middle Iron Age communities of egalitarian households to the highly ranked historic dynasties of the Latest Iron Age is difficult to explain solely in terms of increased trading contacts. He considered it more likely that the Middle to Late Iron Age transition tended to be a violent power struggle rather than a peaceful adoption of new ideas. Using the Maori example again, the *pā* were certainly centres for groups of warriors and European travellers documented many reasons for hostility between communities that led to attacks on New Zealand hillforts.

While John Collis argued that continental *oppida* had developed to a stage where they had central place functions, he questioned such a status being attributable to British hillforts (1984, 2). He acknowledged the planned layout of streets and houses, evidence of trade and industry and its function as a defensive centre that mark Danebury out as a key settlement within its locale. However, he felt that hillforts need more evidence of a commercial centre and a distinctive hierarchy of building types. These would indicate a variety of building functions and perhaps the rank of their occupants. The apparent similarity of the round houses within hillforts makes it difficult to recognise them as towns and, therefore, central places in the economic sense. However, the recent geophysical survey of Hod Hill (see Chapter Nine) provides evidence of a greater variety of buildings, enclosures and outbuildings than has usually been recognised within hillforts.

Excavations within Middle Iron Age settlements do not usually reveal remains that indicate high-status housing. The round houses seem similar in plan and diameter and, therefore, no hierarchy is discernible, but one might argue that the chief person within a settlement was not the man with the largest house but the one who owned the largest herd, or the most storage pits and granaries. In the Late Iron Age, enclosures within settlements, such as Gussage All Saints and Cleavel Point in Dorset, seem to define individual households, but high-status buildings are not clearly discernible in the way that mosaics and wall paintings might indicate the wealth and power of the occupants of Roman buildings. However, John Creighton has highlighted gold and horses as two significant changes in the Late Iron Age that symbolise power and prestige.

The comparison of Middle and Late Iron Age animal bone assemblages from sites such as Gussage All Saints (Wainwright, 1979), Bury Hill (Cunliffe 2000, 62), Danebury (Cunliffe 1995) and Maiden Castle (Sharples 1991) revealed a significant increase in the percentage of horse bones. In addition, there are the remains of horse harnesses found at Bury Hill and Gussage thus indicating that horses were increasingly being used to ride and to pull carts and chariots. This archaeological evidence is supported by Caesar's description of British war chariots in his account of the Roman invasions of 55 BC and 54 BC (*The Conquest of Gaul* IV.33; V.15–16). They had become unfashionable in Gaul by this time and were a novelty to Caesar.

Late Iron Age coins appear in Britain from the early first century BC and are used as evidence for the emergence of tribes and kingly authority, and many include inscriptions of the names of leaders. Caesar recorded the use of gold and bronze coins and also iron ingots of fixed weights in 54 BC (*The Conquest of Gaul* V.12). The iron ingots seem to have taken the form of swords in the Dorset environs before coins were used, 'spit'- and sickle-shaped ingots have also been found in southern Britain. Groups of these currency bars have been found at Hod Hill (see Chapter Nine).

The remains of pottery containers, such as amphorae, reveal that wine and other exotic commodities were being imported. This was made possible by increased trade links with the Mediterranean world and the expanding influence of Rome. Internal markets also developed and new decorated styles of pottery replaced the plain 'saucepan pot' styles.

Oppida like Silchester and Colchester represent the latest and most distinctive high-status settlements in Britain at the dawn of the Roman Conquest. They are proto-towns but may not have developed the range of functions normally attributed to towns. The continental *oppida* tend to be much closer to Roman towns in scale and organisation than those in the British Isles. John Collis (1984) examined the origins and emergence of this new form of settlement in central Europe. He noted that these *oppida* were not planted as colonies by the Greeks or Romans but developed as key territorial centres with urban genesis stimulated by an internal process encouraged by trade with the Mediterranean. They often adopted the names of the communities of which they were a part, for example Paris of the Parisii.

The excavations on the site of the forum-basilica at Silchester revealed that the Roman town of *Calleva Atrebatum* originated as a planned *oppidum* in the Late Iron Age *c.*25-15 BC. Two phases of Late Iron Age settlement were identified, consisting of streets of buildings located beside two trackways forming a T-junction. Less than 1 per cent of the area within the boundary rampart of the early settlement has been examined but it is likely that an early street grid of town-like proportions lies buried beneath the Roman town. The available evidence suggested that the earlier buildings were round houses but in Phase 2, these were replaced by rectilinear structures flanking the streets. Circular and rectilinear structures probably co-existed but pre-Roman rectilinear buildings are rare in Iron Age Britain. They are a sign of continental influence, as are the Iron Age wells found on the site, the oyster shells and the numerous Gallic and Roman ceramic imports (Fulford 2000, 545-581).

Barry Cunliffe (1994, 76) noted the chronological link between the decline of hillforts and the emergence of *oppida* and other new forms of settlement. This change is not clearly understood but the study of the settlement pattern of the Durotrigan zone will provide useful information. Populations within the Dorset environs were only beginning to move away from their hillforts by AD 43. This differs markedly from their eastern and northern neighbours who had abandoned their windswept fortresses long before the Roman Conquest. Therefore, the archaeology of Durotrigan hillforts is significant because the evidence is fixed in time through rapid abandonment following Roman intervention.

The next chapter looks at the historical sources that refer to the Durotriges and considers the Roman local government structures of *pagi* and *civitates*.

2

HISTORY AND THE DUROTRIGES (THE ROMAN *CIVITAS*)

The name Durotriges begins the history of Dorset. The name implies a grouping, a common identity for the peoples of the area, but the name is only known from three Roman sources. These are looked at later in the chapter, but first the context of the Durotriges and other documented group names is considered. Historically these names were used to describe the peoples occupying Roman administrative districts. Can these Roman names be used to describe pre-Roman communities?

Our understanding of the tribal boundaries of Late Iron Age southern England (*2*) is based largely on the surviving inscriptions naming Romano-British administrative divisions (*civitates*). These districts, it is thought, were created from the old pre-conquest tribal areas and some, such as the Iceni, Trinovantes and Atrebates, are named by classical writers before the Roman Conquest.

In the 50s BC, the tribal division of Gaul was described by Julius Caesar (*The Conquest of Gaul*). It is clear from his accounts that leadership and political organisation varied greatly between 'tribes'. Caesar provided an account of the way he felt Gallic society operated at that time (VI.13-15):

> Everywhere in Gaul there are only two classes of men who are of any account or consideration. The common people are treated almost as slaves, never to act on their own initiative and are nor consulted on any subject … The two privileged classes are the Druids and the knights …

> … the Gallic states used to fight offensive or defensive wars almost every year – these all take to the field, surrounded by their servants and retainers, of whom each knight has a greater or smaller number according to his birth and fortune.

Therefore, Caesar depicts the Gallic 'tribes' as hierarchical and consisting of a variety of belligerent groups. He describes the 'tribes' of Britain in a similar way (V.11-12):

> Cassivellaunus' territory is separated from the maritime tribes by a river called the Thames, and lies about seventy-five miles from the sea. Previously he had been continually at war with the other tribes, but the arrival of our army frightened them into appointing him their supreme commander.

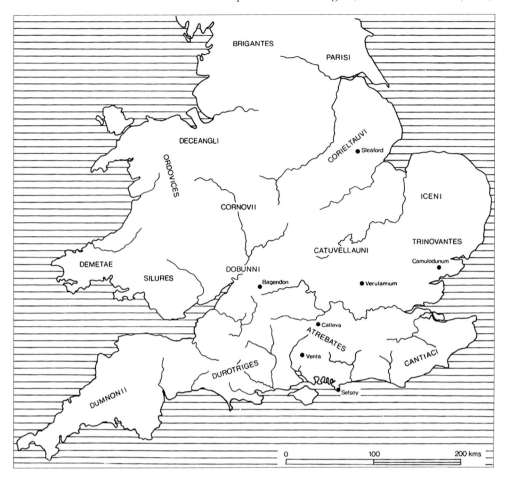

2 Late Iron Age named groups. (Cunliffe 1991, 160)

The interior of Britain is inhabited by people who claim on the strength of oral tradition, to be aboriginal; the coast by Belgic immigrants who came to plunder and make war … nearly all of them retaining the names of tribes from which they originated … and later settled down to till the soil. The population is exceedingly large, the ground thickly studded with homesteads, closely resembling those of the Gauls, and the cattle very numerous. For money they use either bronze or gold coins, or iron ingots of fixed weights.

Cornelius Tacitus, writing about 150 years later, also stated that the British were warlike and described the cynical way the Roman governor Julius Agricola 'civilised' the population:

Agricola had to deal with people living in isolation and ignorance, and therefore prone to fight; and his object was to accustom them to a life of peace and quiet by the provision of amenities. He therefore gave private encouragement and official assistance to the building of temples, public squares, and good houses. He praised the energetic and scolded the slack; and competition for honour proved as effective as compulsion.

Furthermore he educated the sons of the chiefs in the liberal arts, and expressed a preference for British ability as compared with the trained skills of the Gauls. The result was that instead of loathing the Latin language they became eager to speak it effectively. In the same way, our national dress came into favour and the toga was everywhere to be seen.

And so the population was gradually led into the demoralising temptations of arcades, baths, and sumptuous banquets. The unsuspecting Britons spoke of such novelties as 'civilisation', when in fact they were only a feature of their enslavement. (*Agricola* XXI)

CIVITATES

Therefore, the Romans actively encouraged the adoption of Roman ways to facilitate ease of governance. The administration of local districts in Britain, that developed between AD 50 and 80, was based on a pattern already established in Gaul. The Romans adapted the communities they found, promoting the development of towns, often near native centres, and granted the local people the right to administer the area around them – the *civitas*. The authority was given to an *ordo* or council made up of about 100 *decuriones*, elected among citizens, who were normally at least 30 years old and who had a certain level of personal wealth and property.

It will be seen that there is considerable archaeological evidence for settlement continuity within the Dorset environs. Excavations have revealed that many Iron Age farmsteads developed into Roman villas (e.g. in Dorset the villas excavated at Bucknowle, Halstock, Dewlish, Tarrant Hinton & Bradford Down). One might conclude that the heads of these higher ranking households became *decuriones* and that they benefited financially through the influence they exercised at council meetings. Neil Faulkner has argued that although membership of the *ordo* was advantageous in the earlier Roman period, from the third century it became increasingly unpopular and councils and urban living began to decline. This is because central government placed on the council members the responsibility of demanding higher taxes to pay the army. This financial strain impacted on the ability and desire to invest in public building work (Faulkner 2004, 169-171).

Nevertheless, by the fourth century, the Dorset villas had developed to become grand buildings decorated with fine mosaics and wall paintings, demonstrating that the important local families were still wealthy. However, they were investing their money in their country estates rather than the towns which had become fortified strongholds rather than symbols of Roman civilisation.

KEY TEXTS

Classical documents list the names of many towns, settlements and *civitates*. Archaeological confirmation of some of the *civitas* centres has been found on inscriptions excavated from Roman towns, for example *Calleva Atrebatum*, Silchester, *Corinium Dubonnorum*, Cirencester and *Isca Dumnoniorum*, Exeter (i.e. the administrative centres for the Atrebates, Dubunni and Dumnonii).

The key texts for the Durotrigan zone are the second-century *Geography* of Ptolemy (*Geographia Claudii Ptolemei*), the third-century road book known as the *Antonine Itinerary* (*Itinerarium Provinciarum Antonini Augusti*) and the seventh-century list of countries, towns and rivers known as the *Ravenna Cosmography* (*Ravennatis Annonymi Cosmographia*).

It has been assumed that the named *civitates* were based on pre-Roman tribal groups, although new boundaries are likely to have been drawn by the Roman administration. Some disparate communities may have been grouped together to form *civitates* by the occupying power.

THE DUROTRIGES

The group name commonly applied to the Late Iron Age communities centred on Dorset is usually written 'Durotriges', although the name is only known from three sources. These are listed by Rivet and Smith (1979, 352). Ptolemy provided one example, and the other two were inscriptions found on stones from Hadrian's Wall.

The meaning of the word has not been resolved but Rev. John Hutchins suggested:

> The name Durotriges is ancient, and though in sound it bears great affinity to the Greek language, it is entirely of British original, derived probably from *Dour* or *Dwr*, in British water, and *Trig* an inhabitant, *q.d.* dwellers by the water or sea-side. (1774, ix)

Rivet and Smith (1979, 352) suggested an alternative and also divided the name into two elements: *Duro* possibly referring to 'fort' and *riges* being a plural of the word 'king'. However, the temptation to interpret the name as referring to the land of the fort kings is tempered by the fact that the word *Duro* was usually used in Britain to describe low-lying early Roman forts. This interpretation does not appear to be relevant in an area containing so many hillforts. However, by the Latest Iron Age, there was a trend for the principal enclosed settlements to become established beside rivers.

PTOLEMY

The earliest source for the word is Ptolemy, the Greek geographer writing *c.*AD 140-150. Rivet and Smith analysed his *Geography* and assessed commentaries on his work. Although written in the second century, he used earlier sources particularly Marinus of Tyre who mapped the whole known world from Britain to the Malay Peninsula at the turn of the first and second centuries. Ptolemy and Marinus probably never visited Britain and therefore their information on the peoples and places of the area was derived from travellers, such as soldiers, mariners and merchants.

For southern Britain, Rivet and Smith examined the places recorded by Ptolemy and concluded that the information he used dated to the mid-first century. Ptolemy recorded each principal named place within an area as a *polis*. This does not necessarily mean a town but could be no more than a place with a name. However, one assumes that the few named places that Ptolemy chose to include in his *Geography* were distinctive in relation to any other named places that he chose to exclude or had not heard of.

Rivet and Smith's dating of Ptolemy's information on southern Britain was based on which of the known named settlements were included and which were excluded from the document. For example, although the new town of *Noviomagus* (which is considered to be Chichester) was recorded as a *polis*, *Durnovaria*, the accepted Roman name for Dorchester, was not. Excavations in and around Dorchester indicate that it was established *c.*AD 65-70. *Noviomagus* was founded early within a client kingdom that did not oppose the Roman Conquest. Dorchester lay within an area hostile to the Romans and was established later (Woodward 1993, 359). Additional evidence for the date of Ptolemy's information is found in the portion dealing with South Wales. Caerleon and Caerwent were not included but Usk was, and excavation has shown that Usk predated Caerleon as a legionary base before *c.*AD 74. (Rivet & Smith 1979, 115).

Therefore it can be argued that Ptolemy listed the names of the peoples of southern Britain within 20 years of the Roman Conquest and included the principal settlements which were in existence at the time. After describing the Belgae, he noted that:

> … to the west and south of these are the Durotriges amongst whom is the *polis* of *Dunium*.

Mortimer Wheeler (1943, 12) believed *Dunium* to be Maiden Castle because of its size and the later creation of the principal town of Dorchester nearby. Whereas Rivet and Smith (1979, 145) considered Hod Hill to be a better candidate because it lies closer to the latitude and longitude provided by Ptolemy. Hod had an extensive Roman settlement beside the River Iwerne outside its east gate and the evidence for this will be considered below (see Chapter Nine).

It is assumed that Dorchester was the administrative centre of the *civitas* created by the Romans to govern a people known as the Durotriges and the size of Roman Dorchester strongly suggests this. However, the only inscriptions currently known refer to Ilchester not Dorchester.

THE STONES FROM HADRIAN'S WALL

The two other sources containing the Durotrigan name are inscriptions on stones from the central section of Hadrian's Wall. One was found before 1873 'somewhere west of Housesteads' (*RIB* 1673), inscribed *c(ivitas) Dur(o)tr(i)g(um) (L)endin(i)e(n)sis* 'the canton of the Durotriges of *Lendiniae* (built this)'. The other inscription was found in 1882 at the foot of the crags north of the Wall near Cawfields (*RIB* 1672), *ci(vitas) Durotrag(um) Lendinie(n) si(s)* 'the canton of the Durotrages of *Lendiniae* (built this)'.

The inscriptions have been interpreted as stones set up to record the work of a group of masons from the Durotrigan area who repaired this section of wall. Alternatively, a Durotrigan Roman administrative area (*civitas*) provided the funds for the work. *Lindinis* is interpreted as the name of the Roman town at Ilchester, which will be considered in more detail below.

Michael Fulford has brought together the evidence for all the stones from Hadrian's Wall that record *civitates*. There are also two that commemorate the work of the Dumnonii (centred on Devon), one of the Catuvellauni (centred on Hertfordshire) and one of the Brigantes (centred on the north Pennines). None were found in a secure archaeological context and previous commentators have suggested that the stones dated to the third or fourth centuries, when the wall was extensively repaired. However, Fulford commented that by this time Britannia had been split into more than one province and that the governor who managed Hadrian's Wall no longer controlled the peoples of southern Britain. He suggested that if the stones dated to the second century the governor would still have had direct influence over the Durotrigan and Dumnonian *civitates* (Fulford 2006, 65-71).

PLACE NAMES WITHIN THE DUROTRIGAN AREA FROM CLASSICAL SOURCES

The *Antonine Itinerary* and *Ravenna Cosmography* name *Durnovaria* and two other places that probably lay within Dorset. These are *Vindocladia*, probably Crab Farm near Badbury Rings (see Chapter Eleven), and *Ibernio*, possibly near Hod Hill (see Chapter Nine). These surviving names represent principal places along routeways and may give an indication of local power centres within the Romanised Durotriges. If they were names for Hod and Crab Farm, they were already significant places in the Late Iron Age. These settlements may be examples of district administrative centres or *pagi*. Each *civitas* would have included a number of these smaller centres (Burnham & Wacher 1990, 39-40).

The linking of the *Antonine Itinerary* names of *Durnovaria* or *Durnonovaria* with Dorchester is confirmed by later references to the town. In the Anglo-Saxon period, the town was known as *Dornwaracaester* and a Welsh document refers to it as *Durngueir*. Rivet and Smith considered that *Duriano* of the Ravenna list also referred to Dorchester. They noted that Ravenna usually recorded *civitas* capitals but the expected *civitas* designation *Durotrigum* was not added to *Duriano*. Their explanation was that the Ravenna list contains many errors and that, as with Bath (*Aquae Sulis*), the name may have been placed out of context in amongst a list of places that were generally much further west. It is interesting to note, however, that the *Antonine Itinerary* references also omit the Durotrigan suffix.

The archaeology of Dorchester testifies that it was a significant place. Similar sized nearby towns such as Exeter, Winchester, Cirencester, Chichester and Silchester do have the historical evidence for their *civitas* status. Therefore, researchers have concluded that Dorchester was also a *civitas* capital and the location of the Durotrigan *ordo* or local council.

However, the boundaries of the supposed Durotrigan *civitas* may not have remained static during almost 400 years of Roman rule. The town name *Lindinis*, recorded on the Hadrian's Wall inscriptions, is thought to be the walled Roman town of Ilchester in south Somerset and it is argued (Stevens, 1952, 188-192) that by the fourth century, the Durotrigan *civitas* had been split into at least two areas: one centred on Ilchester and the other at Dorchester. Michael Fulford (2006, 69) has suggested that if the inscriptions from Hadrian's Wall are early, then the *civitas Durotrigum Lendiniensis* may already have existed in the second century. It is possible, based on current written evidence, that Dorchester was never a *civitas* capital. However, this seems unlikely given the size of Roman Dorchester in comparison with Ilchester.

Suetonius Tranquillus, Vespasian and Legio II Augusta

From the above, it can be seen that there is historical evidence for a Durotrigan *civitas* but did this derive from a pre-Roman group of that name? One historical text that has been associated with the Durotriges is the life of Vespasian by Gaius Suetonius Tranquillus (*The Twelve Caesars*):

> On Claudius' accession, Vespasian was indebted to Narcissus for command of a legion in Germany; and proceeded to Britain, where he fought 30 battles, subjugated two warlike tribes and captured more than 20 towns (*oppida*), besides the entire Isle of Vectis. In these campaigns he served under Aulus Plautius, the commander of consular rank, and at times under Claudius, earning triumphal decorations. (X.4)

One of the 'warlike tribes' is generally considered to be the Durotriges. In Dorset and south Somerset the evidence for this consists of first-century Roman forts and mutilated human remains. The traditional linkage of this historical source with the archaeology makes Vespasian the first named individual within the history of Dorset and the soldiers of Legio II Augusta as the conquerors of the Durotrigan people. However, it has been claimed that an inscription found at Alchester indicates that Vespasian and the second legion were in Oxfordshire and may not have been in Dorset (Sauer 2005, 168-176). The validity of this new information has been disputed; the grave stone had been redeposited and commemorated a veteran of the legion (Fulford pers. comm. 2006). Amongst the military remains from sites in Dorset there are no objects that can be ascribed to a particular legion, but the evidence still indicates first-century conflict and this will be considered in more detail in Chapter Four.

Suetonius implied that the 'tribes' were large. They were large enough to include many *oppida*. Therefore they were depicted as unified groups of communities, recognised as significant political powers. Their defeat by Vespasian was worthy of praise. The inclusion of *Vectis* suggests that Vespasian's campaign was near the Isle of Wight and this supports the view that one of the 'warlike tribes' lay within the Dorset environs. Recent discoveries of coins on the Isle of Wight are predominantly of the type associated with the Durotriges (Wellington 2001, 39-57), thus supporting the Dorset link to the Isle of Wight and therefore Vespasian. Across the Solent, Hampshire does not contain evidence for first-century Roman forts or conflict and therefore Suetonius' other warlike tribe may have been a group within the Devon or Somerset areas. However, the tribes are unnamed and the Alchester gravestone demonstrates that reinterpretations are possible and that the Vespasian/Durotriges link is based on plausible but inconclusive evidence.

Historical Evidence for Confederacy or the Enlargement of Communities

In 55 BC and 54 BC, the writings of Julius Caesar indicate that there were more political units than existed in AD 43 (*The Conquest of Gaul* IV.20-38; V.8-23). By 55 BC, a power centre was emerging north of the Thames in the area later attributed to the Catuvellauni. The leader of this area, Cassivellaunus, was given command of the united war bands of the other communities 'by common consent' against the Roman army. Cassivellaunus had killed the king of the Trinovantes, the people centred on Essex, which Caesar described as 'about the strongest tribe in south-eastern Britain'. Five other groups are mentioned as surrendering to Caesar during the campaign (Cenimagni, Segontiaci, Ancalites, Bibroci and Cassi) but these names are not recorded again (unless the Cenimagni were part of the Iceni). Similarly, the four Kentish kings that were commanded to attack the Roman coastal supply base in 54 BC suggest that smaller political units still existed at that time, which had been absorbed into the larger kingdom by AD 43.

Until Ptolemy, there are few references to British named groups but the inscription on the triumphal arch of Claudius in Rome (C.I.L. VI 920) may give an indication of the number of political groups that existed in southern Britain in AD 44. It records that Claudius received the submission of eleven British kings. His army had conquered a larger area than that occupied by the forces of Julius Caesar. The purpose of the arch was to celebrate the glory of the emperor and therefore it is likely to exaggerate the number of rulers Claudius had conquered rather than understate his victory. This evidence suggests that in the 98 years since Caesar's campaigns the trend had been for communities to form alliances and create larger groups.

THE BOUNDARIES OF *CIVITATES*

This process of political change, where smaller groups merged, is likely to have been the pattern across southern Britain in the Late Iron Age, including the Dorset environs. The threat from a mutual enemy would tend to encourage alliances, as Caesar implies.

Therefore, the boundaries of territories and the units of administration would have been changing in the Late Iron Age and they are unlikely to have remained static during the Roman period.

Boundaries are difficult to define but distributions of coins enable some boundaries to be suggested for the pre-Roman period. A common currency prevents such definition after the Roman Conquest. Therefore the Roman *civitas* areas have been defined by using pre-Roman evidence and the Iron Age 'tribes' are largely derived from Roman administrative names.

Nevertheless, it is reasonable to assume that the Roman administrative units were guided by a pre-existing group identity. This would enable the Iron Age communities of Britain to be organised through a system of councils based at the new towns and elected from the elite by the local gentry. These towns were built to house Roman 'civilisation' and enable pursuits that would act as 'tender traps' for the pacification of communities.

Having looked at the historical sources, the next chapter considers the archaeological evidence to show how the understanding of Iron Age communities has developed within the Dorset environs.

3

THE DEVELOPMENT OF
IRON AGE STUDIES WITHIN
THE DORSET ENVIRONS

EARLY RESEARCH AND THE NINETEENTH CENTURY

Since the sixteenth century, Ptolemy's Durotriges have been used to provide an ancient identity for the Dorset people. The classical sources we know today were available for study and all were examined in detail and interpreted by historians such as John Leland, William Camden and John Aubrey.

Rev. John Hutchins (1774, ix-xix) reviewed these ancient texts and looked at each source for evidence of the Durotriges. The introductory sentence to his great historical study demonstrates this:

> The county of Dorset was anciently inhabited, according to Ptolemy, by the Durotriges.

In 1861, when the third edition of the book was published, his analysis of the classical sources remained little altered. Indeed, Charles Warne in his *Ancient Dorset* (1872) attributed all the pre-Roman earthworks of the county to the Durotriges:

> … whose hands accomplished works of apparently superhuman power, in an age when the light of civilization had hardly dawned on these benighted shores.

Sir John Evans first described in detail the various types of British pre-Roman coins and their significance as indicators of tribal areas (1864, 101-102). Charles Warne illustrated some of the coins from Dorset and stated 'several of which may be accepted as types of the rude unlettered coinage of the Durotriges' (1872, 154). This established the link, and subsequent researchers analysed the distribution and metallurgy of the coins and classified them into types (see Chapter Four).

Therefore the idea of a distinct Dorset people with a unique coinage was accepted in the nineteenth century and maintained into the twentieth century.

The sixteenth- to nineteenth-century descriptions of Iron Age sites tended to be limited to the large hillforts and concentrated on the romance of past associations. In 1542, John Leland noted that South Cadbury was thought to be Camelot, once occupied by Arthur of the Britons. He provided a useful early description:

The very Roote of the Hille whereon this Forteress stode is more than a Mile in Cumpace. In the upper Parte of the Toppe of the Hille lie four Diches or Trenches, and a baulky Walle of Yerthe betwixt every one of them. In the very Toppe of the Hille above all the Trenches is a magna area or campus of about twenty acres or more by estimation, where in divers places men may see Fundations, and rudera of Walls. There was much dusky blew stone that the people of the villages thereby hath carried away. The top within the upper wall is twenty acres of ground and more, and hath been often plowed and borne very good corne. Much gold, sylver, and copper of the Romaine coins hath been found there in plowing, and likewise in the feldes in the rootes of the hille, with many other antique things and especial by East.

Some 350 years later, Rev. J.A. Bennett was still presenting a romantic image of the place: 'tradition is not wanting, the air of Cadbury is full of legend and romance.'

However, by this time archaeological excavations were taking place to try to fit material evidence with the traditional beliefs. Bennett supervised the cutting of a trench across one of its ramparts and recorded stories of the place retold by the local labourers he employed to do the work.

From the late eighteenth century, plans of archaeological sites began to be published for places like Eggardon Hill (Hutchins 1774) and Hengistbury Head (Grose 1779). In the early nineteenth century, Richard Colt Hoare of Stourhead commissioned some of the earliest detailed earthwork surveys of Iron Age sites in the area. These included the Gussage Cow Down multiple ditch systems and 'banjo' enclosures on Cranborne Chase (1821, 30) and Ham Hill, south Somerset (1827, 39-42), where he recorded the discovery of human remains by quarrymen in 1816.

In 1880, Augustus Henry Lane Fox inherited the Rushmore estates on Cranborne Chase and took the name Pitt Rivers. He had been carrying out archaeological and anthropological research since the 1860s and his inheritance enabled him to study the sites on his land. He concentrated his work particularly in and around Rushmore Park and his carefully recorded excavations set the standard for British field archaeology. Beginning at Winkelbury Camp in 1881, his subsequent excavations were on the sites of the Iron Age and Romano-British settlements of Woodcutts in 1884, Rotherley 1886 and Rushmore Park 1888 (Pitt Rivers 1887; 1888; 1898).

Although many of Charles Warne's conclusions concerning the Durotriges seem outdated now, his tour of ancient Dorset is valuable and some of his observations were ahead of their time. At Hod Hill, for example, he noted the circular banks within the hillfort and believed they were hut sites. Charles Warne, like Hutchins, noted the remarkable survival of settlement remains in the unploughed eastern half of the hillfort. He referred to excavations within the huts:

… on being dug into, the soil is found to be black and discoloured, yielding ashes, pottery and other refuse. Some indeed, have a tolerably regular floor, either on the hard chalk or paved with flints, and a trench surrounding many of them, which was probably a drain to keep the floor dry. (1872, 72)

He concluded that Hod was a large walled *oppidum* and argued that the settlement existed on the hill before the construction of the ramparts because he was able to see hut sites buried or cut by the defences:

> There are proofs that the hill was very thickly populated long before it was converted into a regular Camp. A careful examination of the ground within and without the ramparts, particularly on the North side, will not fail to disclose the sites of ancient dwellings.

Ploughing has since removed the earthwork evidence on the north exterior side of the hillfort.

In contrast to Warne's analytical approach, Henry Durden of Blandford was a collector of objects and left few records. He began his Hod Hill collection in 1841, but most artefacts were recovered after 1858 when the west half of the hillfort was first ploughed, and in 1865 when the interior of the Roman fort began to be cultivated (Longworth & Haith 1992, 151-160). Although he rescued the objects from the ploughsoil, he also dug into the unploughed areas. Professor W. Boyd Dawkins, who in 1897 carried out the first scientific excavations at Hod, was critical of Durden's work:

> Nearly the whole of the area of both fortresses had been ransacked by Mr Durden during the last fifty years, and the rich harvest which he obtained of Roman and Pre-Roman age has now for the most part found its home in the British Museum, without any record of the precise circumstances of each discovery. (Boyd-Dawkins 1900, 57)

Boyd-Dawkin's map of Hod shows the location of his 15 excavation trenches. He created a good stratigraphic record for his day and his conclusions are generally sound, but he followed the contemporary theory that Iron Age people usually lived in pits.

Other Victorian excavators were not so careful at recording their investigations. In October 1894, Edward Cunnington excavated a trench somewhere within the central area of Hambledon Hill. He noted the discovery of Roman and Iron Age finds but not their location.

THE EARLY TWENTIETH CENTURY

In the early twentieth century, archaeological records tended to be kept more systematically but publication still fell short of today's standards. Harold St George Gray carried out numerous excavations in Somerset. He excavated five trenches within South Cadbury and from 1923-30 within the north-west spur of Ham Hill hillfort, but these were only published as interim notes in the Somerset Proceedings.

The discovery of three waterlogged occupation sites on the Somerset Levels led to excavations by Arthur Bulleid and Harold St George Gray. The Glastonbury lake village was almost entirely excavated between 1892 and 1907 (Bulleid & Gray 1911; 1917) and the two settlements 5km to the north-west at Meare were investigated from 1907-1956 (Bulleid & Gray 1948; 1953). The preserved wooden artefacts from these sites are remarkable. Their importance was appreciated and the excavation reports were extensive and published as separate volumes for each site. This pioneer work demonstrated the importance of considering a range of settlement evidence, not just that which lay within hillforts.

Another significant non-hillfort site was excavated in 1911 and is an early example of rescue archaeology. The fortified coastal settlement of Hengistbury Head on the Hampshire/Dorset border was threatened with housing development in 1909-10. Finds of numerous Durotrigan coins, Iron Age and Roman pottery had raised awareness of the significance of the site and an appeal was launched to conserve Hengistbury or make a record before the archaeological evidence was lost. J.P. Bushe-Fox directed the excavations on behalf of the Society of Antiquaries. Over six months, he investigated almost 20ha within the ramparts of the fortified Iron Age harbour. He dug long, narrow strip trenches, which caused minimal damage to the archaeological potential of the site. The speed and thoroughness in which the report was produced was impressive, with full ceramic and metallurgical analyses setting the site in context with other known investigations. The report was a model for its time (J.P. Bushe-Fox 1915).

The first publication devoted to archaeological aerial photography included several sites in east Dorset and south Wiltshire (Crawford & Keiller 1928). The photographs and descriptions of significant earthworks provided pioneering analytical discussion of the evidence for Hanging Langford and Ebsbury settlements on the Nadder-Wylye Ridge, the Gussage Cow Down Settlement on Cranborne Chase and hillforts such as Hod, Hambledon, Buzbury and Badbury Rings. This synthesis of past discoveries with photographs and plans was a forerunner of similar non-intrusive site surveys carried out by Victoria County History in Wiltshire (1957 & 1973) and the Royal Commission on Historical Monuments across Dorset (1952, 1970a, 1970b, 1972 & 1975).

The ABC of the Iron Age, Maiden Castle and Marnhull

In 1931, Professor Christopher Hawkes wrote a key article on hillforts. This divided the Iron Age into categories that would remain in use during the next 40 years (Hawkes 1931, 60-97). Previously, British archaeologists had tried to match excavated evidence with finds from continental Europe, the main sites being Hallstatt in south Germany and La Téne in the Rhineland, both excavated in the mid-nineteenth century. The distinctive Hallstatt material was dated to *c*.800-400 BC and the La Téne *c*.400-100 BC, with a third Belgic category applied to the period of 'Romanisation' from 100 BC until the Roman Conquest (Cunliffe 1991, 1).

Although Hawkes could see links with the Hallstatt, La Téne and Belgic continental influences in the British Iron Age material, he argued that the parallels were not exact and therefore he proposed to divide the British Iron Age using the neutral terms A, B and C. Nevertheless, he still maintained that changes in the archaeological record, particularly changes to the defensive architecture of hillforts, were the result of successive waves of population movement from continental Europe (Payne 2006, 4).

This was the chronological framework used by Mortimer Wheeler during his excavations at Maiden Castle from 1934-37. Wheeler, like Hawkes, explained change in terms of invasion (Wheeler 1943, 381-387). Peoples arriving in Britain from the sixth century BC fused with the native population to form the Iron Age A culture. During this period, it was thought, many of the hillforts were first constructed in southern England. A second wave of invaders arrived in the fourth century BC from Spain and Brittany, initially occupying Dorset and the Cotswolds. The massive multivallate hillforts like Maiden Castle were ascribed to these Iron Age B people. The Iron Age C people were linked to Belgic invaders arriving around 75 BC. These people first occupied the Thames valley and Kent, later spreading into Essex. A few years later, refugees from northern France landed on the Solent coast and moved into central southern Britain. These invasions were linked to Roman military conquests in Gaul and the assertion by Julius Caesar, in his *Conquest of Gaul*, that Belgic incursions had taken place in Britain. Wheeler believed that the result of this Belgic influence, in the Iron Age C areas, was the decline of hillforts and the creation of low-lying defended settlements or *oppida* (Payne *et al.* 2006, 4).

The Maiden Castle excavations were the first to examine a large area within a hillfort in Dorset. Wheeler stated his three reasons for the excavations: first, that the scale of Maiden Castle warranted its examination because it was surely a significant place. Secondly, he noted that apart from Pitt Rivers' work on Cranborne Chase, only the fortified coastal site at Hengistbury Head to the east (Bushe-Fox 1915) and Hembury hillfort to the west (Liddell 1935, 135-137) had previously been subjected to scientific excavation. Therefore central Dorset remained a blank:

> A large and important cultural province thus remained unsystematized, and much miscellaneous material found here and there within its borders was devoid of scientific context.

His third reason was that the excavations at *Verulamium* had just been completed and a trained team of archaeologists was available.

In his epilogue, Wheeler stated that he believed that Dorset lay outside the commercial activity evident to the north and east during most of the Iron Age C period:

> The Durotriges remained self-sufficient, content by force or by choice with its own mineral resources.

Change only happened, he thought, about AD 20-40 when the Belgic insurgents introduced distinctive coinage from the north-east:

> Maiden Castle still owed much to the Iron Age A and B elements in the local tradition. But now for the first time Wessex became a unit in the Belgic complex of south-eastern Britain and forgot much of its westerly orientation.

In 1939, following Wheeler's work at Maiden Castle, members of his team examined two nearby hillforts. Excavations in Chalbury Camp (Whitley 1943, 98-121) and at Poundbury (Richardson 1940, 429-448) revealed contrasting results. The round houses of Chalbury (3) were found to have been abandoned at the end of the Iron Age A period but at Poundbury, trenching across the hillfort revealed no building remains within its interior. Therefore distinctive differences of occupation within hillforts had been recorded.

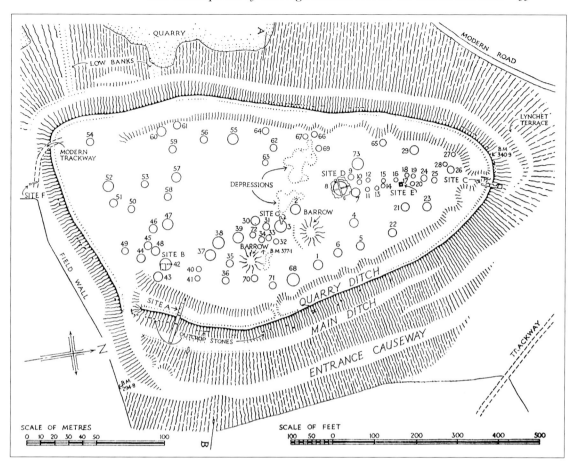

3 Earthwork plan of Chalbury hillfort, Bincombe. (Whitley 1943, 100)

Another important archaeological site excavated 1932-45 was in the Blackmoor Vale parish of Marnhull in north Dorset (Williams 1950, 34-56). An Iron Age settlement was discovered during limestone extraction from Allard's Quarry near Todber. This open settlement site included remains of round houses, pits, burials and four-post structures. Occupation evidence was assigned to A, B and C culture communities. The extensive pottery assemblage from this site was compared with that from Maiden Castle. This led to the adoption of the term Maiden Castle-Marnhull style of pottery to define a group of distinctive Middle Iron Age ceramic forms concentrated within the Dorset environs (Cunliffe 1991, 82-83).

Bernard Calkin published the first distribution map of Iron Age settlement in the Isle of Purbeck (Calkin 1948, 29-59). This was the product of intensive fieldwork from 1931 onwards linked to eighteenth- to nineteenth-century discoveries. Since his first map of prehistoric settlement was published, the data-base has been greatly expanded by field survey and small-scale excavation by local archaeologists R.A.H. Farrar, John Beavis, Tony Brown and Norman Field (Sunter & Woodward 1987, 6).

1950-1970: Hod Hill and the Durotrigan Culture

Renewed ploughing within Hod Hill led to the first excavation by British Museum staff of an English site. The initial trial trenches (Brailsford 1949, 41-50) were followed by eight seasons of excavation between 1951 and 1958. Ian Richmond directed the work and investigated the earthworks of several round houses and cut sections across the ramparts (Richmond 1968). The publication of the work took place after the death of Professor Richmond and this may have been the reason why the analysis remained with the ABC system and that the pottery report contained insufficient detail. However, the earthwork surveys and excavated evidence revealed a high level of archaeological survival, enabling the settlement pattern within the hillfort to be better understood than any previously investigated.

While working on the material from Hod Hill, John Brailsford wrote the article that defined the Durotrigan 'culture'. He described the criteria that set these people apart from those in neighbouring areas (Brailford 1957, 118-121). This will be considered in more detail in the next chapter.

During the 1960s, two other Dorset hillforts were excavated, but their eventual publication was unsatisfactory. From 1963-66, at Eggardon, on the western edge of the chalk, George Rybot excavated various linear banks, pits and round houses inside the ramparts. He died before writing a report on his work but Caroline Wells, who gathered together the records from various sources, was able to publish his results in 1978 (Wells, 54-72). At Pilsdon Pen, in west Dorset, the landowner asked Mortimer Wheeler to find an archaeologist to excavate the site. Peter Gelling was selected and work took place 1964-71. Gelling undertook area excavations within the ramparts and identified the ring gullies for many round houses. Following a disagreement, he left the site before he had completed his investigations. The lack of ceramic evidence from Pilsdon in comparison to Hod and Maiden Castle was significant (Gelling 1977, 263-286).

In Somerset, another campaign of investigation within a hillfort was taking place at South Cadbury. From 1966-73, Leslie Alcock directed excavations on behalf of the Camelot Research Committee. All periods of South Cadbury were examined but the Committee had been formed in 1965 particularly to examine the sub-Roman and early medieval aspects of the site (Alcock 1972).

Early, Middle and Late Iron Age: South Cadbury and Gussage All Saints

Alcock saw the potential of the prehistoric ceramic sequences from South Cadbury and their contribution to the wider understanding of the Iron Age of southern Britain. However, the excavations were taking place as the old ABC cultural hypotheses were breaking down. By 1964, Frank Hodson had demonstrated that associating cultural changes with invasions from the continent could not be sustained. He proposed that the British Iron Age was dominated by indigenous cultural development to which the contribution of continental cultures was limited (Hodson 1964). Therefore, Alcock adopted an 'intrinsic typology' based on the stratigraphic sequence at South Cadbury:

The typological study of the Cadbury material itself without reference to other sites. (Alcock 1980, 682)

The extensive excavations of the interior were a deliberate attempt to reveal the extent and organisation of building activity rather than concentrating efforts on rampart construction. The final publication of the prehistoric and Romano-British phases is a rigorous modern report combining stratigraphic analysis, finds reports with geophysical and earthwork surveys; the chronology was based on 10 Cadbury-specific ceramic phases linked to 'Early Cadbury', 'Middle Cadbury' and 'Late Cadbury' time zones (Barrett, Freeman & Woodward 2000).

Following the abandonment of chronology based on invasion theories and cultures, a new definition of the Iron Age was adopted. Researchers such as Barry Cunliffe and John Collis advocated the division of the Iron Age simply into Early, Middle and Late. This system is currently in use and often amended by adding two additional categories, one at either end of the period: a Latest Bronze Age to Earliest Iron Age (*c.*900-700 BC), to define the period of initial infiltration of iron into society, and a Latest Iron Age to cover the rapid social changes of the first century AD (Cunliffe 1984, 12-45).

The important synthesis of information contained in the Royal Commission on Historical Monument Dorset inventory volumes was published in the limbo period when the Iron Age was being redefined. These books retain the ABC system because, although most of the RCHM volumes were published in the 1970s, they referred to fieldwork mainly carried out in the 1940 and 1960s. This work provided a data set of accurate earthwork surveys and location maps, enabling the Dorset prehistoric sites to be considered within their landscapes. In addition to this, complementary landscape survey work has been published by RCHM staff for Cranborne Chase and south Wiltshire including the contrasting settlement patterns on the Nadder-Wylye Ridge (Corney 1989, 115-119), Nadder-Ebble Ridge (Fowler 1964, 46-57), Oxdrove Ridge (Rahtz *et al.* 1990, 1-49) and Cranborne Chase (Bowen 1990).

The Hod Hill and Maiden Castle evidence for a violent Roman Conquest of the Dorset environs was supported by new discoveries. The Lake Farm fortress near Wimborne Minster was found in 1959 and excavations at various times from 1960-81, together with geophysical survey, confirmed the first-century date and plan of the site (Field 1992, 32-44). In west Dorset, the Waddon Hillfort was extensively excavated from 1959-69 and also dated to the mid-first century (Webster 1979, 51-90).

On Cranborne Chase, excavations of two plough-damaged Iron Age sites took place in 1968 and 1972. Geoffrey Wainwright, who directed this work, wanted as complete a data set as possible. Previously, only part excavations of settlements outside of hillforts had taken place (Wainwright 1968; 1979).

Berwick Down, Tollard Royal was a kite-shaped enclosed settlement, severely affected by ploughing. In 1962, the Ministry of Works employed E. Greenfield to excavate trial trenches across the site. In 1965, the surviving earthworks, including the other enclosed and unenclosed settlement evidence farther north, were surveyed by RCHM. This was followed by ploughsoil stripping of the whole of the kite-shaped enclosure by JCB and total excavation of features within and around the site. Wainwright commented on the value of this methodology as it enabled the total recovery of available evidence for a farmstead established in the Durotrigan period and abandoned in the early Roman period (Wainwright 1968, 102-147).

In the summer of 1972, another plough-damaged enclosure was selected. Dr Wainwright chose the Gussage All Saints site because it was so closely comparable with Little Woodbury near Salisbury. Dr Bersu's 1938 excavations there had been very influential in developing Iron Age studies but had only examined about 40 per cent of the site (1940, 30-111). As with Berwick Down, Wainwright carried out a total excavation. The research revealed that the site had been occupied from the Early Iron Age to the first century AD, in contrast to Little Woodbury which had been abandoned 200 years earlier (Wainwright 1979). The ceramic study included petrological analysis and the ceramic chronological framework was supported by radiocarbon dates.

At this time five Roman villa sites were examined in various parts of Dorset: in 1967-85, Halstock in west Dorset (Lucas 1993); 1968-72 Bradford Down (Field 1982); 1968-84 Tarrant Hinton in east Dorset (Graham 2006); 1969-79 Dewlish in central Dorset (Putnam 1976); and 1976-91 Bucknowle in Purbeck (Light 2009). The excavation of these sites has revealed a pattern of continuity, seen elsewhere in southern Britain, where settlement sites are occupied from the Late Iron Age into the Romano-British period.

HENGISTBURY, CLEAVEL POINT AND THE MAIDEN CASTLE ENVIRONS

From 1979-84, Hengistbury Head was re-examined to bring modern analytical techniques to bear on the developmental sequence of the site and compare the results with the older collections. The work also sought to define the range of settlement structures, to evaluate the overseas contacts of the communities and to obtain data to determine changes to the environment throughout the Iron Age (Cunliffe 1987, 18). The published work demonstrates the range of imported material on the site, particularly Gallic pottery and coinage. The coins were significantly of the type attributed to the Durotriges, indicating that this was an important trading place for these coin users. However, the importance of the settlement seems to have declined in the Latest Iron Age (4).

In 1978, excavations took place at the coastal industrial site at Cleavel Point before an oil gathering station was erected. Here, evidence for a Late Iron Age port, comparable with Hengistbury Head, was found and was published with a review of industrial sites in the whole Purbeck area (Sunter & Woodward 1987). Further oil exploration in the north Purbeck heathland enabled fieldwork, excavation and a synthesis of past research in the area (Cox & Hearne 1991).

The advent of developer-funded archaeology in the 1980s gave rise to numerous new investigations but most significantly in the Dorchester environs. Late Iron Age and Roman cemeteries and settlements were discovered in 1984-87 at Allington Avenue, south of the town (Davies 2002) and in 1986-88, during the development of the Dorchester by-pass (Smith 1997). This body of information could be added to the data from the Poundbury industrial estate excavations. From 1966-82, the work on the east side of the Poundbury hillfort had revealed Iron Age occupation underlying an extensive Roman cemetery (Sparey-Green 1987).

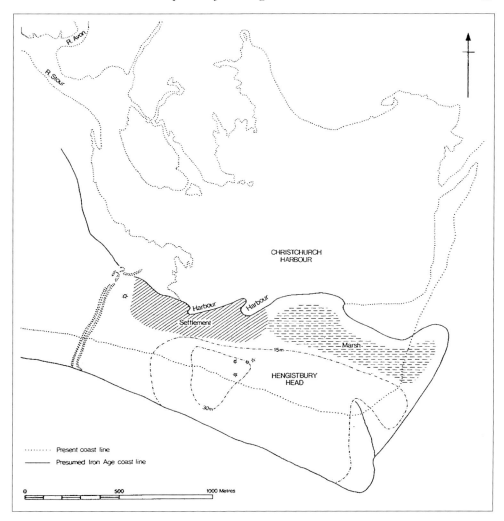

4 Plan of Hengistbury Head showing cross-dykes and settlement area. (Cunliffe 1987, 5)

These broader area research strategies led to investigations that placed sites within the context of their landscape. In neighbouring Hampshire, Barry Cunliffe's extensive excavations within Danebury hillfort were followed by research into the Danebury environs (Cunliffe 2000). This idea of looking beyond the boundaries of the hillfort was also adopted at Maiden Castle, where from 1985-86 some of Mortimer Wheeler's trenches were reopened and cut back to enable new samples to be taken for analysis. The research design highlighted three areas of enquiry. Primarily it was to increase understanding of the changing environment at Maiden Castle from the Neolithic to the Roman period. Secondly, to determine the Iron Age cultural sequence within the hillfort and lastly, to concentrate on understanding the development of the east gate where Wheeler had found an Iron Age cemetery. Following on from the excavation was a landscape survey considering all the available evidence of the Maiden Castle environs using fieldwalking, aerial photographs and geophysical survey (Sharples 1991).

From 1985-91, Niall Sharples considered the available evidence for the Durotriges. His summary of the distribution of Iron Age burials in Dorset and other indicators for Durotrigan identity is particularly significant because it highlighted the differences between areas within the traditional Durotrigan tribal area (1990, 90-93).

In south Somerset, extensive survey work with excavation has taken place at Ilchester (Leach 1982, 1993) and Ham Hill (RCHME 1996; McKinley 1999). These projects have given some consideration to the setting of these places within their landscape but not on the scale of the South Cadbury Environs Project. This research programme began in 1993 with the aim of understanding the chronological development of settlement around the hillfort. South Cadbury lies at the centre of the 10km by 10km study area and the research design included fieldwalking, geophysical survey and targeted excavation. The work continues, and regular articles and bulletins have provided information on the progress of the research (Tabor 2004). Of particular interest are the ceramic distribution maps that indicate the changing influence of South Cadbury within its landscape.

Work is also continuing on Cranborne Chase, where a reappraisal of the prehistoric archaeology took place in the 1980s (Barrett, Bradley & Green 1991) and Chase resident, Martin Green, has continued to involve archaeologists in the investigation of his farm and the surrounding area (Green 2000).

THE SIGNIFICANCE OF THE ARCHAEOLOGICAL RESOURCE

The above selection of the significant research within the Dorset environs emphasises how unusual it is in archaeological terms. There is nowhere in Britain that can boast this level of published Iron Age material. The data sets from Gussage All Saints, South Cadbury, Maiden Castle and Hod Hill are frequently referred to in national reviews of the Iron Age. If there is an opportunity to describe a region in the British Isles and to define the communities within it, as suggested by Niall Sharples (1990a, 93), then the Dorset environs must surely be the place to start. Previous archaeologists, in writing about their Iron Age sites, have concluded their narratives by linking the new evidence with the accepted regional interpretation. This has usually confirmed previous ideas of the Late Iron Age and particularly the Durotriges. The post-processional approach of South Cadbury (Barrett, Freeman & Woodward 2000) is an exception to this but the analysis is generally Cadbury specific and only touches on the regional context of the hillfort.

Since the publication of most of the sites listed above, the old tribal labels have been increasingly criticised. Local variations between communities have been considered instead and the concept of 'regionality' is now discussed. This is one of the key elements of 'Understanding the British Iron Age: an Agenda for Action' (Haselgrove *et al.* 2001). The 'Agenda' encourages the understanding of difference and calls for 'regional syntheses'.

New Archaeological Research

In embarking on this Iron Age research, the author followed the path of many previous researchers into the Dorset environs. This involved looking in detail at a specific geographical area and then considering the settlement pattern in relation to the previously perceived whole. However, as already noted, Badbury now forms one of seven comparative study areas.

I worked on some of the projects described above but my main contribution to Dorset Iron Age archaeology began in 1986 with a historic landscape survey for the National Trust's Kingston Lacy and Corfe Castle Estates. The survey's main purpose, using fieldwork and documentary study, was to record the significance of this archaeological resource. The completed reports provided recommendations for good conservation management of the sites and monuments on Trust land.

As this work progressed, the prehistoric landscape began to be appreciated in a way that hitherto had not been possible. The Bankes family, who had bequeathed Kingston Lacy to the National Trust in 1983, had not encouraged access to their land and archives for research. For this reason, Badbury Rings, at the centre of the Estate, remained the largest hillfort in Dorset where no excavations or detailed survey had taken place.

There had been some research, including work on the Iron Age and Romano-British settlement at Bradford Down north of Badbury (Field 1982). Local archaeologist Norman Field had also discovered smaller settlements at Barnsley and Lower Barnsley, east of Badbury, and had reported the discovery of Roman fort at Crab Farm, south-west of Badbury in 1976 (Field 1976, 280).

In 1988, a BP oil pipeline crossed the Kingston Lacy Estate and unexpectedly cut through a major Iron Age settlement. This lay on the west side of Kingston Lacy Park, south of Sweetbriar Drove.

In 1990, fieldwalking beside the Crab Farm fort site revealed extensive occupation debris, and subsequent geophysical survey and targeted excavation have revealed the plan of a small Romano-British town overlying an Iron Age settlement (Papworth 2004).

By 1998, the National Trust wardening staff had cleared the scrub from the interior of Badbury Rings thus uncovering numerous earthworks. This enabled RCHME surveyor Martin Fletcher to plan these settlement remains and for subsequent geophysical surveys to be carried out.

South-west of Badbury, small-scale excavation had taken place in 1900 and 1952. At that time no structures were found but parch marks seen in the area during dry summers indicated building footings. Geophysical survey and excavation revealed the site to be a Romano-Celtic temple overlying a Late Iron Age site where numerous Durotrigan-type coins have been found (Papworth 2000, 148-150).

It was at this point, in late 2000, that the National Trust agreed to fund a PhD to link together these pieces of research for eventual publication. Since that time, the three large Iron Age settlements within 2km of Badbury Rings have been surveyed using the Trust's resistivity meter and fluxgate gradiometer. Geophysical survey also took place within Badbury Rings followed by small-scale excavations.

In west Dorset, the National Trust had acquired Pilsdon Pen with its abandoned spoil heaps. David Thackray had supervised the levelling of the spoil combined with some additional excavation before the site was returfed (Thackray 1983, 178-179). In addition RCHME had carried out an earthwork survey there for the Trust and some geophysical survey had also taken place. An excavation had been carried out at Lambert's Castle and a landscape survey had looked in detail at the Golden Cap Estate. Little information is currently available for the Iron Age archaeology of west Dorset and therefore this information provides a valuable additional resource.

The opportunity was taken to carry out additional work in Purbeck and analyse information gathered during the Corfe Castle Estate historic landscape survey. Most significant was the geophysical survey and excavation at Norden, north of the Corfe gap, where an Iron Age temple complex was identified following the discovery of Durotrigan coins (Woodward 2006).

Finally, Dave Stewart has surveyed the interior of Hod Hill with a fluxgate gradiometer and created a remarkable plan of the settlement to complement the central Dorset study area (Stewart 2006). This has been combined with survey and excavation work along the Iwerne valley to reveal something of the relationship between the valley floor and hilltop settlements.

To summarise, for four of the study areas, significant new fieldwork has been assembled to add to the information that has already been published or lies within developer-funded 'grey' reports or research dissertations. The task ahead is to bring together this evidence from various sources and seek to determine the similarities and differences between Iron Age communities within the Dorset environs.

Before each of these areas is examined, the next chapter will consider how the Durotriges have been defined in archaeological literature and the types of evidence that have been used to create the 'tribe' and its boundaries.

4

THE DUROTRIGES AS AN ARCHAEOLOGICAL CREATION

In Chapter Two, it was shown that at least one *civitas Durotrigum* existed in the Roman period and that historians and archaeologists have fixed their attention on this named group and created a back-projection. They have attributed the distribution of distinctive, Late Iron Age artefacts to a pre-Roman Durotrigan 'tribe' and defined a tribal area.

Inscribed Coins, Uninscribed Coins and Coinless Societies

Books dealing with Late Iron Age Britain will provide a map showing tribal areas. These boundaries are based on coin and pottery distributions using the names provided by classical sources. As discussed above, they were Roman *civitates*, and archaeologists have assumed they were distinct pre-conquest entities. The 'tribal' boundaries tend to be drawn along rivers or other distinct topographical features that are most likely to have acted as borders near the limits of artefact distributions.

Geographically, it is probably not surprising that in the late second century BC it was the south-east of England that adopted coinage first and contains the best examples of continental ways of living. Barry Cunliffe suggested a model comprising three zones that illustrated the diminishing effect of Roman contact from south-east to north-west (Cunliffe 1991, 130-198).

The peoples of the south-east corner of England, west to Hampshire, north to Oxfordshire and north-east to Norfolk, are described as comprising the 'core zone'. It is in this area that the highest levels of political and economic development can be demonstrated, particularly in the way coinage was used.

Fringing this area to the north and west from Lincolnshire to Dorset, were groups that produced distinctive coins. They differed from the core area peoples in being less altered in their settlement structure and social organisation, either because of deliberate resistance to change or because distance slowed the effect of change. This second area is known as the 'periphery'.

The communities further north and west, Cunliffe placed in a zone termed 'beyond'. These groups did not produce their own coinage and this area contains much less archaeological evidence to indicate social change to distinguish Late Iron Age communities from those of the Early and Middle Iron Age.

Therefore, according to this model, Dorset and land to the north were part of the 'periphery'; land east of Dorset was in the core zone and the area to the west lay 'beyond'.

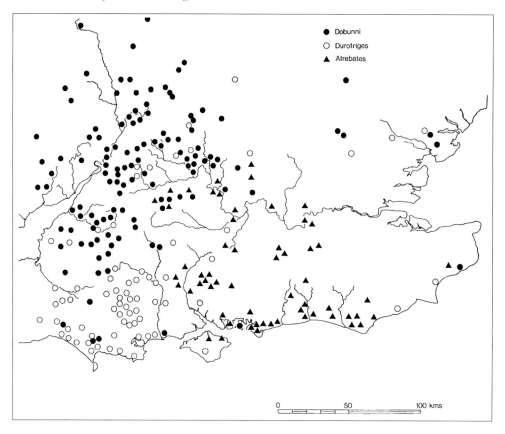

5 Distribution of coins attributed to Atrebates, Dobunni and Durotriges. (Sellwood 1984, 192)

Coin and pottery distribution patterns provide evidence for these three divisions in the areas surrounding the Dorset environs.

To the east and north-east are found coins attributed to the Atrebates and pottery types known as Yarnbury-Highfield and Southern Atrebatic Wares. To the north is the coin zone attributed to the Dobunni, with pottery types known as South Western Decorated and Savernake Wares. To the west is an area where coins were not produced and pottery is sparse, although East Devon Sandy Ware and other types of South Western Decorated Ware are found there. Devon and Cornwall are lumped together to form a Dumnonian tribe based on the Roman *civitas* which had its capital at Exeter (*Isca Dumnoniorum*). Three other *civitates* are known. To the east, the Belgae with their capital at Winchester (*Venta Belgarum*) are thought to be a Roman sub-division of the Atrebates. This group had its *civitas* capital to the north at Silchester (*Calleva Atrebatum*). The Dobunnic *civitas* capital was at Cirencester (*Corinium Dubunnorum*).

Lyn Sellwood (1984, 191-204) showed these zones of usage by plotting where various types of coins have been found (5). Her maps show distribution patterns for coins attributed to the three south-west coin producing communities: the southern series or Atrebatic coins, the western series or Dobunnic coins and the south-west series or Durotrigan coins. This exercise produced distinctive concentrations of coin types and indicated comparative contact between groups.

The western series coinage covers the area of modern Gloucestershire, Worcestershire and north Somerset, extending into parts of Wiltshire and Oxfordshire. This Dobunnic coinage was more static than the Romanised inscribed coins of the southern series/Atrebatic area, but from the late first century BC, some Dubunnic coins were inscribed with named people. The Durotrigan coins do not include the names of rulers and this has led to speculation that there was no supreme leader in their distribution zone.

Lyn Sellwood's distribution map (1984, 192) shows Dobunnic coins within the Durotrigan area and Durotrigan coins within the Dobunnic, but few Atrebatic coins have been found in these zones. This apparent north-south exchange of coinage contrasts with the lack of evidence for exchange from east to west. Although the Dobunnic and Durotrigan issues seem originally to have been influenced by the coins of Atrebatic type, by the Latest Iron Age this influence appears to be minimal. The north to south trade route is supported by analysis of over 3000 coins from the large coastal settlement at Hengistbury Head. The majority of coins found on this site are Durotrigan. Of the non-Durotrigan coins, 20 are Dobunnic and 35 are from communities that inhabited the coasts of Normandy and Britanny (6).

This north to south corridor can be seen to continue into the Roman period. When the distribution of Black Burnished pottery distribution is plotted, clear links with the coastal settlements of Normandy and Brittany are shown, particularly in the areas of the

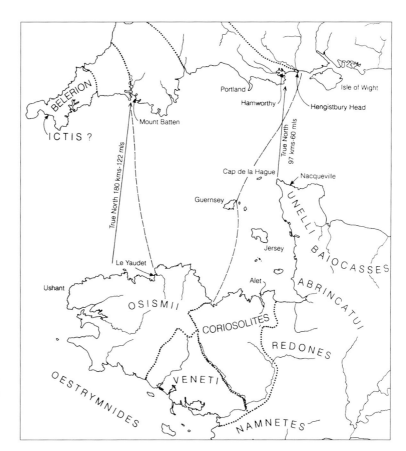

6 Suggested boundaries between named Armorican groups and trade routes to southern Britain (Cunliffe and de Jersey 1997, 52)

Baiocasses Arbrincatui and Coriosolites. The coins from these three groups and the Osismii and Namnetes of Britanny are found at Hengistbury Head. The coins attributed the Coriosolites are most numerous (Sellwood 1987, 138-139).

PERAMBULATION OF THE DUROTRIGAN ZONE

The following brief tour around the Durotrigan zone is based on distribution maps of finds like those described above. The boundaries archaeologists have drawn around a Durotrigan territory vary and in some places are derived from meagre evidence.

South Boundary

The south boundary is the coast and may include the Isle of Wight. On the mainland it includes the trading settlement of Hengistbury and further west the industrial sites of Poole Harbour and Purbeck. At Portland and around Weymouth Bay, finds of exotic coins suggest that another important trading port awaits discovery there. The Bridport area and West Bay mark the western limit of coastal occupation sites containing artefacts attributed to the Durotriges.

West Boundary

The west boundary for the Durotriges tends to be drawn either along the line of the River Axe in Devon (Cunliffe 1991, 201) or along the Dorset border from Lyme Regis (Frere 1978, 13). However, it will be seen from the study of this area (see Chapter Seven) that Durotrigan pottery and coinage is rarely found this far west. Perhaps archaeologists have drawn the boundary there because of the long historical link between Dorset and the Durotriges.

North-west Boundary

The evidence for Iron Age settlement activity is also sparse for north-west Dorset but becomes more concentrated in south Somerset around Ilchester, Ham Hill and South Cadbury. The geography of this area sets it apart from the Marshwood Vale of west Dorset and the chalkland surrounding Dorchester. The rivers Yeo, Parrett, Tone and Brue drain north-west towards the Bristol Channel rather than south-east into Poole and Christchurch harbours. The change between two different watersheds coincides with a change in the archaeological signature of their Late Iron Age populations.

The Somerset Levels lie north of Ham Hill, bounded by the high ground of the Quantocks to the south-west and the Mendips to the north-east. The River Parrett follows the foot of the Quantocks and the Brue runs beside the Mendips, both converging and flowing into the Bristol Channel near Bridgewater. This corridor of land was the subject of a survey of Iron Age settlement sites (Miles 1969, 17-55) which highlighted the sudden decline of South Western Decorated Ware in this area and its sudden replacement with Durotrigan pottery in the last decades before the Roman Conquest.

Barry Cunliffe (1991, 159) suggested that the pottery evidence indicated that the Durotriges had a narrow outlet to the Bristol Channel in the Latest Iron Age. The distribution map of ceramics found in this area supports this and the results from the excavation at

Westonzoyland uncovered Late Iron Age pits containing South Western Decorated Ware that pre-dated the Durotrigan pottery from the site.

Two areas of settlement, at Meare (Gray & Bulleid 1948), and 5km south-east of them, at Glastonbury (Gray & Bulleid 1911 & 1917) were found in waterlogged conditions on the Somerset Levels beside the River Brue. The preserved wooden artefacts from these sites include bowls decorated in the same styles as the South Western Decorated Ware. This ceramic style was found in the latest Glastonbury and Meare deposits but Durotrigan pottery was not found. These places are at the northern edge of the traditional Durotrigan zone but the suggestion that they acted as a market centre between the Dobunni and Durotriges (Cunliffe 1991, 159) is unlikely as there is no evidence for significant Durotrigan influence at the time of their abandonment.

North-east Boundary

The landscape between Somerset and Wiltshire, approaching Warminster from the west, provides a clear impression of the topographic changes probably utilised by Iron Age communities as boundaries between groups. The chalk escarpment to the south dominates the lower lying land between Shepton Mallet and Frome. The chalk outlier of Cley Hill can be seen, and further along the escarpment the Westbury White Horse reveals the position of Bratton Camp hillfort on the western edge of Salisbury Plain.

Passing through Longleat Forest, overlooked by Cley Hill, one has the impression of a natural gateway into the Wylye valley and at this point an artefact distribution threshold is crossed. Although the Late Iron Age settlements to the north and north-west include Durotrigan coins and pottery, the finds there are predominantly of Dobunnic type. A good example of this is the Late Iron Age settlement at Camerton near Bath, where excavations have uncovered typical Dobunnic pottery and coinage.

At Warminster, the Wylye turns south-east into the chalkland, carving a 25km-long valley before it joins the River Nadder at Wilton and further east meets the rivers Avon, Bourne and Ebble at Salisbury. These united rivers continue south as the Avon for 40km as far as Christchurch Harbour and Hengistbury Head.

Jim Gunter (2004, 50) has plotted coins from all groups in south Wiltshire and south Somerset and demonstrated that the main river valleys, such as the Avon, Wylye and Stour, were key trade routes where exotic coin issues from distant groups are most likely to be found.

North of the Wylye and west of Salisbury and Yarnbury as far as Bath and Camerton, there is little ceramic evidence to indicate a boundary between the Dobunnic and Atrebatic zones. Barry Cunliffe examined pottery from north Somerset sites and concluded that the large bead-rimmed bowls and necked jars found there were quite unlike those of the Durotrigan area but closely comparable with the Atrebatic pottery. Therefore the north Somerset communities were influenced from the east but in time developed their own styles.

Philip de Jersey described an unusual group of Iron Age coins found north of the Wylye and he suggested that a separate group occupied the central Wiltshire area. Lyn Sellwood (1984, 202) suggested a 'Sub-Dobunnic zone here.

Finds of Durotrigan coins occurring separately or mixed with Dobunnic coin hoards are frequent enough in east Somerset and west Wiltshire to confirm the links between these two coin issuing groups.

East Boundary

South-west of Salisbury, Bokerley Dyke is a massive linear bank and ditch 30m wide and up to 3m high that marks the Dorset-Hampshire border. It is traceable for 6km, aligned north-west to south-east, with its ditch on the north-east (Hampshire) side.

Collin Bowen (1990) produced a careful survey and analysis of the archaeology around Bokerley Dyke and concluded that the dyke originated as a territorial divide in the Late Bronze Age-Early Iron Age and was subsequently modified at various times into the sub-Roman period. He compared the types of enclosure that were known on both sides of the dyke through fieldwork and aerial photograph analysis and concluded that there was a significant difference. Ovoid enclosures are present on both sides of the dyke but 'banjo', multiple ditches and linked paired enclosures or 'spectacles' only exist on the Dorset side.

Little excavation has been carried out north-east of the dyke, but the settlement change either side of Bokerley gives weight to Bowen's hypothesis that Bokerley formed a long standing boundary between Iron Age communities. This is supported by the similar 'sauce-pan pot' style Late Iron Age pottery from the settlements near Salisbury and the lack of Durotrigan coinage known from this area.

South of the hillfort of Whitsbury Castle Ditches, the Avon flows through the poorer heathland soils of Damerham, Edmonsham, Alderholt and Verwood. Collin Bowen's distribution map of prehistoric features demonstrates the concentration of field systems and settlements on the agriculturally prized chalk compared with the lack of archaeology on the tertiary soils further south. Evidence for settlement continues to be sparse down to the coast until the Stour and Avon flow into Christchurch Harbour. This is where the Iron Age port of Hengistbury Head became established.

East of Hengistbury and the River Avon is the New Forest. This is also an area of heath-land where few coins have been identified. It seems to have acted as buffer zone between the Atrebatic and Durotrigan distribution zones. This area as far as the Solent may have been part of a sub-Durotrigan group according to Lyn Sellwood.

This perambulation around the edges of the Durotrigan zone has demonstrated that archaeological evidence can be reinterpreted to create differences of definition and indicates that the boundaries were not static but changing during the Latest Iron Age.

Durotrigan Ethnicity

Early historians established the idea of the ethnic root for the people of Dorset. Their traditional romanticised image was of a proud independent race fighting bravely against the Roman invaders, but was there a distinct community with a clear identity?

In prehistoric archaeology, much has been lost from the original identity of a group of people. The essential definition that was once clear to a visitor, such as the stories the inhabitants told of themselves, their dances, songs and fashions cannot be recovered.

With the exception of waterlogged places, like the Meare and Glastonbury lake villages, most of the decorated wooden artefacts have gone, along with the leather objects, wicker work and the clothes people wore. The archaeologist is forced to rely on ceramics and metalwork.

Using these more durable materials, a sense of identity for Iron Age Dorset has been built around a Durotrigan nation and the review of its supposed boundaries has demonstrated this.

The challenge is to examine the archaeological record objectively and to determine local similarities and differences. The Iron Age inhabitants were probably as diverse as the geology of the county, but they may still have considered themselves linked to a communal concept. This could have been no more than a background consciousness, perhaps in the sense that the people of Bournemouth and Lyme Regis consider themselves to be part of Dorset rather than Hampshire or Devon.

CONFLICT AS EVIDENCE FOR DUROTRIGAN IDENTITY

The documentary source referring to Vespasian's campaign in the west has been quoted in Chapter Two. This historical evidence for a unified political power that opposed the Roman army is supported by archaeological discoveries in Dorset, Somerset and perhaps Wiltshire.

The people of this area do not seem to have capitulated easily and one might argue that each local leader co-ordinated the defence of his community as the Roman army moved west. The number of first-century conflicts represented in the archaeology of this area is nationally rare (Whimster 1981, 420-425) but this does not mean that all communities within the Durotrigan zone opposed the Romans. The evidence from Poole Harbour may suggest the collaboration or acquiescence of at least one group of people.

Finds from excavations at Maiden Castle, South Cadbury and Hod Hill indicate that first-century battles were fought at these places. Battle-scarred burials at Spetisbury Rings and Ham Hill and possibly from Battlesbury Camp, Wiltshire may also date to the conquest and subjugation period (AD 43-61). Some of this evidence has been reinterpreted and it is difficult to provide an exact date for the conflicts represented by the remains.

In south Somerset, the South Cadbury 'massacre deposit' is a good example of this. Previously, researchers had tried to link the remains with historical conflicts dated to AD 43-44, AD 47 or AD 60-61. When the excavation was finally published, the analysis of the deposits provided an earlier first-century date. However, Ann Woodward concluded that the archaeological evidence enabled key questions to be asked but could not link the massacre to a specific historic event:

> We have covered many issues in our detailed contextual studies of the deposits in the gateway. These relate to how the gate was attacked, how the occupants of the hillfort attempted their defence, how the bodies of both factions might have been treated immediately after the assault, how and why the deposited remains may have been reworked or displayed, why the deposits were sealed with such care, and how the aggrandised entrance passage was constructed over these remains. Such questions as these surely are the principal subject matter of our enquiry. We are glimpsing the actions of people undertaken in the face of disaster, mourning and glorification in the aftermath of internecine conflict. The exact moment within the 1st century AD when this stage of stress may have occurred is not only unknowable; it is largely irrelevant. (Woodward 2000, 116)

The ideal would still be to gain an exact date for the massacre deposits if it was possible, and in rare circumstances it is achievable. For example, dendrochronology has recently provided a construction date of AD 44 for the first-phase Roman fort at Alchester, Oxfordshire. However, in the absence of waterlogged timber deposits such fine dating is currently unavailable for South Cadbury.

In east Dorset, the mutilated skeletons found in the ditch of Spetisbury hillfort are also difficult to link to the Roman Conquest. Some finds from the ditch filling are Middle Iron Age and others are typical of the Saxon period.

The combined archaeological evidence for community defence within the Dorset environs indicates a cultural cohesiveness that led Niall Sharples (1990b) to suggest that certain industries were established within the territory to act as tribal emblems to unify the various peoples of the confederacy. Can the type and distribution of the material evidence define a Durotrigan homeland?

Traditional Archaeological Definition of the Durotriges

The archaeology of the Durotriges was analysed by J.W. Brailsford (1957, 118-121). He listed six types of evidence that could be used to define the Durotrigan 'culture'. These were pottery, metalwork (particularly brooches and swords), coins, farmsteads, burials and hillforts.

From Brailsford's identifying characteristics, four have been generally termed Durotrigan in subsequent archaeological publications and therefore before considering any other distinguishing characteristics they deserve a closer examination.

Durotrigan Pottery

The ceramic evidence is an important dating tool but it is generally not refined enough to determine the transition from latest pre-Roman to the earliest Roman period. The fabrics and forms of pre-Roman and post-Roman products are indistinguishable (7). The influence of Poole Harbour pottery moves from its source to the periphery of the Durotrigan zone from the late Middle Iron Age to the Latest Iron Age. For example, in ceramic Phase 6E at Maiden Castle (fourth to second century BC) Maiden Castle-/Marnhull-style pottery with Poole Harbour fabrics amounted to 20 per cent of the group. By ceramic Phase 7 (first century AD), these fabrics accounted for 93 per cent of the assemblage (Brown 1991).

At South Cadbury, Poole Harbour pottery became dominant later than at Maiden Castle. 'Late Cadbury' encompassed both ceramic phases 9 and 10 to include the whole of the Romanisation process (Woodward 2000, 41-43). It has been suggested that the dominance of Poole Harbour Ware in south Somerset to the exclusion of other locally produced material was very late and only achieved around the time of the Roman Conquest (Woodward 2000, 218).

It has been argued that Durotrigan pottery was one of the means by which society was defined by the standardisation of a range of products (Sharples 1990b, 303) and therefore the distribution of Poole Harbour pottery demonstrates the range of Durotrigan political influence.

Lisa Brown (1997, 41) noted that the published literature includes over 40 Late Iron Age types produced in Wareham/Poole Harbour Ware, in contrast to the small group of principal forms identified by Brailsford. Copies of 'Belgic' forms derived from across the Channel and eastern Britain are noted, including tazze, butt beakers, cordoned cups and platters. Roman products were reaching the area before the Roman Conquest and therefore some Romanised forms of black burnished pottery may also be copies of these early imports.

This evidence indicates successful marketing, with the Purbeck potters willing to adopt new stylistic fashions and to know the requirements of their customers. One can speculate about the power and status behind the success but the evidence does not support a Durotrigan branding that promoted traditional native forms and excluded outside influences or new ideas, as advocated by Sharples (1990b, 303). He noted the lack of imported pottery at inland sites and suggested that Hengistbury, Cleavel and the Purbeck industrial sites were deliberately different and kept on the edge of the tribal area. Foreign goods were held at these ports but were largely excluded from the core zone. He suggested that imported commodities may have been transferred into Durotrigan vessels from Armorican containers at the ports, thus explaining the lack of imported pottery at prestigious sites like Maiden Castle and South Cadbury.

The first-century dominance of the Late Iron Age Purbeck pottery industry has been explained by noting the early adoption and use of the products of the industry by the Roman army. The rapid takeover of a successful industry may have been with the compliance of the producers, whose experience of Roman market potential and military strength may have persuaded them to capitulate easily.

Not all of the Durotrigan-style pottery was produced in Purbeck and certainly by the later first century petrological analysis has shown that Black Burnished Ware was being produced in kilns further west. Lisa Brown suggested that the ribbed bowl, Brailsford's type 1a, may derive mainly from kilns in the Exeter area.

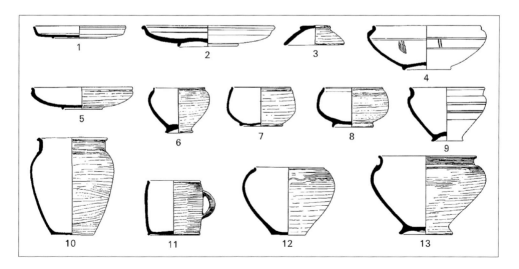

7 Examples of Durotrigan pottery, Cleaval Point and Hengistbury Head. (Sharples 1991, 124) *Copyright English Heritage*

To conclude, the Durotrigan pottery was being made mainly around Poole Harbour and imitated Roman and Belgic styles and it in turn was later imitated in kilns further west. It was made within the Durotrigan zone and its market success rather than its 'emblematic function' is likely to have enabled it to exclude other ceramic industries from the area and to form a sizeable percentage of ceramic assemblages from sites further north and east. However, its presence reveals political as well as economic contact and therefore implies social significance not only where it is found but where it is not found. Pilsdon Pen, west Dorset, is closer to Maiden Castle and Purbeck than South Cadbury, but at Pilsdon very little Poole Harbour Ware was recovered. Nevertheless, Poole Harbour pottery dominates the Latest Iron Age assemblages from South Cadbury. Therefore, pottery distribution does have the potential, when combined with other material remains, to define a cohesive identity.

DUROTRIGAN FARMSTEADS

The total excavation of an enclosed farmstead on Berwick Down, Tollard Royal, was described as a 'complete picture of a Durotrigan farmstead' (Wainwright 1968, 139). This was because unlike other farmstead sites on Cranborne Chase, like those at Woodcutts and Rotherley (Pitt Rivers 1887), the occupation at Tollard had shifted to a new site in the Romano-British period, leaving the Late Iron Age farmstead undisturbed by later features. Although the site had been heavily ploughed, the excavation revealed the plan of a kite-shaped enclosure of about 1ha within which was a round house and four granaries interpreted from arrangements of four to six post-holes. There were four irregular areas scooped out of the chalk described as 'working hollows' and 35 storage pits, some of which were cut into the 'working hollows'. Most of the occupation lay near the single enclosure entrance, which was on the south side. The northern 50 per cent of the enclosure contained few features and was interpreted as an area to hold livestock. The site was occupied for about 50 years in the first century AD and is comparable with other Latest Iron Age creations in the Durotrigan zone like that at Dorchester First School (Bellamy, Graham & Richards 1993, 152).

In contrast, other Durotrigan farmsteads evolved from earlier enclosed Iron Age sites that contained all the Durotrigan farmstead elements in the Early and Middle Iron Age. At Gussage All Saints farmstead, for example, the enclosure with its granaries round houses and storage pits was occupied for almost 500 years.

The pioneering work at Little Woodbury, Wiltshire (Bersu 1940, 30-111), clearly demonstrated the presence of similar enclosed Iron Age farmsteads outside the Durotrigan zone and the range of Iron Age farmsteads is demonstrated in regional surveys.

Ian Powlesland's (2004) work in classifying farmstead and settlement sites of the Bristol Avon region is an example of this. He identified 446 probable later prehistoric enclosures of which his largest group is rectilinear enclosures of Tollard Royal size under 1.5ha in area. However, there were also a range of other farmstead sized sites which included those with multiple enclosures, ovoid enclosures (including the distinctive 'banjo' enclosures) and also unenclosed sites.

Therefore the definition is no longer used because it is difficult to distinguish Durotrigan farmsteads from other farmsteads outside the Durotrigan zone.

Nevertheless, there is a Latest Iron Age phase of new enclosed farmsteads on 'green field' sites to which Tollard Royal and Dorchester First School belong. These contain ceramic assemblages that are almost exclusively from Poole Harbour.

DUROTRIGAN BURIAL

Rowan Whimster's book on burial practice in Iron Age Britain (1981, 37) includes a chapter devoted to the Durotrigan burials of south Dorset. The area is exceptional in representing a distinct regional sub-tradition of funerary practice. This form of crouched inhumation burial emerged in the last decades of the first century BC and continued to the end of the first century AD. Many of the Durotrigan burials found around Dorchester are dated to the mid to late first century AD and therefore this native tradition appears to be most visible following the Roman Conquest.

A typical Durotrigan burial (*8*) was deposited in a shallow oval earth grave or more rarely (but particularly in Purbeck and Portland) within a cist lined with stone slabs. The body was usually placed in a crouched position on its right side with the head to the east and often the burials were grouped into cemeteries like those found at the east gate of Maiden Castle and Jordan Hill near Weymouth. Another important element of these unusual burials is the provision of grave goods, suggesting individualism and belief in an afterlife. Chambers (1978) showed that there were no grave goods in almost half the adequately recorded burials. In the remainder, joints of meat and pottery were most common with other items occasionally being included.

The pottery vessels, as might be expected, were usually items manufactured around Poole Harbour, particularly bead rimmed bowls and handled tankards but a variety of forms are

8 Durotrigan burial at Poundbury with pottery vessels and joints of meat. (Woodward 1993, 7) *Copyright Dorset County Museum*

found. Occasionally imported Samian Ware and Gallo-Belgic Ware were included.

The joints of meat were usually pork, mutton or beef and Chambers (1978) stated that while sheep bones have been found equally with both male and female burials, pig bones tended to be placed in female graves and cattle in male. However, in a group of 12 burials found at Allington Avenue, Dorchester, bones of pig and domestic fowl were included in both male and female graves.

Personal items were deposited with some inhumations, like the gaming counters found at Pins Knoll, Litton Cheney. The range of grave goods can indicate ranking and status within society. For example, the grave goods of a woman found buried at Portesham included a decorated bronze mirror, three brooches, a toilet set, a bronze strainer, an iron knife, a ribbed bead rim bowl, a high shouldered jar and joints of mutton and pork. The grave of a man was excavated within a small Durotrigan grave group of 11 inhumations from Whitcombe near Dorchester (see *22*, page 81). The grave goods included a sword, a scabbard mount, iron and copper rings, iron spearhead and iron file and a copper alloy brooch. Warrior burials have been found on the Channel Islands but they are rare in Dorset.

Durotrigan burials are distinctive, but are concentrated in south Dorset (*9*). Crouched burials associated with settlements but without grave goods have been found at Tollard Royal, Rotherley and Woodyates. Although Niall Sharples included them as part of this group, Rowan Whimster classified them as pit burials typical of this Cranborne Chase area. However, more recently a crouched Late Iron Age burial in a shallow oval grave, typical of the south Dorset type, has been found at Tarrant Hinton in east Dorset. It is unclear whether crouched inhumations without grave goods like this example can be considered as outliers of the Durotrigan form of burial. Other examples include Perrott Hill School, south Somerset and Tinney's Lane, Sherborne. Records from Purbeck and Tolpuddle indicate changes to the normal Durotrigan burial practice east and north of the core area. Outlying burials tend to exclude joints of meat from the graves. There were certainly individualised forms of south Dorset burial, for example the body found with an array of animal bones placed around the skull near the shrine at Portesham, west of Weymouth.

The Late Iron Age Durotrigan form of burial seems to have British origins. Rowan Whimster looked for continental parallels and compared inhumations found in Brittany and the Channel Islands to those found in Dorset but these tend to be extended burials rather than crouched. The closest parallels lie in Devon and Cornwall where crouched inhumations in stone-lined cists have been found in cemeteries such as Stamford Hill, Harlyn Bay and Trethellen Farm near Newquay and above Mount Batten near Plymouth. These also have grave goods although most of the discoveries at these sites took place in the nineteenth and early twentieth centuries and were poorly recorded. Their date range extends from the Middle Iron Age until the end of the first century AD and therefore they originate well before the emergence of Durotrigan burials. Whimster concluded that the comparable burials in Dorset were local inventions but there may have been influence from the west. The contact between Dorset and Devon is clearly demonstrated at Mount Batten, a site that was a port with coin evidence for trade with Armorica, Cornwall, Dorset and Somerset.

There is some evidence for the chronological development of this burial tradition around Dorchester. East of the town at Flagstones, pit burials were found to be interspersed with

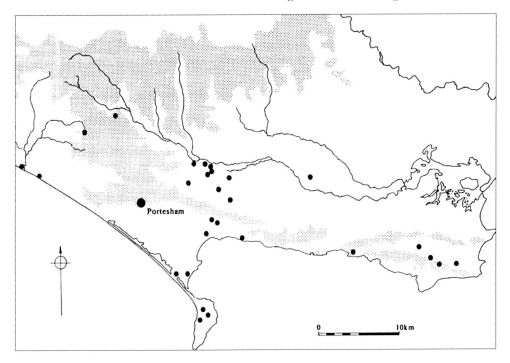

9 Distribution map showing Durotrigan burials. (Fitzpatrick 1996, 52) *Copyright Dorset County Museum*

unaccompanied burials in graves and one grave cut a pit containing a burial of possible first-century BC date. This indicated that, in this community, the transition from pit to grave burial occurred in that century. Burials accompanied by Durotrigan pottery and joints of meat were found at Max Gate and Allington Avenue and indicate a later extension of the Flagstones cemetery towards the east (Smith 1997, 291-292).

   Therefore, at the end of the Iron Age, south Dorset people were laid to rest as though asleep, apparently accompanied by food and drink and sometimes by special possessions. The finds indicate a belief in an afterlife that is not generally seen in contemporary burial practice elsewhere in Britain. Perhaps the south Dorset burials are evidence of a new religion or they may represent a reinterpretation of old ideas concerning eternity.

DUROTRIGAN COINAGE (*COLOUR PLATE 1*)

Of all the cohesive 'tribal' indicators, mapping the distribution of specific coin types is the most persuasive. By the mid-nineteenth century, a link had been made between certain types of pre-Iron Age coinage and the Durotriges (Evans 1864, 101-102; Warne 1872, 154). Following on from this early work, Derek Allen (1968, 43-57) brought together the coins found at Hod Hill in the nineteenth and twentieth centuries and used this opportunity to publish a general description and analysis of Durotrigan coinage, making comparisons with neighbouring coin producing areas. His work provides a base that has been developed by other specialists as new discoveries are made. In addition to Allen, Durotrigan coinage has been categorised by R.P. Mack (1953), Robert Van Arsdell (1989, 347-351) and Melinda Mays (forthcoming). However, as already noted, Colin Haselgrove (1994) has rejected the 'tribal' designation and renamed them 'south-western series' coins.

Few stratified Durotrigan coins have been found during archaeological excavations and therefore the precise dating of Durotrigan coin types is still difficult. However, the earliest coins contained gold and a high (80 per cent) silver content and the latest were of cast or struck bronze, the latter sometimes with a silver coating.

The Durotrigan coins were very conservative in design (*10*) and were originally based on Greek staters of Philip II of Macedon. The design was imported from the continent and had gradually changed as eastern British groups recast the coin. Gallo-Belgic coin types C and D had the most influence on the British coins, which in turn inspired the south-west series. Apart from stray finds, the earliest type of coin from Dorset is termed British B and is usually found in the Cranborne Chase area. Van Arsdell (1989b) categorised the British B coins as Durotrigan (V.A. 1205) but they have a distribution pattern centred on Wiltshire and Hampshire. He also considered British C (V.A. 1220), British D (V.A. 1215) and British O (V.A. 1225) coins as Durotrigan issues but other numismatists would not include them. Therefore amongst specialists there is disagreement over what a Durotrigan coin is. The earliest generally accepted Durotrigan issues are more closely comparable with British A, which also has a distribution centred to the east within Hampshire and Sussex (de Jersey 1996, 22). The British O coins, with a distribution pattern extending from the Solent as far as south-east Dorset, are thought to have been the prototypes for the smaller south-west issues known as quarter staters.

Melinda Mays divided the south-west series into three basic coin types: staters, quarter staters and 'starfish' coins. The earliest staters are of very pale gold and silver with more intricate designs than the later struck and cast bronze staters. The quarter staters also appear in several varieties and the earlier pale gold and fine silver examples were replaced by debased silver examples. The 'starfish' coins are named after the starfish-like design on these rare issues. They are smaller than a stater but larger than a quarter stater and are of two main types. The superior 'starfish' design is most common and both designs occur early in the south-west series.

On the basis of progressive debasement and weight loss of the Durotrigan coinage, Colin Haselgrove and Melinda Mays (2000, 249) divided the series into earlier and later coins. However, they are uncertain 'to what extent the later and cruder overlapped chronologically with the earlier and finer'.

The current difficulty in providing a close date for the earlier Durotrigan coins is demonstrated from two key groups, one ploughed up at Le Catillon, Jersey in 1957 and the massive find of about 850 coins from near Badbury Rings discovered by metal detectorists in 1983. Both were dispersed without archaeological recording.

Fitzpatrick and Megaw (1987, 44) analysed the various types of coins and associated finds and dated Le Catillon from between 56 BC and 20 BC. Van Arsdell (1989, 347-351) gathered the available information for the Badbury hoard and compared it with Le Catillon. He created a dated range for various types of early Durotrigan coins of stater, quarter stater and 'starfish' varieties and believed that the earliest Durotrigan staters (his Durotrigan A = British B) were produced from 68 BC. The other coins from the hoard (including examples

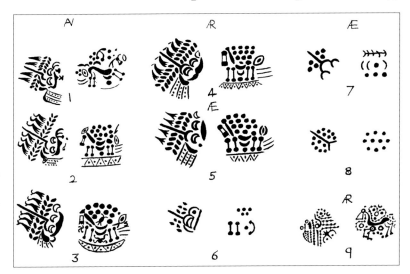

10 Proposed development of south-west uninscribed/ Durotrigan coin types.
1 Gallo-Belgic C (gold); 2 British A (gold); 3 British B (gold); 4 SW/ Durotrigan stater (silver); 5 SW/ Durotrigan stater (bronze); 6-8 Durotrigan cast bronze issues. (Allen 1961, 106)

of Van Arsdell Durotrigan E, G, H and I) were, he believed, minted at roughly five-year intervals with a declining percentage of silver content.

Van Arsdell's date for the Badbury hoard was 35-30 BC. Mays and Haselgrove (2000, 250) were more cautious, stating that while it is possible to place the very earliest coins around 50s-40s BC, there is no evidence to date the later issues:

> They may have been struck fairly soon after the finer ones or there may have been some gap in time: all that we can say for certain is that they have a wider date distribution than the finer coins, and that they were in circulation longer, occurring in Claudian and later contexts.

The distribution of the finer earlier coins lies within Cranborne Chase extending as far west as the River Stour, being found both at Hod Hill and Badbury and as far south as Corfe Common, Purbeck. The later issues have a wider circulation but apart from the Dorchester-Maiden Castle area the finds are noticeably sparser (*ibid.*, 249) (see *61*, page 175).

The best excavated groups of Durotrigan coins are from Maiden Castle, South Cadbury, Waddon Hill and Norden. However, at Waddon the coins were recovered from a Roman fort. The coin distribution in west Dorset and south Somerset, as with the pottery, has been affected by the use of this material by the Roman army. The context of coin discoveries generates doubt as to their original use, as many finds occur as hoards or as religious offerings at sacred sites like the temples at Corfe Common, Norden, Badbury, Bath and Hayling Island.

Niall Sharples suggested that by the early first century AD the common late bronze issues, like those found in great quantities at the port site of Hengistbury Head, were used by the Durotriges like Roman coinage. That is to buy and sell goods, and Sharples believed that their continued use into the Roman period supported this. However, Philip de Jersey (2000, 7) described a coin group found beside the Avon at Downton Wiltshire which included both cast Durotrigan bronze and worn second-century Roman coins. He questioned whether similar cast coins were produced in the Iron Age. He suggested that

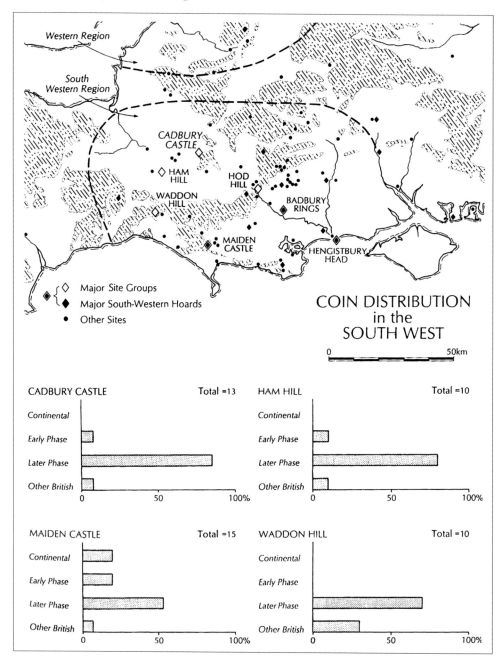

**COIN DISTRIBUTION
in the
SOUTH WEST**

0   50km

11 Coin hoards of the Dorset environs. (Haselgrove & Mays 2000, 249) *Copyright English Heritage*

the evidence from around Hengistbury Head, where they are most commonly found, indicated that they may not have been produced until the late first century. He wondered why they were apparently produced with the approval of the Roman authorities and what their use may have been.

Mays and Haselgrove suggested a three-phase progression of Durotrigan coinage (*11*). It began in Cranborne Chase, then was adopted in the Maiden Castle area, and finally it was used in south Somerset around the time of the Roman invasion. This can be compared with the gradual dominance of Poole Harbour pottery and supports the case for subdivisions within the Durotrigan zone and the progressive adoption of Durotrigan coinage and pottery from east to west.

Durotrigan?

These last four Durotrigan indicators have been described in more detail to highlight the elements of doubt surrounding their Durotrigan title.

Farmsteads may contain Durotrigan pottery and perhaps a Durotrigan coin, but apart from this they do not have distinctive Durotrigan attributes. Poole Harbour pottery was a successful product that dominated the market but although manufacture was centred around Poole Harbour, on the edge of the Durotrigan zone, it was not an emblem of native design promoted by powerful leaders to create a cohesive tribal identity. The Purbeck potters were not averse to extending their repertoire to include new design influences. Durotrigan burials are distinctive but limited in distribution, and Durotrigan coinage seems only to spread to the traditional limits of the Durotrigan tribal area shortly before the Roman Conquest. The Latest Iron Age distribution pattern may in part have been displaced by post-conquest coin usage by Roman soldiers. The occurrence of Iron Age and Roman coins found in the first-century forts at Hod and Waddon hills is evidence of their use by the Roman army.

Modern excavation reports still refer to Durotrigan burials but because of their restricted distribution within the area Colin Haselgrove, as with Durotrigan coinage, has removed the tribal label and renamed them 'Dorset tradition burials' (1994, 2).

Other types of distinctive find that might identify a Durotrigan site are the types of bone weaving comb which are concentrated in Dorset and Somerset and perhaps shale objects, but the distribution of neither of these artefact types is limited to the Durotrigan area. Finds of Iron Age shale radiate over 80km from its geological source at Kimmeridge in the Isle of Purbeck. Finished objects as well as rough-out bangles have been found in Glastonbury, Hengistbury, Danebury, the Channel Islands and northern France. Therefore, although always quarried and traded from the Durotrigan zone, shale does not identify a site as Durotrigan but as a place that had trade links with the area.

Bearing all this in mind, only coins and pottery can be used to define the Durotrigan zone and these can only be adopted with health warnings attached. All the other indicators, such as types and designs of manufactured objects, settlement morphology and burial rite, vary across the region. This variation gives a clear indication that the population was made up of differing groups of people. Nevertheless, their common coinage and the evidence

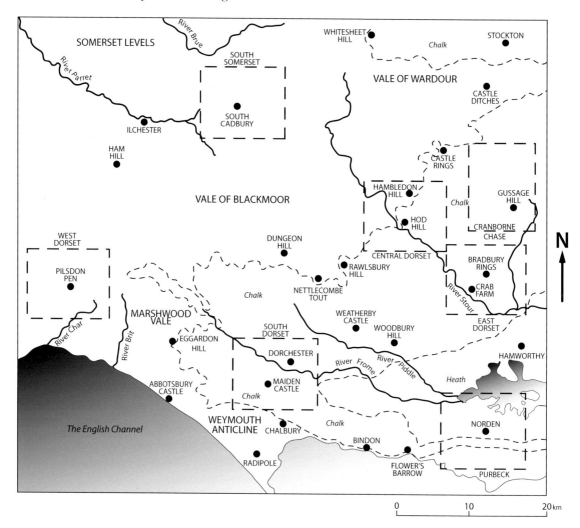

12 The Durotrigan zone, showing the seven study boxes and other prominent locales.

that most areas resisted the Roman invasion may indicate that, at least on the eve of the Roman invasion, the people of this area were linked economically and politically.

The following chapters are a tour of the landscapes of the Durotrigan zone (*12*). The survey starts at Hengistbury Head continues along the coast west to the Devon border and returns inland via south Somerset and Wiltshire. It then crosses Cranborne Chase to the Stour and heads south-east to Christchurch Harbour. Each chapter includes an 80 square kilometre study area, starting with the Isle of Purbeck (*colour plate 34*).

5

PURBECK AND POOLE HARBOUR

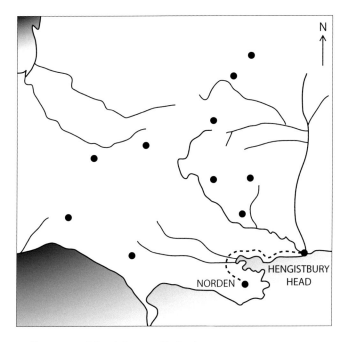

13 Tour map 1: Hengistbury to Purbeck.

SOUTH-EAST DORSET

Towards the south-east edge of the Durotrigan zone is Christchurch Harbour and Hengistbury Head, an important trading port for the area. The rivers Avon and Stour flow into the harbour, used as trade highways into the heart of Dorset and Wiltshire.

Hengistbury is flanked by the Isle of Wight and the Isle of Purbeck. The Iron Age coin finds across both of these places are dominated by south-western series/Durotrigan issues.

East of Hengistbury and the River Avon is the New Forest, which is heathland where comparatively few Iron Age sites have been identified. Similarly the heathland around Bournemouth, west of Hengistbury, contains little settlement evidence. There are numerous occupation sites along the Stour corridor and the coast around Poole Harbour.

The first hillfort along the Stour is at Dudsbury. It is bivallate and encloses about 3.5ha. Further along the Stour, to the north and west, settlement increases as the geology changes to chalk.

POOLE HARBOUR

The Hamworthy peninsula, on the north side of Poole Harbour, contains much evidence of Iron Age occupation. Excavations at various times from 1925-2006 have revealed Late Iron Age and first-century Roman coins and pottery on the east side of the peninsula, including the ditches of a probable harbour-side military base (see Chapter Eleven). Salt was produced here and the site was probably a port by the end of the Iron Age as sherds of various types of imported pottery have been found. These include early amphorae from Spain and Gaul and other pottery imports including Terra Nigra and Breton Black Cordoned Ware (Coles & Pine 2009, 63-98).

The rivers Frome and Piddle enter Poole Harbour from the west and between them is a coastal strip of land, east of Wareham, known as Bestwall. Extensive archaeological excavation in advance of gravel extraction has revealed many phases of occupation across the site (Ladle 2009).

Further west around Wareham, other Iron Age and Roman pottery production sites have been found. The rivers provided a route for producers, east to Poole Harbour or west to central Dorset and Maiden Castle. However, more important than the ease of transport was the diverse geology of the Isle of Purbeck that enabled this area to become an industrial centre during the Late Iron Age.

STUDY AREA 1: ISLE OF PURBECK

Peter Woodward (Sunter & Woodward 1987, 7) divided Purbeck into seven zones A-G, from the southern sea cliffs to the northern shores that form the south side of Poole Harbour; they are:

A   Kimmeridge shales
B   Portland/Purbeck limestone
C   Wealden clays
D   Chalk ridge
E   Eocene gravels and clays
F   Eocene gravels and clays (harbour edge)
G   River gravels

Topographic Description
The first 10km by 8km study area includes parts of Woodward's zones A-G. Its south-west corner touches the south coast of Purbeck at Kimmeridge Bay and its north-east corner includes Green Island and part of Furzey Island at the south edge of Poole Harbour.

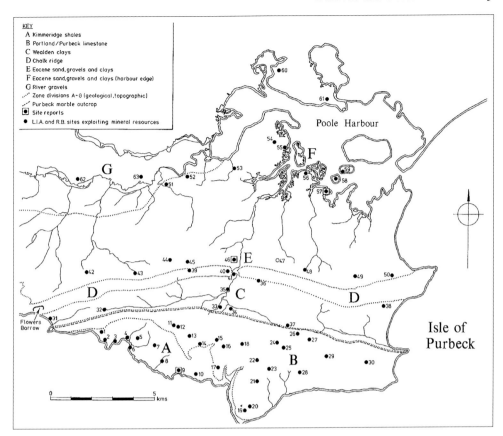

14 The Isle of Purbeck, showing topographic zones. (Sunter & Woodward 1987, 7) *Copyright Dorset County Museum*

Crossing the centre of the area from east to west is the chalk ridge of the Purbeck Hills which is cut near its centre by two streams, the Byle Brook and Wicken Stream. These flow either side of a natural mound of chalk now occupied by Corfe Castle (*colour plate 3*). On the north side of the ridge, the streams converge to form the Corfe River that meanders across the heathland and flows into Poole Harbour on the south side of the Middlebere peninsula.

The study box includes the north Purbeck coast south and west of Green Island which consists of a series of promontories and bays, including part of the Goathorn peninsula, Newton Bay, Cleavel Point, Fitzworth, Middlebere and the south side of the Arne peninsula. The north-west corner includes the section of the River Frome south-west of Wareham (*colour plate 2*).

Many Purbeck farms and settlements have names recorded in Domesday Book and were established near Romano-British and Iron Age sites. These places are sited at the harbour edge, for example Arne, Slepe, Middlebere, Ower, Wytch and Newton, or beside the rivers across the heath, such as Stoborough and Ridge near the Frome and Scotland Farm near the Corfe River. The heathland is characterised by poor agricultural soils and a poor water supply and therefore settlement is sparse.

A string of farms are found along the spring-line at the northern foot of the chalk ridge, for example Creech, Norden, Brenscombe, Rollington and Rempstone. However, the sunnier south side of ridge is the preferred spring-line, where villages like Steeple, Church Knowle and Corfe, and farms like Woolgarston, Ailwood, Knitson and Godlingston are sited.

On the south side of the Purbeck Hills there is good farmland. Here, the Wealden vale slopes up to the Purbeck limestone plateau. Farms and settlements lie across this area and particularly at the junction of the clays and sands of the Wealden beds and valuable limestone strata on the slope north of the plateau. The woodlands near Wilkswood, Downshay and Quarr farms all contain ancient evidence of quarrying where the Purbeck Marble and Burr stone beds outcrop.

The south-east corner of the study box is just north of the Purbeck limestone village of Langton Matravers but includes Kingston further west. In its south-west corner, the study area takes in the vale and village of Kimmeridge. Here, the oil-rich shales, for which it is famous, are exposed in the coastal cliffs.

Chronological Development

The distribution of known Iron Age and Romano-British sites in Dorset indicates that the Isle of Purbeck contains the greatest concentration of occupation in the county. This may partly be due to the conspicuous nature of the archaeological remains but it is also a reflection of the industrial value of the geological diversity of the area.

The salt industry produced enormous quantities of orange-red briquetage, the remnants of rough pottery containers used for evaporating brine. The Durotrigan and Black Burnished Ware potteries are evidenced by numerous sherds, many of them half finished and warped waste products of the industry. The hand-cut and lathe cores known as 'coal money' and broken armlets, trays and other products of the shale industry are frequently found across Purbeck and particularly around the geological source at Kimmeridge Bay. Evidence of the Purbeck limestone industries is less obvious although Purbeck Marble offcuts and half-finished *mortaria* are frequently encountered on archaeological sites.

The pattern of change of settlement north of the chalk ridge has been summarised by Peter Cox and Carrie Hearne (1991, 226-231), building on the chronological evidence derived from earlier excavations (Sunter and Woodward 1987, 6-8).

Although the heathland north of the ridge was occupied in the Early Bronze Age there is no settlement evidence from this area dating to Late Bronze Age and Early Iron Age. However, the environmental data from pollen analysis indicates that the land was not abandoned to become scrub woodland but remained rich in heathers and grasses. Therefore land management through grazing and controlled burning and cutting of scrub was being carried out by people who either commuted from sites further south or occupied sites north of the ridge that have not been recognised. Cox and Hearne suggest (1991, 228) that these settlement sites lie buried under colluvial deposits on the north spring-line of the ridge. However, they may have lived at a higher altitude as excavations in 1956-57 on the crest of the chalk ridge west of Corfe Castle at Knowle Hill revealed Early Iron Age occupation associated with a group of cross-ridge dykes. Another Early Iron Age site near the heathland lies beneath the Roman villa at Bucknowle. This was sited just south-west of the Corfe gap but the pottery evidence indicates that this was not established until towards the end of the Early Iron Age (Light and Ellis 2009, 173-174).

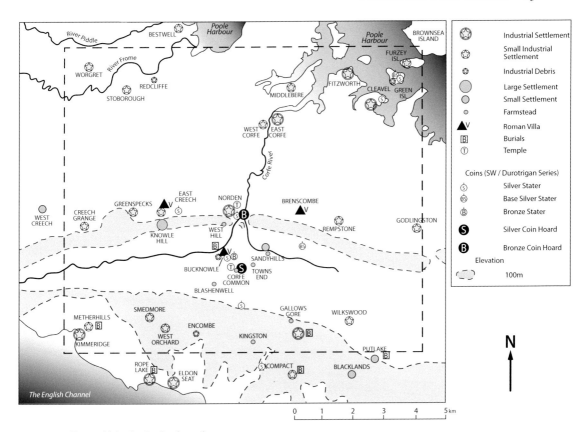

15 Sites within the Purbeck study area.

Most of the evidence for Early Iron Age activity is concentrated further to the south on the Purbeck limestone plateau. There have been finds of Early Iron Age pottery near the village of Kingston and at Blashenwell and Wilkswood farms but extensive settlement evidence was excavated at Gallows Gore near Worth Matravers. Bernard Calkin recorded features revealed during limestone quarrying and found remains of a hand-cut shale industry and of the 14 storage pits examined, 6 were dated to the Early Iron Age.

In the earlier twentieth century, the pottery from Iron Age Purbeck sites was described as belonging to A, B and C cultures. Iron Age B pottery is rarely identified, indicating a lack of evidence for settlement in the Middle Iron Age, but Bernard Calkin argued for continuity of settlement into the Late Iron Age at Gallows Gore. He believed that the Purbeck potters were conservative and insular and continued using similar styles until the Late Iron Age. Gallows Gore East lay only 300m away from the western site, with ceramic evidence suggesting a similar date range from *c.*800 BC until the Romano-British period.

Another pair of sites lie further south on the Purbeck limestone plateau beside the coastal cliffs. These are Eldon Seat, excavated by Barry Cunliffe, and Rope Lake Hole, excavated by Peter Woodward and his team. We lived in tents at the cliff edge for a few weeks in 1979 and in the evenings walked along the coast and across the fields to the Scott Arms at Kingston.

Occupation at Eldon Seat and Rope Lake Hole, like Gallows Gore, began about 2800 years ago and was continuous until the Roman Conquest. The ceramic sequences from these sites have been extremely valuable in determining local Iron Age chronologies. Peter Woodward (1987, 146) suggested that the sites with their field systems were organised and managed in tandem. Rope Lake Hole contained more evidence of industrial activity than the primarily agricultural Eldon Seat. Both sites continue to the cliff edge and Eldon Seat lies only 500m east of Rope Lake Hole. The original extent of these sites and their access to the shore is unknown because of subsequent coastal erosion but the importance of the proximity of the sea was revealed by increasing evidence for salt production found as briquetage in the Middle Iron Age deposits.

In 1993, David Hinton of Southampton University directed excavations just south of the study area at Compact Farm near Worth Matravers. This work confirmed the Early Iron Age settlement concentration on the limestone plateau. The site may have been abandoned in the Early Iron Age and then reoccupied in the Late Iron Age However, excavations from 2007-08 by the East Dorset Antiquarian Society have revealed that the settlement was larger than originally thought and Middle Iron Age occupation evidence may exist there. The finds included round houses with stone footings and stone-lined vertical sided pits with paved floors. One had a stone path leading to it and contained large amounts of Late Iron Age pottery, animal bone and worked shale. Nearby was a Late Iron Age crouched inhumation with a joint of pork placed on the person's knees.

North of the limestone plateau, evidence for Early Iron Age occupation is limited. At West Creech, west of the study area, at the foot of the north slope of the chalk ridge, Middle and Late Iron Age ceramics were associated with ditches, pits and post-holes. The excavation indicated occupation from the fourth century BC until the early first century AD. The site may have been continuously occupied but this was unclear from the small area of the settlement that was excavated. Bucknowle, just south of the Corfe Gap, became established slightly earlier than this.

About 2300 years ago, people moved north again. Settlements became established on the southern shore of Poole Harbour on the Fitzworth peninsula and on Furzey Island. At that time it was part of the mainland and linked to the Ower peninsula. Peter Cox and Carrie Hearne (1991, 229) suggested that these sites were established initially to enable an increase in salt production. The developing importance of this industry is indicated by the briquetage evidence found at Rope Lake Hole on the limestone plateau. The colonisation of land on the heathland on the west side of the Corfe River at the end of the Middle Iron Age was thought to have taken place as an expansion inland from the initial Poole Harbour coastal settlements.

A number of new settlements were established from the first century BC, by which time external trading contacts had become well established with northern France. The evidence for this is increasing amounts of Armorican pottery and Mediterranean amphorae found at places like Cleavel Point and neighbouring Green Island. The central Purbeck industrial site at Norden, on the north side of the Corfe gap, may also have been established at this time as metal-detected hoards of Durotrigan coins indicate a Late Iron Age significance for this site.

In 2006, Peter Woodward organised an excavation and we carried out geophysical survey based on these finds (*17*). This identified the site of a Late Iron Age temple within concentric ditched rectilinear enclosures 60m across. A foundation burial of Durotrigan pottery, coins, two spearheads and other iron metalwork was deposited within the construction trench of the 4m square central stone temple building.

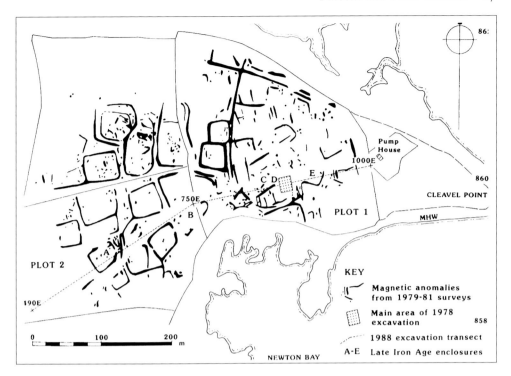

16 Cleaval Point plan of geophysical anomalies. (Cox & Hearne 1991, 71) *Copyright Dorset County Museum*

A group of Durotrigan coins was also found beside wall foundations on the highest part of Corfe Common overlooking the site of the Bucknowle settlement. This would be another good site for a temple as numerous Roman coins have been found here and these indicate that coin offerings continued to be made at the site until the end of the fourth century. The Durotrigan coins from the common had a high silver content compared with those at Norden which were copper alloy staters, while the six Celtic coins found on the Bucknowle settlement included both high silver content and predominantly bronze issues.

In 1978, as newly qualified archaeologists from Weymouth College, we helped Peter Woodward excavate some evaluation trenches in advance of oilfield development works by BP. This revealed the large Late Iron Age and Roman industrial trading settlement at Cleaval Point (*16*). One evening we walked to the end of the harbourside promontory and looked at the strange causeway beneath the water that extends out towards Green Island. A similar causeway extends from Green Island towards Cleaval. In 2001, the longer Cleaval Point structure was examined by Bournemouth University staff and students. This revealed an earlier origin for trade here than had previously been considered. The causeway was discovered to be a sophisticated construction of timber, gravel, sand and limestone and is now interpreted as a mole to enable boats to shelter behind and unload cargoes on to a quay. It may also have acted as a security barrier guarding access through this channel. The timber piles for the causeway structure provided a radiocarbon date of *c.*250-200 BC (Markey, Wilkes & Darvill 2002, 7-11).

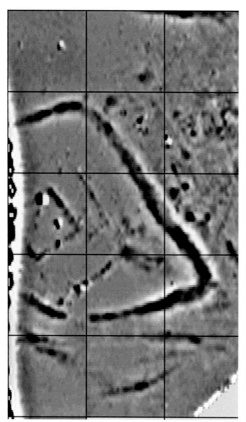

Norden Romano-Celtic temple complex. Plots
divided by 20m grids.
Left 17a Fluxgate gradiometer survey.
Below 17b Resistivity survey (site of 5m square
stone temple footings second row down, left square).

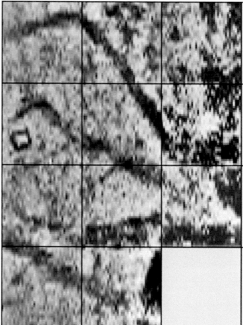

Cleavel Point and Green Island with Fitzworth, East of Corfe River, Middlebere and
Shipstal Point, produced large quantities of salt, pottery and shale items during the Iron
Age. The influence of Purbeck and Poole Harbour pottery production is revealed when
contemporary sites are excavated in the wider Durotrigan area. When the relative proportions of pottery fabrics are analysed it becomes clear that local pottery production declined
as a result of the increasing adoption of Poole Harbour products.

The continued success of the Purbeck industries following the Roman Conquest and
the lack of evidence for military occupation may suggest that the population embraced
the opportunities of expanded economic markets. Purbeck pottery has been found in
the Dorset Roman forts at Waddon Hill and Hod Hill; also Purbeck Marble was used in
the temple of Claudius in Colchester before AD 60 (Allen & Fulford 2004). Nevertheless,
there seems to be evidence for a shift in the Purbeck settlement pattern by the end of
the first century. By this time some settlements around the edge of Poole Harbour had
been reduced in size or abandoned. For example, parts of the settlements of East of Corfe
River and Cleavel Point reverted to arable agriculture for a time (Cox & Hearne 1991,
228-230). These Late Iron Age settlements had a distinctive system of contiguous rectilinear ditches presumably marking allotments of land for households (*16*). These boundary
ditches were backfilled around the time of the Roman Conquest and this is seen at

other sites within the Durotrigan zone where there is a similar settlement plan (e.g. Bradford Down and Sweetbriar Drove near Badbury, also Barton Field, Tarrant Hinton – see Chapter Eleven).

However, the large settlement north of the Corfe gap at Norden developed after the conquest. It grew as an industrial centre producing objects of shale, mudstone, Purbeck Marble and also chalk tesserae and pottery. Around Norden, three villas developed which were all about 2km from the settlement and each may have evolved from Late Iron Age sites. This is certainly true of the large Bucknowle villa on the south side of the ridge and probably also for East Creech that lies on the spring-line to the west. Brenscombe villa, east of Norden, is only known from the chance discovery of mosaics associated with sherds of pottery that dated the building to the second to fourth century. Deeper excavations would be needed to discover the origin of the site.

It has been suggested (Cox & Hearne 1991, 232) that the industrial wealth of Purbeck was taken away from the area and therefore it may have been part of an imperial estate with local officials managing production for the emperor. The contract for Purbeck to supply pottery to the Roman army is revealed by the concentration of Black Burnished Ware along the northern military frontiers of Britannia. This near monopoly of coarse ware pottery for the army was surely very lucrative. It has been argued that the size of the villas indicates that their occupiers were not particularly wealthy and therefore they were not gaining significantly from the success of the Purbeck industries. However, the extents of Brenscombe and East Creech villa are not known and the excavation of Bucknowle reveals it to be a good sized home.

Bucknowle was a courtyard villa and its excavated plan compares well with other villas in Dorset. Finely worked shale furniture was being produced in the villa's workshops and perhaps here, generations of Purbeck entrepreneurs were profiting substantially from the local industries. Pottery from Bucknowle included Terra Nigra platters and other Gallo-Belgic and Armorican fine wares. These are rare imports to find on a non-coastal site. It suggests that this family was of high status in the Late Iron Age and continued to occupy Bucknowle into the Roman period and benefit from Roman trade.

CONCLUDING REMARKS

A focus of settlement, large enough to be considered a central place, only emerges at the very end of the Iron Age. This is Norden on the north side of the natural gateway through the Purbeck Hills at Corfe. A range of goods was produced there and the three villas spaced around it indicate Norden's local dominance in the Roman period.

This focus may have developed from a sacred site because of the concentration of ritual evidence around Corfe's Castle Hill. The topography of this locale is evocative and appears to have been significant for the local Iron Age people. Perhaps Castle Hill was the focus and an important shrine lies buried beneath the medieval royal castle. Alternatively, it may have been the gaps through the ridge or the confluence of the Byle Brook and Wicken Stream that enhanced the sanctity of this area. This apparent religious significance is emphasised by the locations of the Corfe and Norden temples with their south-western series/Durotrigan coin hoards, the concentration of Roman coins to the west of Castle Hill and the coins and ritual deposits at Bucknowle.

A zone of larger industrial settlements became established along the south shore of Poole Harbour, particularly at the Furzey Island/Green Island/Cleavel Point peninsula. This settlement began on Furzey towards the end of the Middle Iron Age and shifted south to Cleavel Point in the Late Iron Age when the peninsula was breached and the islands were formed. The Cleavel Point settlement continued into the Roman period although the settlement shrank in size, while further south at Norden an industrial settlement grew.

There was apparently industrial continuity between the Late Iron Age and Early Romano-British periods. This is a feature of Purbeck and the archaeology does not seem to reflect the conquest and submission of a hostile people. The resources of Purbeck were rapidly exploited, with mud stone, shale and Purbeck Marble used at Fishbourne, Chichester and Colchester within 20 years of the Roman takeover. It seems likely that pre-conquest trade had already alerted Roman businessmen to the economic potential of the area and local producers would see the value of expanded markets.

There appears to be a hiatus between the Late Bronze Age and Early Iron Age in some parts of the study area, particularly on the heathland north of the chalk ridge. A lack of evidence for occupation in this period will also be seen in south Dorset. On the Wealden beds there is also limited evidence for Early Iron Age settlement. At Bucknowle the Earliest Iron Age pottery dates from around the fifth century BC but occupation then continues. Large settlements are known with continuity of settlement from the eighth century BC to the Roman Conquest but these lie on the Purbeck limestone plateau. At Rope Lake Hole/Eldon Seat and Gallows Gore, Early Iron Age and Middle Iron Age styles of pottery are similar and indicate a conservative local pottery tradition. The early records, which only recorded Early Iron Age pottery, may have left Middle Iron Age material unrecognised. Fabric type as well as form needs to be analysed to determine relative dates.

The concentration of Early Iron Age settlement on the limestone plateau is followed by a late Middle Iron Age reoccupation of the heathland and littoral zone on the north side of the study area. In the Late Iron Age, there is a rapid rise in industrial activity and settlement, not only around Poole Harbour but on other sites across the study area. It will be seen that south Dorset also demonstrates settlement shift at this time. Bucknowle is of particular interest where an Iron Age settlement developed into a villa. It occupied a key position close to the Corfe gap, and was perhaps a forerunner of Norden.

In the Latest Iron Age, there is evidence for strong links with south Dorset as the two areas adopt the same burial practice. Crouched inhumations in graves, accompanied by Poole Harbour pottery and occasionally joints of meat, indicate a shared belief system. In Purbeck the graves tend to be lined with limestone slabs. Burials have been found at Bucknowle and within several settlements on the limestone plateau where the calcareous soils preserve bone.

There also appear to be links between the Purbeck people and the population of east Dorset. In both areas, the larger settlements were developed to create an extensive network of conjoined rectilinear enclosures.

Following the Roman Conquest, these enclosure ditches are backfilled but the Purbeck industries increase productivity. Norden, north of the Corfe gap, developed into a specialised redistribution centre. Its success perhaps eclipsed the role of some of the Poole Harbour coastal sites, such as Cleavel Point, resulting in their partial decline.

PURBECK TO SOUTH DORSET

Flowers Barrow lies outside the study area and is the only true hillfort in Purbeck. Covering 6.3ha, it occupies the west end of the chalk ridge and its southern ramparts have eroded into the sea (*colour plate 2*).

Further west, beside Lulworth Cove, Bindon Hill challenges Ham Hill, Somerset, as the largest hillfort in Britain but it is more truly a rampart and ditch using the topography to secure a coastal area of over 162ha. Mortimer Wheeler dated the rampart to the Early Iron Age.

Along the River Frome and on the chalkland south to the coast, a scatter of Iron Age occupation traces and 'Celtic' field systems have been recorded but the next area with a concentration of evidence is around Dorchester, Weymouth and Portland.

6

SOUTH DORSET

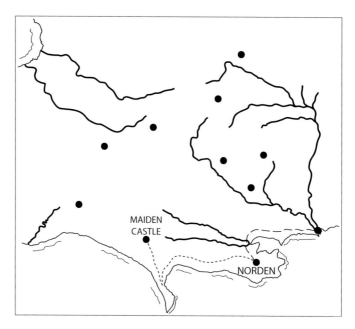

18 Tour map 2: Norden to Maiden Castle.

WEYMOUTH AND PORTLAND

There are many sites on Portland. The archaeological records are mainly the result of chance discoveries during quarrying and building work, usually in the nineteenth century. These include accounts of crouched burials in cists, most of which date to the Late Iron Age.

A distinctive feature of Portland's nineteenth-century discoveries were the Late Iron Age 'beehive chambers' made of corbelled slates of limestone cut into the bedrock then buried and sealed with a flagstone cap. A number of these chambers were found on the highest point of Portland, near the Verne prison. They contained various items but predominantly carbonised grain and therefore they are probably a localised type of grain storage pit.

There was probably an important port at Weymouth from the Iron Age but there are only poor records from the Radipole area to indicate this. There are reports of pottery and Durotrigan burials from Broadwey, north of Weymouth, and other burials may have been unearthed during clay digging for the Putton Brickworks at Chickerell west of the town.

In 2009, part of a large settlement was excavated and this was closely comparable to Rope Lake Hole/Eldon Seat in Purbeck. The excavation was directed by Vix Hughes of Oxford

Archaeology and took place during the construction of the Weymouth Relief Road. This Southdown Ridge settlement occupied a spur of land on the south side of the Ridgeway. It was defended by a cross-ridge dyke and occupied from the Late Bronze Age to the early Romano-British period. Remains of several round houses were found, some with footings constructed of local limestone. Kimmeridge shale armlets were made there and these may have been produced from local shale outcrops. Burials from the earlier settlement phases were placed in pits and ditches but those dating to the Late Iron Age were crouched inhumations accompanied by Poole Harbour bowls. A stratified copper alloy south-western series/Durotrigan coin was found on the site (Peter Woodward pers. comm.).

Jordan hill above Bowleaze Cove, near Preston, was a sacred place. This was probably in use from the Late Iron Age until the fifth century AD. In 1872, Charles Warne recorded a cemetery of crouched inhumations associated with Durotrigan pottery. The burials were found north-east of a square building interpreted as a Romano-Celtic temple.

Chalbury

Chalbury is the nearest hillfort to Weymouth and Portland. It lies north of Preston and dates from the Early Iron Age (see *3*, page 35). It will be considered in more detail in the next study area which is to the north across the chalk escarpment of the South Dorset Ridgeway. This divides the varied geology of the Weymouth Anticline from the chalkland around Dorchester and the Winterborne and Frome valleys.

Study Area 2: South Dorset, Dorchester and Maiden Castle

This study area contains one of the most exciting archaeological landscapes in the country. At its centre lies the modern county town of Dorchester, which was also the principal town in the medieval and Roman periods. Immediately to the north-west is Poundbury Camp and 1.5km to the south-west is the massive hillfort of Maiden Castle.

Both Dorchester and Maiden Castle overlie and are surrounded by a grand assemblage of Neolithic and Bronze Age ceremonial monuments, and south and west of them hundreds of Bronze Age burial mounds form the vast cemetery of the South Dorset Ridgeway.

Topographic Description
The valley of the River Frome enters the study box at its north-west corner and meanders south-east between the villages of Stratton and Bradford Peverell and past the northern edge of Dorchester. The river crosses the centre of the east boundary of the study area flanked by the villages of Kingston Maurwood on its north and West Stafford on its south bank. The River Cerne joins the Frome from the north, passing through Charminster and Wolfeston before its confluence at Frome Whitfield.

The geology and topography of the area is characterised by a chalkland landscape. This consists of a pattern of chalk spurs and coombes sloping towards the Frome valley from the South Dorset Ridgeway to the south-west (*colour plate 5*) and the ridge between the Frome and Piddle rivers to the north-east. There are alluvial deposits in the river valleys, and gravel capping on the chalk in the south-west corner of the study box at Bronkham Hill, which is the highest point. There are also heathland soils at the eastern fringes of the area within Puddletown Forest, West Stafford and West Knighton.

Chronological Development

The excavations in and around Dorchester and Maiden Castle tend to confirm the pattern of occupation proposed by Niall Sharples (1991). The Late Bronze Age settlements, farmsteads and field systems of the area seem to be abandoned by the Early Iron Age. Very little of Middle Iron Age date has been found beyond the hillforts of Poundbury and Maiden Castle.

Maiden Castle was densely occupied in the Middle Iron Age but the surrounding landscape is archaeologically blank for the period 800 BC to 100 BC. Roland Smith (1997, 299) summarised the evidence following the Dorchester by-pass excavations:

> … the absence of evidence for settlement from the Earliest Iron Age through to the first century BC adds weight to the view that from c.600 BC there was near wholesale occupation of the Maiden Castle and Poundbury hillforts within the study area. The By-pass excavations produced only a handful of unstratified possible Iron Age sherds. At present there is no evidence from c.800-200 cal BC between the Maiden Castle and Poundbury hillforts and this is in contrast to the later Bronze Age, represented by the settlements at Middle Farm, Fordington Bottom, Poundbury and Coburg Road/Middle Farm Poundbury Development. This last named site is the latest and probably dates within the period 10th-9th century cal BC. This leaves a period of perhaps over two centuries where there is at present an absence of settlement within the study area prior to the construction of the two hillforts.

Poundbury

Poundbury hillfort occupies a ridge of land beside the River Frome to the west of Dorchester (*colour plate 7*). On the east side of the hillfort there is excavated evidence of settlement from the Bronze Age to the Romano-British period but this is on a small scale in comparison with Maiden Castle. The position of the site at a river crossing has led Christopher Sparey-Green, the director of the Poundbury excavations, to suggest that it was an outwork or complementary site within the Maiden Castle territory. Poundbury was a secure place for cattle grazing in the meadows beside the river, whereas Maiden Castle was where crop storage was concentrated (1987, 146).

A group of three Early Bronze Age burial mounds lie within the Poundbury hillfort enclosure and a Middle Bronze Age ditched enclosure has been found on its north-west side. The hillfort itself is thought to date from the Late Bronze Age when it consisted of a single bank and ditch with an entrance on the south-east side. The excavations of 1939 (Richardson 1940) found no occupation evidence within the hillfort despite 38 test pits dug 1m square every 30m. However, parch marks visible in 1976 revealed a cluster of about 10 circular features in the south-east corner of the hillfort that indicate a small settlement in an area sampled by only one of Miss K.M. Richardson's test pits.

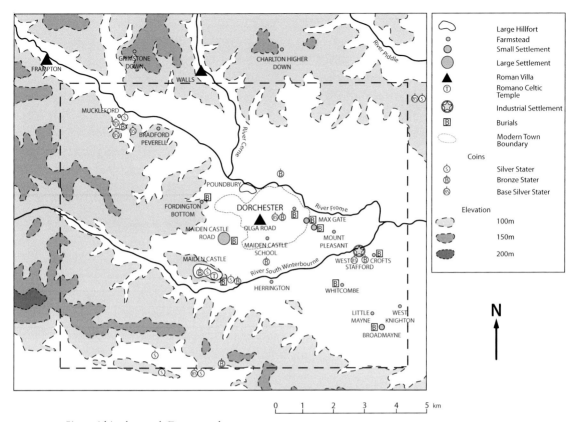

19 Sites within the south Dorset study area.

Chrisopher Sparey-Green compared Poundbury to Abbotsbury hillfort, situated 13km to the south-west. Unlike Poundbury it has never been ploughed and the earthworks of about 6-10 round houses can be seen clustered on its east side. A similar sized hillfort lies 7km south of Poundbury at Chalbury (see *3*, page 35). This has evidence for more numerous hut sites within it (Whitley 1943) but these were abandoned in the Early Iron Age. Niall Sharples (1991, 84) suggested that the abandonment of Chalbury was linked to the expansion of Maiden Castle. Once Maiden Castle had become the dominant settlement, any competing fortified settlements were deliberately closed down.

At Poundbury, the Middle Iron Age evidence came from within a ditched enclosure beside the river on the south-east side of the hillfort. Here there were several phases of occupation continuing into the Late Iron Age although only two or three huts seem to have been occupied at any one time. The hillfort was refurbished in the Late Iron Age when the inner rampart was converted from box rampart to glacis style and an outer rampart and ditch constructed. A hornwork was also added to the south entrance at this time.

The evidence from Poundbury is for a small community that maintained the hillfort as a secure place and insurance against trouble, but which tended to live outside the hillfort beside the river. Although Maiden Castle hillfort began as an enclosure surrounding a similar area to Poundbury, it developed into the principal place, and to date the only other settlement that has been found within the study area dating to the Early and Middle Iron Age.

Maiden Castle

An abiding memory of the summer of 1985 is the visit to see the reopening of Mortimer Wheeler's excavations at Maiden Castle (*colour plate 6*). One trench showed a cross section spanning 5000 years where the hillfort rampart could be seen overlying part of the 546m-long Middle Neolithic bank barrow which in turn covered the Early Neolithic causewayed enclosure.

The hillfort was built around 600 BC, later than the proposed construction dates for Chalbury and possibly Poundbury. It initially enclosed 6.5ha occupying the east knoll of the hill and was enlarged to the west to enclose 19ha in about 450 BC (*20*). Around 300 BC, there was a reorganisation of the settlement within the hillfort and the round houses were rebuilt in rows. Niall Sharples suggested that this implied that those who controlled the hillfort had 'increasing power over the fundamental structure of social life'.

From about 100 BC the excavated evidence suggests a gradual breakdown of occupation of the hillfort. The rows of houses were replaced by occupation of a more random type. One of the excavated Late Iron Age houses had been constructed over a previously important road within the settlement. The western part of the hillfort was largely abandoned and settlement was concentrated in the eastern half. At the eastern entrance many of the ditches of the outworks were infilled and the settlement spread out through the entrance. An industrial area concerned with ironworking was found there and also an extensive cemetery. This covered most of the flat land between earthworks that surround the eastern

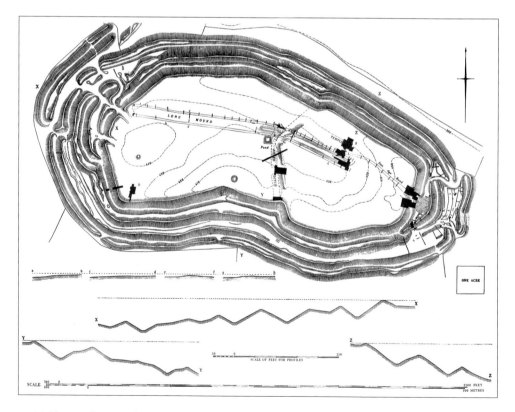

20 Maiden Castle, Winterborne St Martin. Earthwork plan showing excavated areas, 1930s. (RCHM 1970a, 498) *Crown Copyright*

entrance. Mortimer Wheeler (1943) interpreted the cemetery as evidence for a battle at the hillfort in AD 44. However, of the 52 excavated burials only 14 showed signs of mutilation and Niall Sharples suggested that the bodies may have been brought to an established cemetery from a battlefield remote from the hillfort (see *21*, page 81).

The Late Iron Age significance of the east end of Maiden Castle Hill is supported by the discovery of a scattered hoard of Durotrigan silver staters in the field beyond the gateway.

The hillfort may have been temporarily occupied by the Roman army after AD 44 and had been abandoned by the local people around AD 70. By this time, Dorchester (*Durnovaria*) had been established, probably as the regional capital of the Durotrigan *civitas* (Woodward 1993, 359-362; Smith *et al.* 1997, 300-302).

Frome Valley Settlement

In the Late Iron Age, the reduction of the occupation within Maiden Castle was matched by increasing numbers of farmsteads becoming established in the surrounding landscape. The earliest evidence of a trend for settlement outside the hillfort dates towards the end of the Middle Iron Age. Two sites have slight evidence of occupation in this period. These are Mount Pleasant on the east side of Dorchester, where a round house and a few scattered pits may date to the end of the Middle Iron Age, and at nearby Allington Avenue (Davies 2002, 34), where two Middle Iron Age pit burials were found beneath Late Iron Age settlement evidence.

Several Late Iron Age farmsteads associated with Durotrigan pottery and crouched burials have been found in and around Dorchester. These sites include a group of burials discovered by Thomas Hardy while building his home at Max Gate on the south-east outskirts of the town. Other settlements are Poundbury on the north-western outskirts, Fordington Bottom 2km to the west and Whitcombe Hill, 2km south of Dorchester. Concentrations of Durotrigan coins indicate other settlements in the Frome valley at Muckleford and West Stafford (see *19*, page 75).

A ribbon of settlement evidence is visible on aerial photographs 1km north of Maiden Castle and 2km south-west of Dorchester. It may have become the interim focus of occupation between the Latest Iron Age and earliest Roman periods. The Dorchester by-pass cut through the eastern part of this site at Maiden Castle Road and revealed early Roman occupation including a Durotrigan burial (Smith 1997, 65). Fieldwalking across this area revealed pottery evidence to show that settlement continued and developed here up to the fourth century.

Further east, at Maiden Castle School, two enclosures were discovered in 1992. The northern enclosure was excavated in 1993 by Peter Bellamy and Alan Graham and consisted of an external ditch 1.5m deep enclosing a sub-rectangular area (0.5ha) with an entrance on the south side. The former position of the interior bank was apparent in the absence of features in a clear zone of slightly raised protected chalk. Three round houses were found on the west side of the enclosure facing into an open area, partly metalled with flint gravel, interpreted as a courtyard that lay immediately inside the gateway. The north-eastern part of the enclosure appeared to be an open space with evidence of storage pits ranged along the back against the enclosing bank.

The concentration of occupation around Dorchester in the Latest Iron Age suggests that there was a focus there. Perhaps an *oppidum* pre-dated the Roman foundation but there is very little evidence for pre-Roman settlement from excavations within the town apart from occasional coins and brooches and some pottery (Woodward 1993, 359). A concentration of burials at Fordington, poorly recorded in the eighteenth and nineteenth centuries, may have a Late Iron Age element. Particularly the horse and human burials found under Fordington church which may indicate the site of a chariot burial. There are also references to burials with swords and at least one crouched burial under Fordington High Street to the north-west of the church. One of the swords was described as being over 2.5ft (0.8m) long, perhaps a warrior burial like the Late Iron Age example found at Whitcombe.

Sacred Spring

Peter Woodward (1993, 361) has suggested that the Durotrigan burials around Dorchester are concentrated around a sacred spring that occupied a coombe leading down to the Frome. This lay under Wollaston Field, within the east part of the later Roman town and west of Fordington. The Roman town baths, discovered in 1977, occupied this site but the excavations did not penetrate below the Roman structures and therefore an Iron Age origin cannot be demonstrated. However, the site may have been like the spring at Bath, where the Roman bath was constructed on the shrine to the Iron Age deity Sulis. Dobunnic and Durotrigan coins were found at the lowest excavated level. Evidence of Late Iron Age continuity of worship into the Roman period is also found locally at Jordan Hill near Weymouth, referred to above.

Oppidum?

The possibility of an *oppidum* at Dorchester was suggested by Christopher Sparey-Green who considered Poundbury and Maiden Castle in a wider defensive context. He linked the Late Iron Age refurbishment of the hillforts with lengths of substantial Iron Age ditches found in the Dorchester environs. He thought that Dorchester might once have had *oppidum*-like ditch systems similar to those found around Late Iron Age Chichester and Silchester. If the Fordington evidence indicates high-status burial at Dorchester it would support *oppidum* status for the site. For example, rich burials are associated with *oppida* like *Verulamium* and *Camulodunum*.

CONCLUDING REMARKS

Maiden Castle and Dorchester represent preferred locations for human activity, the relative importance of each shifting over time. In the Early Neolithic the centre appears to be Maiden Castle with its causewayed enclosure and bank barrow. From the Middle Neolithic to the Early Bronze Age the focus shifted to Dorchester and the construction of a cluster of ceremonial monuments.

Following a Late Bronze Age to Earliest Iron Age hiatus, from about 600 BC Maiden Castle became the exclusive settlement within a hinterland extending from the north side of the Ridgeway to the Frome valley. This area has benefited from a range of well-published modern excavations and they have confirmed the lack of settlement outside the hillfort in the Early to Middle Iron Age. The exception is the settlement beside Poundbury hillfort at the ford across the Frome. The assessment of the functions of this occupation, as an outwork, guard post and secure haven for stock linked to the Maiden Castle settlement, is a persuasive explanation of its continuing existence at this strategic location.

Several other settlements were eventually located beside the Frome but they only become occupied in the Late Iron Age when settlement begins to disperse from Maiden Castle.

Farmsteads have been excavated at Quarry Lodden, near Chalbury, 7km south of Dorchester, on the south side of the Ridgeway and at Pins Knoll, Litton Cheney, 14km west of Dorchester. Both occupation sites, in contrast to those closer to Maiden Castle, contained ceramic assemblages that indicated continuity of settlement from the Early Iron Age to the Roman period. Both farmsteads included examples of Durotrigan burial suggesting that their inhabitants were linked to the Maiden Castle area belief system in the Latest Iron Age. However, these farmsteads operated outside Maiden Castle's zone of depopulation.

Niall Sharples (1990, 92) discussed the depopulation of the Maiden Castle area in the Early to Middle Iron Age and linked it to the lack of field system evidence. He suggested a communal land holding centred on Maiden Castle during this time. The evidence of the re-emergence of farmsteads and the practice of Durotrigan inhumation burial indicates that a more independent society of warrior farming families was becoming established in the Late Iron Age. A good example of this being the Whitcombe farmstead and cemetery which includes an adult male buried with his sword (*22*).

Such a model for change would be similar to the abandonment of farmsteads and the concentration of populations in villages that took place in the late Saxon period when open field systems were created under the control of manorial lords. Later, this power diminished due to a range of factors including climate change, disease and the redistribution of land following the Dissolution of the monasteries. These circumstances allowed the rise of a new class of wealthy yeoman farmers who established new farms on enclosed land between the sixteenth and nineteenth centuries.

The evidence for a change from an insular population to a period of contact, particularly with the Purbeck pottery producers, has been demonstrated by the analysis of pottery assemblages at Maiden Castle (Brown 1991, 185-203). By the third century BC, 'saucepan pots' were being imported from the north-east, and South Western Decorated Ware from the west and north-west. However, significant amounts of Maiden Castle/Marnhull style pottery were also being brought to the hillfort and fabric analysis showed that this pottery was produced in the Poole Harbour area. By the late third to early second century, Poole Harbour Ware accounted for 20 per cent of the Maiden Castle assemblage. The percentage of Poole Harbour pottery fabrics rose to 60 per cent in the late second-century assemblage, 77 per cent by the mid-first century BC and 95 per cent by the mid-first century AD. Therefore the sudden shift of pottery use coincided with the resettlement of the Maiden Castle environs.

The Iron Age coin evidence demonstrates that the area was certainly within the south-western series/Durotrigan distribution. Their silver content suggests coin adoption at a later stage than Cranborne Chase. The 50 per cent silver content of the coins found outside the east gate at Maiden Castle is the highest recorded for the area.

The non-Durotrigan find spots indicate the places where contact with traders in the Late Iron Age is most likely to have taken place. The Celtic Coin Index records two Armorican coins and a Trinovantian coin from Maiden Castle. Six non-Durotrigan coins are listed for Dorchester, including Atrebatic and Dobunnic issues. Elsewhere within the study area, all the reported coins are Durotrigan and mainly base silver and bronze.

The Late Iron Age movement of farmsteads toward the Frome valley, apart from the obvious attraction of a more convenient water supply, may also be linked to a sacred spring. The cluster of burials including a possible chariot burial around Fordington and the site of the later bath complex at Wollaston Field might imply a high-status cemetery and shrine.

There is currently not enough evidence to support Christopher Sparey-Green's theory that there was a developing *oppidum* at Dorchester (perhaps Ptolemy's *Dunium*) at the Roman Conquest but Late Iron Age high-class burial would provide a stronger case and future excavations in and around Fordington church might add substance to this hypothesis.

The pre-Flavian evidence excavated from Dorchester has been linked to the debate concerning the position of a Roman military site in the Dorchester area. Peter Woodward set out the slight evidence for a fort beneath the town, perhaps occupied from *c*.AD 44-65, and concluded that the establishment of the Durotrigan *civitas* of *Durnovaria* took place over the abandoned fort no earlier than AD 65, presumably after this area of the province had been subdued following the Boudican revolt.

Durotrigan Burials and Settlements North and East of Dorchester

Durotrigan burials associated with settlement features have been found east of Dorchester at Broadmayne and as far north as Tolpuddle. The distribution pattern indicates that the Piddle valley lay near the edge of the area where this form of burial rite was adopted.

The Tolpuddle Ball settlement was located during the construction of the Tolpuddle to Puddletown by-pass. This site was occupied in the Middle Bronze Age and a few Early Iron Age sherds were found there but there were very few other finds of this date along the route of the by-pass. Carrie Hearne suggested that the local population occupied Weatherby Castle, the bivallate hillfort 2km north of Tolpuddle Ball (*23*). If this were the case it would be further evidence of a general move into hillforts in southern Dorset at this time. Weatherby Castle has not been excavated and therefore there is no evidence to confirm this hypothesis. Tolpuddle Ball was reoccupied in the third century BC and the settlement continued until the late Roman period.

Further east, and astride the Ackling Dyke, is a large Romano-British settlement at Bagwood Copse, Bere Regis. Parts of this site were excavated in the 1960s and traces of Late Iron Age occupation were found. Metal detector finds from across this site have included over 20 Durotrigan coins. The univallate Woodbury hillfort lies 2.5km south of this site but, like Weatherby, it has not been excavated and the relationship between Woodbury and Bagwood has not been determined. Miles Russell of Bournemouth University began examining the settlements in this area in 2009-10 (*colour plates 15 & 16*).

21 Durotrigan burial with iron projectile head in the spine, Maiden Castle. (Wheeler 1943, Plate XVIII)

22 Durotrigan burial excavated at Whitcombe, male crouched inhumation with sword. (Aitken 1990, 65) *Copyright Dorset County Museum*

DUROTRIGAN BURIALS AND SETTLEMENTS WEST OF DORCHESTER

The distinctive south Dorset style of Late Iron Age burial can be seen as far west as Burton Bradstock and West Bay near Bridport. Perhaps the River Brit was the western boundary of the distribution. Six Durotrigan inhumations were found at Pins Knoll, Litton Cheney. They lay within a settlement on the chalk escarpment above the east side of the Marshwood Vale. One grave contained the skeleton of a young man and buried with him was a set of gaming counters and an iron stylus. Further south, at Portesham, a richly furnished grave of a woman was found. The grave goods included a decorated bronze mirror (the handle of a bronze mirror has also been found at Bridport). Other grave goods included a Durotrigan jar, several bowls and presumably food for the afterlife, including joints of pork and mutton.

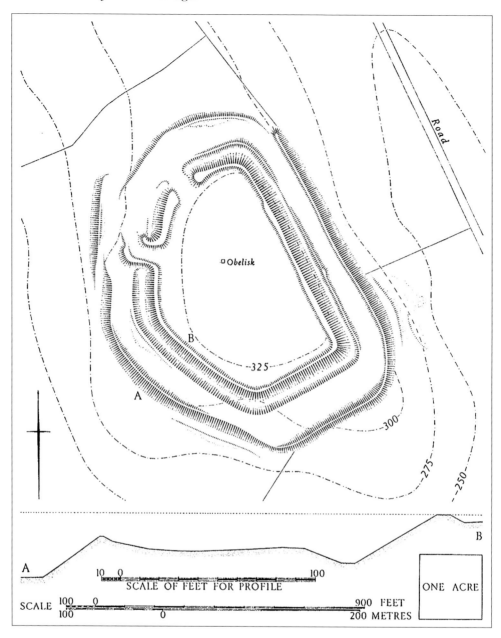

23 Earthwork plan of Weatherby Castle, Milborne St Andrew. (RCHM 1970b, 180) *Crown Copyright*

In 2000, John Valentin excavated other Durotrigan burials at Portesham on the north side of the present village. They were associated with a circular structure which he cautiously interpreted as a temple.

Pins Knoll is central to four Iron Age hillforts or hilltop enclosures, Eggardon 4km to the north, Chilcombe 1.5km to the north-west, Shipton Hill 3.5km to the west and Abbotsbury Castle 4km to the south (*colour plate 10*). These, like Pins Knoll, are sited above the west-facing chalk escarpment. Shipton occupies a ridge of Upper Greensand connected to the escarpment by a neck of land much like Castle Ditches above the Vale of Wardour (see Chapter Ten).

Only the largest of the four, Eggardon, has been the subject of a well recorded archaeological excavation and this revealed storage pits and ditches containing occasional sherds of Middle Iron Age and Late Iron Age pottery (*colour plates 8 & 9*).

At Shipton Hill, occupation evidence was found in the 1950s which dated from the Bronze Age to the Romano-British periods. Near the escarpment edge, a dump of about 1000 pebbles, presumably sling stones, was found above a dark soil containing Early Iron Age pottery decorated with finger print impressions.

A further 2km west of Shipton Hill lies a place called 'Chesils', on a hilltop east of Bridport. The site was built above a steep escarpment and overlooks the mouth of the River Brit at West Bay. Numerous finds of Durotrigan pottery mixed with Romano-British material were found in the ploughsoil in the 1950s. The ceramic assemblage included ribbed bead rim bowls and jars with counter-sunk handles. This site is probably near the boundary between two communities divided by the River Brit.

The archaeology quickly changes further to the west.

7

WEST DORSET

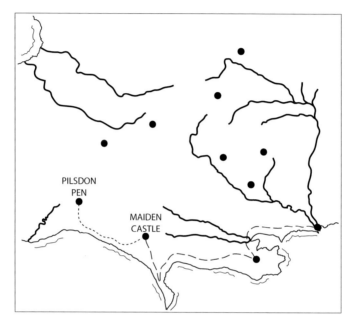

24 Tour map 3: Maiden Castle to Pilsdon Pen.

This is an area where few archaeological excavations have taken place and few finds have been reported. Once the chalk escarpment is crossed, the number of known archaeological sites drops dramatically. Even the route of the Roman road from Dorchester to Exeter becomes unclear after Eggardon Hill. This is an area of Jurassic geology where Lias beds are capped by Upper Greensand. Much of the land is now pasture but it has been heavily ploughed in the past.

The coastal belt from Bridport west to the Devon border contains only a few fragments of evidence that indicate this area was occupied during the Iron Age and Romano-British periods. Within the structure of Whitchurch Canonicorum church there are bricks which are thought to have been reused from an unlocated Roman building. Three other find spots are from the cliff edge.

In 2003, we carried out a salvage excavation of archaeology threatened by coastal erosion at Thorncombe Beacon, Symondsbury (*colour plate 11*). There are stunning coastal views from here. To the east, Chesil Beach curves towards the wedge-shaped Isle of Portland and to the west, and the eye is drawn to Golden Cap and the sweep of Lyme Bay as far as Start Point in Devon. A few sherds of Late Iron Age and Romano-British black burnished pottery were found at Thorncombe but these had been disturbed and mixed with earlier prehistoric material, perhaps when an armada beacon was constructed here in 1588.

Further west, on the Golden Cap Estate at Doghouse Cliff, Chideock and at Broom Cliff, Stanton St Gabriel, a thin scatter of abraded Iron Age and Romano-British pottery has been found since the 1970s. However, our geophysical survey of parch marks within the coastal field at Broom Cliff revealed no significant patterns. The movement of soft clays and sands into the valleys tends to bury archaeology deeply in this part of Dorset. This may be the reason finds are only made at the cliff face where they are seen in rotational slip lines up to 1m deep beneath the turf.

Inland, to the north along the Devon border and across the Marshwood Vale, the survey enters the next study area.

Study Area 3: West Dorset, Pilsdon Pen

Topographic Description

This 10km by 8km study box is divided by the Upper Greensand escarpment, with the south-east half of the area occupied by the small pasture fields and clumps of woodland of the Marshwood Vale and to the north-west by the high ground beyond the escarpment.

The Marshwood Vale is crossed by small streams which drain into the River Char. The settlement pattern consists of hamlets or farmsteads such as Stoke Abbot, Monkwood, Pilsdon and Bettiscombe. They are linked by narrow meandering lanes.

The larger settlements lie in valleys draining north from the escarpment; these are Broadwindsor in the north-east corner of the study area and Thorncombe to the north-west.

The geology is Lias Clays capped by layers of Gault Clay and Upper Greensand sand and Chert beds. The land along the summit of the escarpment is capped with the Chert and these high points at Waddon Hill, Lewesdon Hill, Pilsdon Pen, Coney's and Lambert's Castle have distinctive level surfaces rather than the domed summits of the chalkland. Lewesdon and Pilsdon are the highest hills in Dorset and provide clear views to the coast or inland across Dorset, Somerset and Devon.

Chronological Development

In sharp contrast to Purbeck and south Dorset, this area contains few Iron Age sites that have been recognised. There is very little evidence to suggest that this area fell within the Durotrigan zone because very few artefacts have been recovered.

The character of the archaeological finds and the terrain and geology are more closely related to east Devon than the areas north and east of the study box. Hembury hillfort, near Honiton, is similar to Pilsdon and the excavation records of the two sites will be compared below.

There is evidence of early occupation predating the construction of the hillforts. At Coney's Castle, two round barrow sized mounds are shown on William Woodward's map of 1769 but one of these sites has since been levelled by cultivation and the other quarried for Chert. A mound within Lambert's Castle may originally have been a round barrow before being altered to build a market house for the fairs that were held there from the eighteenth century. Two burial mounds survive as earthworks within Pilsdon Pen hillfort and flint

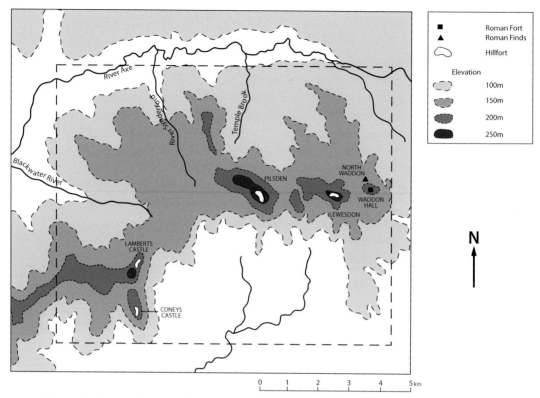

25 Sites within the west Dorset study area.

tools dated to the Upper Palaeolithic and Mesolithic periods have been found there. Struck Upper Greensand Chert fragments have been found on the west summit of Lewesdon Hill and flint flakes have been recovered from ploughed fields north of the hill.

Therefore each of the hillfort sites has traces of pre-Iron Age significance but Pilsdon contains most evidence for this and remained the largest and most elaborate Iron Age earthwork in the study area. The nearest hillforts of comparable size are Eggardon 15km east and Hembury 30km to the west. The much larger hillfort of Ham Hill lies 17km to the north.

Pilsdon Pen

Pilsdon Pen is the key site to enable understanding of the nature of prehistoric occupation in this area (*colour plate 12*). The owners in the 1960s knew Jaquetta Hawkes and Mortimer Wheeler and asked them to find someone to lead an excavation on the site. They eventually chose Peter Gelling of Birmingham University who carried out eight seasons of excavation. He was frustrated because although he found many archaeological features, dateable artefacts were scarce.

Pilsdon is a multivallate hillfort of 3.2ha partially overlying an earlier enclosure (*26*). The long oval shaped earthwork consists of two sets of ramparts and ditches with an additional outer rampart on the long north-east and south-west sides. There are five breaks in the ramparts but only those to the north-east and halfway along the south-west side are thought to be original entrances. Two very distinct phases of defences are apparent at the north end of the hillfort. The identifiable remains of the early defences comprise two low, spread ramparts separated by a ditch flanking a wide central entrance with long inturned entrance banks similar to those dated to the Early Iron Age at Bindon Hill, Purbeck.

These ramparts display a considerable contrast in form either side of the entrance causeway. To the west they appear well finished, separated by a well-defined ditch, but on the east, the ramparts and ditch are shallow features by comparison. In 1964, Peter Gelling started his excavation campaign here. He sectioned the early entrance rampart and causeway (his trenches A-C) (*27*) and concluded that this first grand entrance phase of the earthwork was never completed. Instead of being levelled while the later hillfort was constructed, it was retained for some special function.

We carried out a resistivity survey of this area in 2000 and this revealed two anomalies that may be relevant. The inner rampart readings were generally very high because they were made of Chert rubble, but a distinct 15m-wide section at the centre of the north inner rampart had much lower resistance readings. This indicated that this section was infilled with a less dense material. The readings suggest that an earlier hillfort entrance was blocked when the earthwork was redesigned as a multivallate fortification. This entrance would have aligned with the causeway through the early 'unfinished' fortification. Another

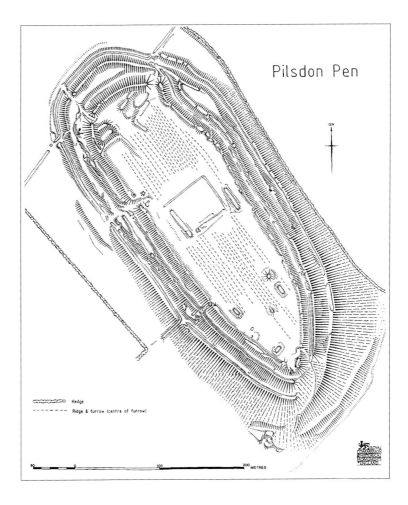

Pilsdon Pen

Hedge

Ridge & furrow (centre of furrow)

26 Earthwork
plan Pilsdon Pen.
(RCHM 1995)
Crown Copyright

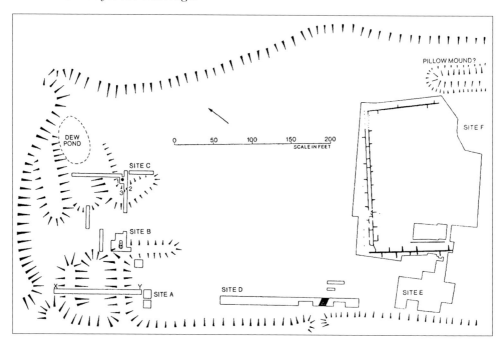

27 Plan of Pilsdon interior showing excavation locations. (Gelling 1977, 265)

interesting feature was an isolated circular anomaly 10m in diameter between the cause-way and the north rampart, perhaps evidence for a significant building. This separated area at the north end of Pilsdon may have been reserved for a special function. The smaller enclosed area at Coney's Castle may also be interpreted in this way. It might be interpreted as a space for a high-status individual or for a sacred or ceremonial function but without excavation it is difficult to do more than speculate.

There were no dateable artefacts from the Phase 1 earthwork in 1964 and subsequent excavations, first at the west entrance (trench D), then further south against the rampart (trench E) and in the centre of the hillfort (trench F) produced very few sherds of pottery. Trench E covered an area 25m by 15m and trench F eventually extended over an area about 50m square. Fourteen round houses were identified, principally from their ring gullies, which ranged from 7-10m in diameter (*28*).

Rings of post-holes lay within the ring gullies. There was little evidence of later round houses cutting earlier constructions and this led to the conclusion that the Iron Age occupation took place over a short period of time (Gelling 1977, 283). However, hut 13, partly excavated on the north-east edge of trench F, seems to have three phases of ring gulley construction cutting the bedrock and many of the excavated post-holes were not interpreted as forming part of a building. The leached sandy soils of the site made identification of stratigraphy difficult and the interior of the hillfort had been ploughed in the post-medieval period which had disturbed the later deposits.

Huts 10a, 10b and 11 were part of a contiguous group and may have been a single homestead with curving ditches extending from their gullies like antennae. Similar groups of round houses can be seen in the earthwork plan and geophysical survey plots of Hod Hill.

At Hod, Ian Richmond interpreted the ditches branching from the ring gullies as stables attached to homesteads.

It is clear that the settlement evidence extended over a wider area than that excavated, because the edges of round houses are shown on the excavation plans continuing into the baulks of trenches E and F.

The round house drainage gullies and post-holes were cut by long parallel ditches that formed a rectilinear plan about 50m square and lay under low earth banks. In the 1960s, these were interpreted as forming an Iron Age temple or sacred site but in 1982, David Thackray's excavation proved that these were much later features. They were probably part of a post-medieval rabbit warren, the ditches constructed as rabbit runs within the mounds.

Most of the pottery came from trench E and this included South Western Decorated Ware (*29*) and what was termed Durotrigan pottery but there was no fabric analysis of the group and the illustrations indicate a range of forms. The lack of pottery in relation to the number of occupation features leads to the conclusion that local pottery manufacture was limited if it existed at all. Pottery was only occasionally used at Pilsdon and most of this appeared to

28 Plan of Pilsdon round houses site F. (Gelling 1977, 269)

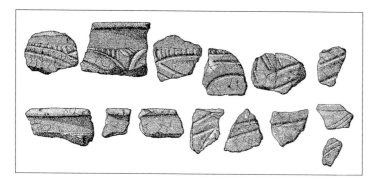

29 South Western
Decorated Ware
excavated from Pilsdon.
(Gelling 1977, 285)

come from Somerset to the north or from Purbeck to the east. Ann Garvey has examined
the small amount of pottery from the National Trust excavation of 1982 and concluded that
although some of the forms are similar to Poole Harbour jars, the fabrics are generally not
from Poole Harbour. Her fabric analysis has demonstrated that most of the pottery was made
with a 'fine sand' fabric comparable with Fabric J identified from the South Cadbury hillfort
excavations (Barrett, Freeman & Woodward 2000, 325). It is currently not possible to source
this fabric although it may be local or from further west. Iron Age pottery in east Devon is
also sparse but there is evidence for some local manufacture. The department of archaeology
at Exeter University has recently carried out a 'diachronic' study of prehistoric pottery in
Devon and Cornwall and this may determine where this 'fine sand' ware was made.

The acid soils meant that no bone survived at Pilsdon. Only three metal objects were
found. An earthenware crucible fragment from trench E had traces of gold, silver, copper
and either lead or arsenic adhering to it. A single gold coin identified as Gallo-Belgic XB
from hut 6 was dated to about 80-40 BC. The third find was an iron projectile point interpreted as a Roman ballista bolt lying above a cobbled surface that lay across round houses in
trench F. No other Roman material has been identified from Pilsdon.

Lambert's Castle

The other site that has been the subject of an excavation is Lambert's Castle, south-west
of Pilsdon. This is a univallate hillfort of about 3ha with an entrance on the south-west
side. Field boundaries and remains of a post-medieval fair have disturbed the interior of
the hillfort.

The severe storm of January 1990 blew over a number of trees on this site. One fell and
tore up part of the north-west rampart. Michael Lester and I cut back the disturbed ground
to record a section across the rampart and ditch. The phases of rampart were constructed of
Chert rubble with evidence of a box rampart replaced by a stone revetted 'glacis' or dump
construction rampart. This work confirmed the general lack of pottery within west Dorset
hillforts; no dateable finds were made apart from nineteenth-century bottle glass found in
the field boundary wall built on top of the rampart (Lester 1990, 115).

Coney's Castle

At Coney's Castle, 1km south of Lambert's, a minor road runs through the hillfort. This is
probably where the original entrance or entrances existed at the north and south ends. In

all, about 2.5ha is enclosed and this includes a small enclosure, probably an extension of the main enclosure on its north side. No dateable finds have been recovered from the site. Coney's Castle appears to have an association with Lambert's Castle as they lie on hilltops either side of a lower shoulder of land, used today as a crossroads. They were perhaps built to defend this access point. A number of similar univallate forts lie to the west including Musbury, 9km to the south-west, Membury, 10km to the north-west, and Blackbury Castle, 19km to the west. In 1955, a section through the rampart of Blackbury Castle dated the earthwork to *c.*400-300 BC but there are no other dates from these sites.

Lewesdon Hill

The last of the hillfort sites is Lewesdon Hill, which lies east of Pilsdon.

Of the four in this study area, it has the least evidence for prehistoric activity but occupies the highest position. It covers an area of about 1.5ha and has an entrance at the narrow west end, protected by a cross-ridge dyke. There are traces of an inner rampart on the north side of the flat-topped interior but Chert quarrying may have removed much of the evidence.

Unlike the Portland and Purbeck limestone quarries, quarrying for Chert at Coney's Castle, Lewesdon Hill and Pilsdon Pen in the nineteenth century led to no reports of discoveries at these sites. This despite the vigilance of the antiquarian Charles Warne who protested at the damage being caused to Pilsdon's ancient Chert ramparts. However, quarrying at Waddon Hill, 1km east of Lewesdon, led to the reporting of Roman finds in 1893.

Waddon Hill

Graham Webster's excavations of 1959-69 revealed the plan of a fort occupied from about AD 50-60 (*30*). The report records no pre-Roman features but there was evidence of tree clearance and levelling before construction (Webster 1979, 55). The evidence for Iron Age occupation was limited to Durotrigan coins and pottery traded or looted from the area. These finds are the best evidence that this study box once lay within the Durotrigan zone of influence, but there was also a Dobunnic coin and a coin from Kent found on the site. Many Iron Age coins have been found on Roman military sites and the distribution pattern they create should be treated with caution rather than be used to define tribal boundaries.

Most of the other first-century Roman forts within the Durotrigan zone lie within or close to significant Iron Age forts such as Hod Hill, South Cadbury, Ham Hill and perhaps another near Maiden Castle. The reason for siting Waddon Hill outside the ready-made fortification of Pilsdon Pen is unclear. It was also constructed in an area where the available evidence indicates a low Iron Age population. Perhaps this impression is wrong and for various reasons the Iron Age of west Dorset is difficult to detect. Traces of tesserae found on the north side of Waddon Hill may indicate that a Roman occupation site overlies an earlier settlement here but further fieldwork is needed.

East Devon

The west Dorset topography and geology is very similar to that of east Devon and the hillforts are closely comparable.

One of the largest hillforts in east Devon is Hembury. It is thought to lie within the Dumnonian zone of influence and has three rings of ramparts and ditches enclosing an

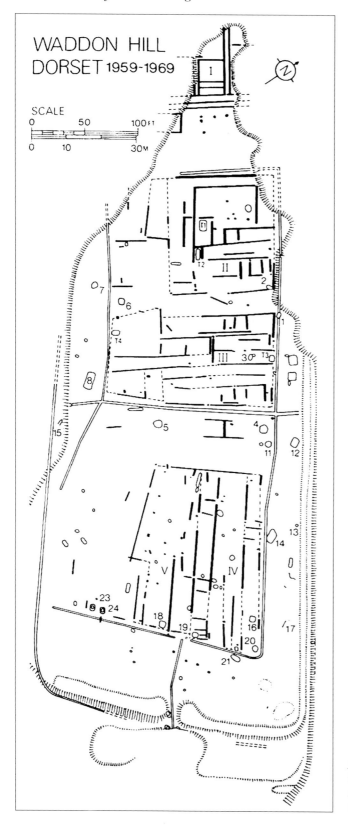

30 Plan of archaeological features at Waddon Hill, Stoke Abbott. (Webster 1979, 52) *Copyright Dorset County Museum*

area of about 3.5ha, with entrances on the east and west sides. Hembury is similar in plan to Pilsdon Pen. Excavations were carried out at Hembury in 1930-35 (Liddell 1935, 135-175). This work revealed a causewayed enclosure and other Neolithic features overlain by the hillfort inner rampart. The earliest rampart was of timber framed box construction and this was replaced by one of dump construction. There were no finds from the earlier rampart but two sherds of South Western Decorated Ware were recovered from the later phase.

Inside the hillfort, traces of only one round house was found and no storage pits. The latest occupation was first-century Roman. Rectilinear beam slots and associated pottery and coins indicated a fort site contemporary with Waddon Hill AD 50-60. Three Claudian coins but no Iron Age coins were found.

The lack of pottery from the earliest phase of construction is similar to Pilsdon. When pottery does reach the area it tends to be occasional fragments of South Western Decorated Ware. This style of pottery was in production from about 250 BC to the earliest years of the first century AD. This is ceramic Phase 8 at South Cadbury, where South Western Decorated Ware was replaced by Durotrigan pottery in ceramic Phase 9 with little overlap.

CONCLUDING REMARKS

Based on this survey of the available evidence, it can be seen that currently it is difficult to create a chronological framework for the Iron Age of west Dorset. The earliest phases are aceramic and from the later Middle Iron Age, rare fragments of dateable material reach the area from outside. In the Latest Iron Age, Durotrigan material is recorded but most of this is found within the Roman fort at Waddon Hill.

The Purbeck study area contained 31 sites, many with dense concentrations of artefacts. West Dorset has four sites that were probably occupied in the Iron Age, only one of which has produced dateable Iron Age material. However, it is fortunate that so much of the interior of Pilsdon was excavated because it revealed numerous occupation features, despite the lack of artefacts.

In contrast to the eastern areas, the Iron Age archaeology of west Dorset is inconspicuous. For example, in the autumn of 2005 the water pipes across the National Trust's Golden Cap Estate needed to be renewed and an archaeological watching brief was carried out during the work. Despite the inspection of several kilometres of pipeline no dateable Iron Age material was found. This is presumably because organic materials have been destroyed by the acid soils and pottery was generally not in use. The leaching of the sandy soils makes stratigraphic identification difficult. Flint objects would need to be brought from a distance, worked Chert is difficult to identify and use of other types of stone or industrial processes have not been recorded. Depth of burial may be another factor.

West Dorset has probably always had a lower population than the chalklands to the east and perhaps our excavation on Golden Cap demonstrates this. In 1993, we put a trench through a Bronze Age burial mound at the cliff edge, which was threatened by coastal erosion. It produced a pollen sequence that showed that oak woodland still covered this area before the land was cleared to build the barrow cemetery. Charcoal provided a construction date for the barrow of around 1900 BC. The chalkland would have been more open by that time, with more land cleared of trees for agriculture. The comparative density of burial mounds on the chalk reveals the apparent difference in population sizes compared to the land west of Bridport. This is still a quiet area of small towns, villages and farmsteads.

Nevertheless, although it cannot be claimed that this was a densely occupied area in the Iron Age, there are probably many undetected farmstead and settlement sites. Those on the lower ground of the Marshwood Vale to the south, and sited on valleys and ridges north of the Upper Greensand escarpment, will be buried by colluvium with few dateable finds to draw the attention of archaeologists. The rare finds by walkers examining the coastal erosion further south indicate that the evidence is there but difficult to identify. In 2009, a Bronze Age cliff-edge site was excavated at Doghouse near Chideock. This revealed that the finds lay at a depth of 0.7-1.2m deep below the hillwash.

No storage pits have been recorded from these western sites. This may be because the acid soils or type of geology made this form of grain storage impractical, but it should be noted that at Pins Knoll (Bailey 1967, 151), on the east edge of the Marshwood Vale, storage pits cut into Greensand were recorded and, therefore, the lack of pits may be significant as an indicator of differences between communities.

The fort at Waddon Hill suggests that the first-century Roman military commanders were aware of a significant, potentially hostile population in west Dorset. The Durotrigan finds from this site (in contrast to the lack of Durotrigan finds from Hembury Roman fort) may indicate that by the Latest Iron Age west Dorset was within the Durotrigan sphere of influence. However, this seems unlikely. The evidence suggests that the Iron Age population was influenced by groups of people further west. The types of hillfort and lack of storage pits, ceramics or other durable material culture in the west Dorset study area is similar to the east Devon sites. It should also be noted that when south Somerset came under Durotrigan influence it became inundated with Poole Harbour pottery, in sharp contrast to the occasional sherds found amongst the round houses of Pilsdon Pen.

The boundary of the Durotrigan zone may lie only 2km east of the study area. In August 2003 Brian Darch metal detected a hoard of 160 Durotrigan base silver staters. These were found 3km east of Waddon Hill, at Beaminster, near the source of the Brit and at the foot of the conical Coombe Down Hill. This hoard may once have been a boundary marker and sacred site perhaps comparable with Cold Kitchen Hill near Warminster (see Chapter Eleven).

Near Bridport lies the most westerly settlement site with a conspicuous ceramic presence. This is 'Chesils', above West Bay, where numerous sherds of Durotrigan pottery have been found. The current western limit of known Durotrigan burial is also marked by the Brit. The two burials with Durotrigan jar, mirror handle and other bronze objects were found after a cliff fall at the mouth of the Iron Age course of the river.

Lack of coinage, pottery and the distinctive south Dorset burial rite indicates that, in the Late Iron Age, west Dorset contained a community that lay outside the Durotrigan sphere of influence.

8

NORTH-WEST DORSET AND SOUTH SOMERSET

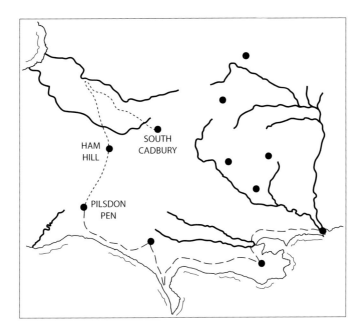

31 Tour map 4: Pilsdon to South Cadbury.

Travelling north from Pilsdon Pen and into the landscape bordering Somerset and Dorset, Iron Age settlement seems sparse until the large hillforts of Ham and South Cadbury are reached. The rivers flow toward the Bristol Channel rather than the south coast and the archaeological evidence seems to indicate a corresponding change in regional affiliation and cultural identity.

HALSTOCK

The Roman villa of Halstock lies on the north slope of the North Dorset Downs. From 1967-85, Ron Lucas directed excavations that revealed the villa had been built on the site of a Late Iron Age farmstead. However, occupation ceased here from the mid-first century until the mid-second century. Ron Lucas wondered whether this was due to the disruption caused by the Roman Conquest. The Romano-British village of Catsgore beside the River Carey has also been shown by excavation to have become established during this period.

Catsgore and Halstock, therefore, are not examples of continuity through the Roman Conquest period in this area. Another site that provides evidence for disruption of occupation is Perrott Hill School, North Perrott. This is in Somerset close to the border with Dorset, 7km north-west of Halstock and 10km south of Ham Hill.

PERROTT HILL SCHOOL AND SHERBORNE

Charles and Nancy Hollinrake excavated this site in 1997. They showed that people lived here from about 300 BC until the mid-first century AD. Storage pits, enclosure boundaries and round houses were excavated. In the last phase of the settlement, the buildings were deliberately destroyed by burning. Within the settlement, there were three Late Iron Age crouched burials placed in oval earth graves. It was thought that one of them had been disturbed by ploughing soon after burial as the articulated skeleton had been torn in half and the remains dragged partly out of the grave pit. Nancy Hollinrake compared the site with human remains found at Ham Hill and South Cadbury where there is also evidence for violence in the mid-first century.

Crouched burials without grave goods of Late Iron Age date (see also South Cadbury below) were also found in oval earth graves at Tinney's Lane, Sherborne, associated with some evidence of contemporary occupation.

HAM HILL

North-west of Sherborne and north of Yeovil lies Ham Hill and this can be claimed as the largest hillfort in the country if Bindon in Purbeck is discounted. The rampart and ditch enclose a plateau of 85ha (210 acres), roughly oval in plan with a narrow finger of land projecting north from its north-west side. Early surveys of this part of Ham Hill recorded inturned entrances typical of the Iron Age on its east and west sides. The spur may once have been divided from the main plateau by a rampart and ditch. This would have created a more defensible annexe to the main hillfort, but subsequent quarrying and building construction have removed the evidence for this.

The quarrying of the famous Ham Hill stone since the Roman period, but particularly in the nineteenth and twentieth centuries, led to many of the early discoveries on the hill. The northern projection has produced most finds, including Iron Age skeletal material and Roman military artefacts. Richard Colt Hoare visited in 1816 and recorded the discovery of 'British chariots' and human bones by the quarrymen. One of the human skulls was 'transfixed with an iron dart'. This recalls the image of the Maiden Castle body with a ballista bolt through its spine and is evidence for a Roman assault on Ham Hill.

In 1987, Elaine Morris examined the pottery from the site and divided it into three periods. The earliest consisted of pottery mainly made from local calcareous fabric; the middle period pottery was made from fabrics from various sources, including the Mendips, Devon and Cornwall and Poole Harbour. In the latest period Durotrigan / Poole Harbour pottery dominated the assemblage with the virtual exclusion of all else.

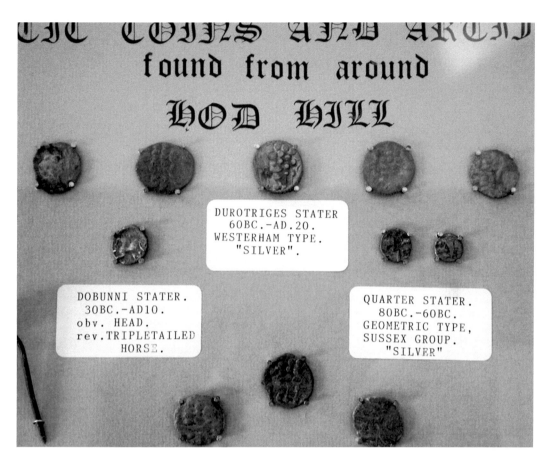

1 Silver (upper) and bronze (lower) Durotrigan or south-western series uninscribed coins, and a Dubunnic or western series silver coin found on the Iwerne settlement near Hod Hill. *Photograph by Martin Papworth*

2 Purbeck view north from the central chalk ridge across heathland to Poole Harbour, Cleavel Point, Green Island and Brownsea. *Photograph by Martin Papworth*

3 Purbeck view north through Corfe gap. Corfe Common and the site of the temple lie in the centre of the picture. *Photograph by Martin Papworth*

4 Flower's Barrow hillfort, Purbeck, looking west. *Copyright F. Radcliffe 1994*

5 South Dorset, view north to Dorchester from the ridgeway. *Photograph by Martin Papworth*

6 Maiden Castle hillfort, south Dorset, looking east. *Copyright F. Radcliffe 1991*

7 Poundbury hillfort, South Dorset, looking east. *Copyright F. Radcliffe 1989*

8 Eggardon hillfort, south Dorset, looking west. *Copyright F. Radcliffe 1989*

9 Interpretation drawing depicting Iron Age Eggardon. *Illustrated by Nick Skelton. Copyright the National Trust*

10 Abbotsbury hillfort, south Dorset, looking north. *Copyright F. Radcliffe 1989*

11 Excavation at Thorncombe Beacon, west Dorset, in 2003, looking west to Golden Cap. *Photograph by Martin Papworth*

12 Pilsdon Pen
hillfort, west Dorset,
looking east.
*Copyright F. Radcliffe
1989*

13 South Cadbury
hillfort, south
Somerset, looking
south-east towards
Sigwells settlement.
*Photograph by Martin
Papworth*

14 South Cadbury
hillfort, south
Somerset, looking
south-west through
the 'massacre'
entrance towards
the Somerset Levels.
*Photograph by Martin
Papworth*

15 Winterbourne Kingston, central Dorset. A storage pit from a 'banjo' enclosure excavated in 2009. *Photograph by Martin Papworth*

16 Winterbourne Kingston, central Dorset. A crouched inhumation placed in a storage pit, excavated in 2009. *Photograph by Martin Papworth*

17 Hod Hill, central Dorset, looking north-east. *Copyright F. Radcliffe 1995*

18 Hod Hill, central Dorset, as it may have looked *c.*AD 44-45 after construction of the Roman fort and clearance of the Iron Age settlement. *Illustration by Nick Skelton. Copyright the National Trust*

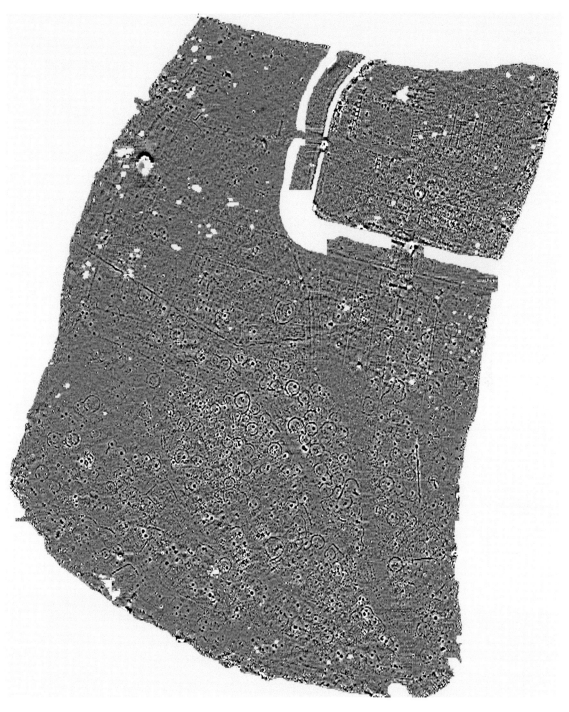

19 Complete geophysical survey of the interior of Hod Hill, central Dorset, showing the layout of tracks, round houses, enclosures and post-holes. *Copyright David Stewart*

20 Hambledon Hill, central Dorset, looking south. *Copyright F. Radcliffe 2005*

21 Banbury hillfort, central Dorset, looking north. *Copyright F. Radcliffe 2001*

22 Cley Hill, south Wiltshire, looking north-west along the Wylye valley from Battlesbury hillfort. *Photograph by Martin Papworth*

23 Middle Hill, south Wiltshire, with Scratchbury Hill beyond, looking west from Battlesbury hillfort across the mouth of the Battlesbury Bowl. *Photograph by Martin Papworth*

24 Badbury Rings, east Dorset, looking north-east. *Copyright F. Radcliffe 1997*

25 Badbury Rings, east Dorset, how it might have looked in the Late Iron Age. *Illustration by Liz Induni. Copyright the National Trust*

26 Badbury Rings, east Dorset. The location of trench I, excavated 2004, against the inner rampart, looking south-east from the west entrance. *Photograph by Martin Papworth*

27 Clay sling-shot excavated from trench I, Badbury Rings, east Dorset, in 2005. *Photograph by Martin Papworth*

28 Poole Harbour Ware. Bead rim jar excavated from trench I, Badbury Rings, east Dorset, 2005. *Photograph by Martin Papworth*

29 Spetisbury hillfort, east Dorset, looking north–east along the Stour. *Copyright F. Radcliffe 1989*

30 Crab Farm settlement, east Dorset, in 2004, looking south. Trench E: Late Iron Age boundary ditch in the foreground, with a Roman well (backfilled in the fourth century) in the background. *Photograph Martin Papworth*

31 High Wood, east Dorset. Excavation across the bank and ditch of a Late Iron Age enclosure, in 2008. *Photograph by Martin Papworth*

32 High Wood, east Dorset. Excavation of
Middle Iron Age pottery beneath a Late Iron
Age enclosure bank, in 2008. *Photograph by
Martin Papworth*

33 Rawlsbury hillfort, north Dorset, looking west. *Copyright F. Radcliffe 1991*

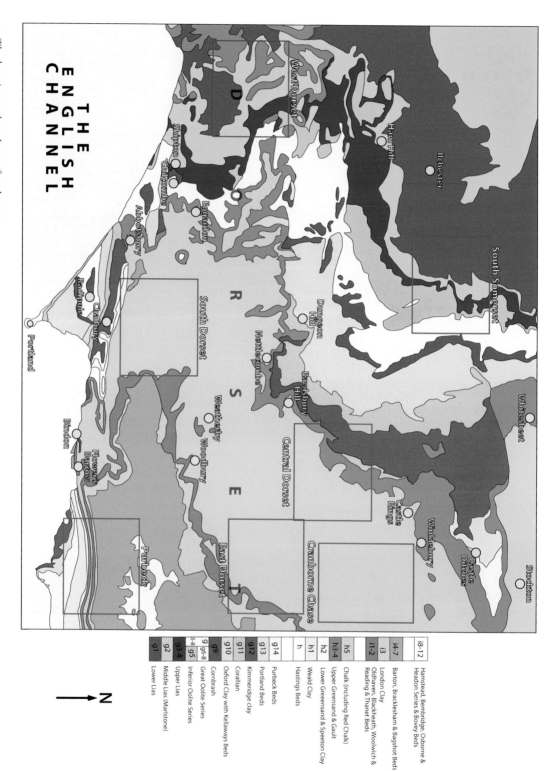

THE ENGLISH CHANNEL

N →

D O R S E T

West Dorset
Hamm Hill
Ilchester
South Somerset
Shipton
Chilcombe
Eggardon
Abbotsbury
Dungeon Hill
Nettlecombe
Rawlsbury Hill
Whitesheat
Radipole
Chalbury
South Dorset
Weatherby
Woodbury
Central Dorset
Castle Rings
Winklebury
Portland
Blindon
Flower's Barrow
Purbeck
East Dorset
Cranborne Chase
Castle Ditches
Stockton

i8-12	Hamstead, Bembridge, Osborne & Headon Series & Bovey Beds
i4-7	Barton, Bracklesham & Bagshot Beds
i3	London Clay
i1-2	Oldhaven, Blackheath, Woolwich & Reading & Thanet Beds
h5	Chalk (including Red Chalk)
h3-4	Upper Greensand & Gault
h2	Lower Greensand & Speeton Clay
h1	Weald Clay
h	Hastings Beds
g14	Purbeck Beds
g13	Portland Beds
g12	Kimmeridge clay
g11	Corallian
g10	Oxford Clay with Kellaways Beds
g9	Cornbrash
g9-6-8	Great Oolite Series
g5-8 g5	Inferior Oolite Series
g3-4	Upper Lias
g2	Middle Lias (Marlstone)
g1	Lower Lias

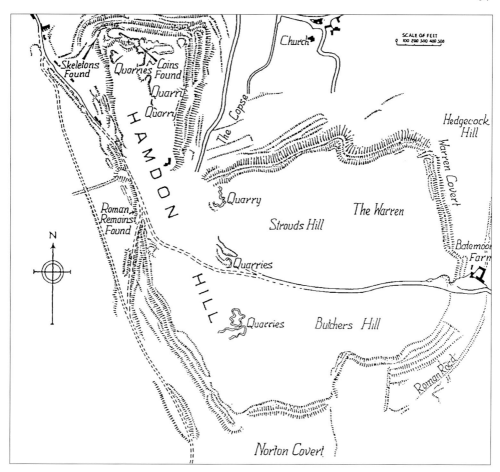

32 Earthwork plan of Ham Hill. (RCHME 1997, 6) *Crown Copyright*

There has not been a careful study of the environs of Ham Hill and therefore it is not possible to compare the changing settlement patterns around this place in comparison with South Cadbury. However, one would expect to find a similar density of occupation hidden beneath the predominantly pasture fields that surround it. An example of this is the previously unknown Montacute Iron Age settlement, discovered in 1991 by Wessex Archaeology during an archaeological watching brief.

North of Ham, Ilchester and South Cadbury, the Brue/Parrett Corridor

North-west of Ham Hill, Iron Age sites have been identified along the corridor of land between the rivers Brue and Parrett which flow into the Bristol Channel. These include Cannington hillfort and West Huntspill settlement. Crandon Bridge near Puriton, beside the Parrett, became an important Roman port and indicates potential for a Late Iron Age settlement here linked to coastal trade. Further south-east, Durotrigan pottery assemblages have been found at Westonzoyland and two sites near Somerton at West Wood and Littleton, which lie south of the small unexcavated hillfort of Dundon.

Meare and Glastonbury Lake Villages

The Meare and Glastonbury settlements lie beside the River Brue on the Somerset Levels. The unusually preserved wooden artefacts from these sites have been referred to in Chapter Four. Carvings can be compared with the designs on South Western Decorated Ware. Lack of Poole Harbour pottery indicates abandonment before the Latest Iron Age.

Ilchester and Environs

The walled Roman town of Ilchester is 7km north-east of Ham Hill, 11km west of South Cadbury and 11km south of Dundon Hill. It was established on the south bank of the River Yeo, slightly west of its confluence with Brearley Brook. It is located at a river crossing on the line of the Fosse Way.

Stratified Early Iron Age pottery dated to the eighth to seventh century bc has been excavated within the town. Middle Iron Age ceramics and South Western Decorated Wares are lacking although there have been numerous finds of first-century Poole Harbour pottery.

About 300m south of the walled town is a stone revetted bank with an outer ditch that encloses a 16ha area. Peter Leach has interpreted this evidence as indicating that there may have been an *oppidum* or valley fort here in the Late Iron Age. This may have been the reason why first a Roman fort and then a Roman town were built at Ilchester in the first century.

Study Area 4: South Somerset, South Cadbury

About 18km south-east of the Glastonbury Lake Village and 11km east of Ilchester is the multivallate hillfort of South Cadbury. The publication of the excavations within the hillfort in 2000, and the ongoing research into the settlement history and archaeology of the land surrounding it, provides valuable information to enable the comparison of this area with other parts of the Durotrigan zone.

Topographic Description

The land of the study area varies in height from almost 200m to less than 50m OD. Most of the higher land lies on its east side and consists of Inferior Oolite and Fullers Earth overlying Upper Lias sand. This forms an escarpment with the Middle and Lower Lias deposits on the low land to the west. Along the top of the escarpment from south to north are Corton Ridge, Corton Hill, Sigwells and Pen Hill. Cadbury hillfort occupies the summit of an isolated remnant of Inferior Oolite, with a 0.5km-wide vale separating it from the escarpment summit of Sigwells.

On the north-west side of Cadbury Hill, the River Cam crosses the area from its source in the escarpment near Yarlington flowing south-west. It runs between Cadbury Hill and

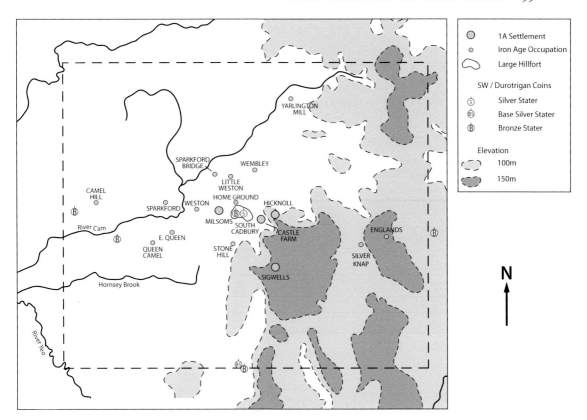

33 Sites within south Somerset study area.

an east-west ridge of Rhaetic clay known as Camel Hill before leaving the area via the villages of Queen Camel and West Camel. A network of other springs and streams emerge from the escarpment and meander across the vale of Middle and Lower Lias Clays.

The area has many farms and settlements, only the lower clay land in the north-west corner of the study box and the higher downs in the south-east are sparsely occupied. The modern villages of Charlton Horethorne and Corton Denham occupy coombes within the downs. To the north-west, Yarlington, Woolston, Blackford, Compton Pauncefoot, South Cadbury and Sutton Montis are spring-line settlements, listed from north to south and located along the foot of the escarpment. Further north-west, North Cadbury, South Barrow, Sparkford, Queen and West Camel, West Bampfylde and Marston Magna, along with other farms and hamlets, occupy the Lower Lias Clays.

The main route to the south-west, the A303, crosses the centre of the study area from east to west and numerous lesser roads, tracks and paths form a network linking the numerous settlements and farms.

Chronological Development

The combined fieldwork, both within South Cadbury and the land surrounding it, pro-vides the data for a more detailed narrative of the occupation of the area than would normally be possible for a hillfort and its environs.

South Cadbury

The 7ha South Cadbury hillfort, enclosed by four sets of ramparts and ditches, has been built on a steeply scarped limestone hill (*colour plates 13 & 14*). Access to the summit is gained via entrances to the north-east and south-west. A third gateway on the east side was blocked at some stage (*34*). The inner rampart is the oldest and the outer ramparts were added between 300 BC and AD 50.

Fieldwork and excavation have revealed that there was considerable occupation on South Cadbury hill during the Neolithic period but little was found that dated to the Early Bronze Age. This is in contrast to the area around the hill where test pits and excavations have shown dispersed settlement linked to field systems and burial mounds; particularly at Milsom's Corner to the west, Sigwells to the south-east and around South Cadbury village to the east.

There was a move towards the top of South Cadbury hill from the Late Bronze Age. The Late Bronze Age and Iron Age ceramic assemblage from the hillfort is considerable

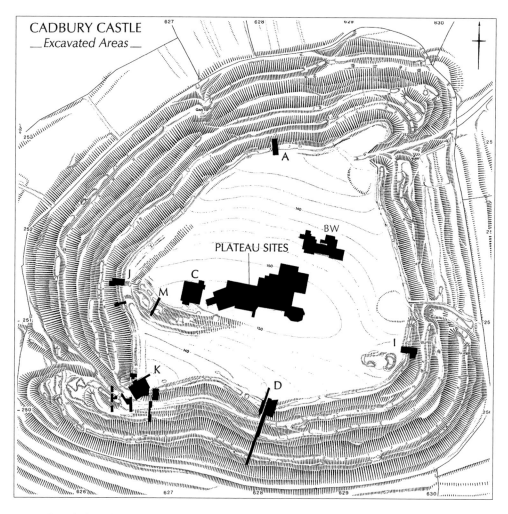

34 Earthwork plan of South Cadbury showing sites of excavations 1966-73. (Barrett, Freeman & Woodward 2000, 156) *Copyright English Heritage*

and, next to the 20 seasons of excavation at Danebury, is the second largest such group ever recovered by excavation in Britain (Woodward 2000, 24).

The occupation of the hill around 1000 BC began with a cluster of buildings established on the plateau associated with a small number of pits and a spread of occupation debris, including finds of Late Bronze Age metalwork.

Outside the hillfort, the distribution of Late Bronze Age pottery becomes less dispersed and is concentrated on the east and west slopes of the hill. At Milsom's corner, a Late Bronze Age shield was found in the upper filling of a Middle to Late Bronze Age boundary ditch which cut through an Early Bronze Age grave. The burial of the shield on the route up to the hill summit from the south-west gave it a 'threshold quality' at a time when the hilltop was newly settled. Richard Tabor thought that its burial was unusual because other shield burials of the period have been found as ritual river or bog deposits. The burial of such a valuable item at a key point of access was interpreted as a symbol of the foundation of a significant place.

The earliest episodes of enclosure of the hill are slight in comparison to the later massive ramparts. These Late Bronze Age features overlay Neolithic deposits and, at the south-west gateway, consisted of a fence and lynchet bank overlain by a soil bank.

The settlement nucleus developed throughout the Late Bronze Age and Early Iron Age with the establishment of circular buildings and four- and six-post rectangular buildings. These flanked the line of an east to west road which probably ran into a hollow-way leading down the slope to the north-east entrance. A series of deposits, seemingly derived from metalworking but including evidence of other industrial activity, lay north of the road. These deposits were built up as a series of cobbled working floors from the Late Bronze Age to the Middle Iron Age.

In the Early to Middle Iron Age (*c.*700-400 BC) the pottery distribution map around South Cadbury is almost blank but with a concentration of excavated pottery from Milsom's Corner at the south-west gate and a few sherds from test pits at Chissell's Green near South Cadbury village. In sharp contrast, the interior of the hillfort became densely settled. Richard Tabor compared this situation with the periods of settlement nucleation demonstrated within Maiden Castle during the Early to Middle Iron Age and Danebury in the Middle Iron Age.

Within the hillfort, round houses were built and re-built across the eastern plateau and alongside the developing hollow-way on the northern slope of the hill. The geophysical survey revealed that round houses and pits covered most of the interior. It is in the Early and Middle Iron Age period that most of the rock cut storage pits were dug and infilled. Some of these may have been associated with particular residential buildings like those identified at Hod Hill (see Chapter Ten); others were dug on to the more exposed and seemingly unoccupied parts of the western plateau.

Throughout the period, the debris and cobbling associated with industrial activity on the plateau continued to develop and the evidence indicates that this area was fenced off from the settlement. In the later Middle and Late Iron Age the settlement activity becomes visible again outside the hillfort as increasing amounts of pottery indicate more dispersed settlement. Pottery from this period has been found within test pits and from excavated features at Sigwells, West Bampfylde and Hicknoll Stait, Milsom's Corner and from the fields around South Cadbury village.

The excavation at the south-west gate revealed how often the ramparts were repaired and renewed. The amount of traffic that passed through the gateway eroded a deep hollow-way between the guard chambers that flanked the gateway.

The excavations within the hillfort indicated that the settlement was beginning to decline during the first century AD. The changing character of the site is hinted at by the lack of buildings and fewer pits which belong to the late period, and by the burial of a number of calf and cattle carcasses in the area of the plateau which had previously been associated with industrial activity. However, the defences of the hillfort were maintained. The ramparts and the south-west gateway were refurbished during this period.

Cadbury Environs

The distribution map of the first-century pottery around the hillfort shows additional sites from the Middle to Late Iron Age. These lie west and east of the hill and at Sigwells, where a sequence of Iron Age settlement features, excavated by Richard Tabor in 2003, included Middle and Late Iron Age storage pits and enclosure ditches.

Pits at Sigwells containing Poole Harbour pottery of the first century AD include ritual deposits with human burials. One pit contained an ox skull with yellow sandstone inserted in the eye sockets, another had a horse skull and mandibles placed on the pit floor, another contained an articulated dog burial. A pit containing an infant burial had four near complete Poole Harbour Ware vessels with it, including jars with a counter-sunk lug and a bead rim. A crouched inhumation of an adult male had been placed on the floor of another pit.

It has also been noted that many boundary ditches were backfilled in the Late Iron Age and that they often contained whole pots that had been broken or crushed into the upper fillings. Jaws and long bones have also been noted at ditch terminals and junctions. These types of finds are located throughout the Cadbury environs but particularly around the open settlements of Milsom's Corner and West Bampfylde and the enclosed settlements at Sigwells. They are interpreted as deliberate structured ditch deposits that are a distinctive feature of the area.

In 2003, a burial of an adult male associated with Poole Harbour pottery was found near South Cadbury village at Eastcombe Farm beside a stream. This burial was not in a pit but had been placed in an oval earth grave. However, it was placed on its left side rather than the usual right side for a Durotrigan burial. The evidence from this grave and the infant burial at Sigwells might be interpreted as signs of a Latest Iron Age ritual influence from the south. More recently, another trench, 250m further along the stream, located an adult inhumation buried without legs, head bent back and body folded forward. The close proximity of the two Eastcombe burials, revealed in small evaluation trenches, raises the possibility that they were once part of a cemetery.

In the Latest Iron Age and earliest Roman period, there is some disagreement between the chronologies provided by the archaeologists describing the hillfort interior and the landscape of the Cadbury environs.

Ann Woodward assigns Cadbury ceramic Phase 9 (the Poole Harbour 'Durotrigan' pottery) to 'Late Cadbury', which begins AD 40-50, and the Cadbury ceramic Phase 8 pottery (South Western Decorated or 'Glastonbury' Ware) to the end of Middle Cadbury, 400 BC-AD 50. This was to place 'Late Cadbury' within the period of 'Romanisation' without assigning pre- or post-conquest pottery assemblages. Richard Tabor has become increasingly convinced that the Poole Harbour pottery came to dominate the ceramic assemblages of the area before the Roman Conquest. The problem is that the present archaeological dating is not refined enough to divide the rapid social changes of this period. The Poole Harbour ceramic dominance and the Roman Conquest may have taken place within a decade of each other.

Within the hillfort, in the mid-late first century AD, a period of destruction occurred at the south-west gateway associated with a spread of fragmentary and partly burnt human remains, weaponry and dress fittings. All the indications are of a Roman attack against the local inhabitants and the dead included men, women and children. The bones were scattered the length of the excavated part of the gateway and remains of at least 22 individuals were present. Another mass grave of 'men and boys' was found at a place called Westwoods Field (Bennett 1890, 18) at the foot of the hill beyond the western end of the ramparts. No dating evidence was recorded and therefore the find cannot be reliably linked to this phase of the hillfort's history. Nevertheless, the remains found at the south-west gate, when considered with the burials from Ham and Perrott Hill School, are evidence for an episode of first-century conflict that affected the south Somerset area.

Richard Tabor noted that the first century AD began with an intense period of activity around South Cadbury followed by a sudden lull that may have continued well into the second century. Within the hillfort, a roadway was laid over the remains of the dead at the south-west gate, four phases of gateway refurbishment took place and a group of Roman timber barrack blocks was constructed within the interior. Final destruction of the gateway by fire took place probably in the second century.

One structure built on the Cadbury plateau and belonging to the mid-late first century, is interpreted as a small timber shrine and there are indications of at least one Roman masonry structure from earlier accounts and from the excavations of 1966-73. This may have been a temple erected on the hill in the earlier Roman period.

Concluding Remarks

The archaeological research in and around South Cadbury tends to confirm its role as a prominent locale to which the local population gravitated in the Neolithic and again from the Late Bronze Age to Late Iron Age. In the Early and Middle Bronze Age, settlement was dispersed and not focused on the hill, and in the Latest Iron Age the hillfort's population began to decline.

During the Early to early Middle Iron Age, South Cadbury can lay claim to be a central place in the same way that Maiden Castle (Sharples 1991, 259-260) and Danebury (Cunliffe 2000, 182) have been presented as centralised populations. Settlement outside of these hillforts seems to have been severely restricted for a period.

At Danebury this settlement concentration is thought to have taken place *c.*270-100 BC but at Maiden Castle it is from 600-200 BC, compared with South Cadbury where the lack of settlement around the hillfort lasted from *c.*700-350 BC, Cadbury ceramic phases 4-6.

Therefore Danebury is different, as the centralising forces that contained the population began later and lasted for a shorter period. South Cadbury compares more with Maiden Castle, but Maiden Castle still stands out as the remarkably contained focus of a controlled social system.

At South Cadbury, through most of the Middle Iron Age, significant settlement evidence can be found surrounding the hillfort. The cohesive force of the hilltop settlement was in decline by the start of the first century AD, although the defences were maintained.

Was this area part of the Durotrigan zone at this time? Based on the evidence from the sites considered in north-west Dorset and south Somerset, the answer must be no. There were trade links with the south because shale and pottery imports have been found in south Somerset. However, the distinctive South Western Decorated Ware was in common use and the distribution of this lies across Somerset, Devon and Cornwall. The distinctive ceramic decoration is matched on wooden objects preserved within the waterlogged conditions of the Mere and Glastonbury lake villages. These decorations are likely to be an ethnic expression of communities who identified with each other.

The sudden ending of the use of this pottery and the swamping of the market with Poole Harbour Ware seems more than a change of fashion and is probably the result of dominance from the south. This change can be combined with the arrival of coinage in this area. There are some western series/Dobunnic issues introduced from the north but nearly all of the remaining coins are south-western series/Durotrigan. Melinda Mays' distribution maps of Phase I and Phase II Durotrigan coins clearly demonstrate that the south Somerset/north-west Dorset area lies within Mays' Latest Iron Age Phase II distribution. There are generally fewer coin finds and these tend to be bronze issues. This was true for the four coins from the study area found outside the hillfort. However, 6 of the 11 south-western series/Durotrigan issues found within the hillfort had up to 79 per cent silver content. Therefore one could argue that the hillfort was a higher status settlement, attracting individuals at an earlier period with coins of higher value/silver content than elsewhere.

Crouched burials in oval earth graves have also been found associated with Poole Harbour sherds. This indicates an influence of Durotrigan-style burial but nothing exactly comparable with the burials of south Dorset.

Is it possible to say whether this was a Durotrigan takeover or a Roman military imposition of imported ceramics and coinage into the area? The evidence for control by the Iron Age people of the south is plausible. It would have enabled the southerners to gain access to the Bristol Channel between the rivers Brue and Parrett, thus opening up markets for Purbeck products along the western coast of Britain.

Waddon Hill and Pilsdon Pen demonstrate that the presence of the Roman army did not necessarily cause a sudden ceramic change. At Waddon Hill, the Poole Harbour pottery and Durotrigan coinage is contained within the Roman fort. In south Somerset it is found in various levels of settlement across the countryside. Some settlements, like that at Halstock, begin with a Durotrigan phase.

The change is very late and sudden. At Maiden Castle the fabric analysis demonstrated a gradual percentage build-up to dominance of the Poole Harbour pottery over a period of 200 years, becoming increasingly rapid toward the end of the period. At South Cadbury, the change happens so quickly that there were only seven pits, of the many excavated within the hillfort, where ceramic Phase 8 (South Western Decorated) and Phase 9 (Poole Harbour) pottery were found together.

A modern comparison may be the way the Safeway supermarket was absorbed by Morrisons in Warminster. The process in which the town's only large supermarket had its brand completely changed took place in under a year. The signs, the carrier bags and the own-brand goods all now bear a different logo. The Cadbury ceramic evidence suggests a similar takeover.

Perhaps in south Somerset, at the Roman Conquest, this was a newly annexed area, with a population dissatisfied with its Durotrigan brand. In these circumstances they might not oppose the Romans and in return the new authority might grant them client status and allow them to retain temporary power in the same way that the Iceni maintained independence for a while. Perhaps by AD 60 their remaining independence was removed, their territory was forcibly controlled by Rome and therefore they sympathised with Boudicca, joined her uprising and were defeated.

In southern and eastern Dorset, the excavated material suggests conflict then peace, with the products of Purbeck adopted rapidly by the Roman authorities. There is a distinct contrast between the cemetery at the east gate of Maiden Castle and the scattered bones through the south-west gateway at South Cadbury.

At Ham Hill, South Cadbury and North Perrott there is evidence of severe measures against the local people by the Roman army. Consistently, south Somerset archaeologists record a hiatus in the third quarter of the first century AD, where the land seems to have been largely abandoned and not reoccupied until the second century AD. Ilchester seems to have been founded later than Dorchester, and Peter Leach speculated about the Boudiccan revolt and the evidence for unrest in the south-west that prevented the II Legion Augusta marching from their fortress at Exeter to join the hard-pressed forces of the Roman governor Suetonius Paulinus. Dorset archaeologists, with the exception of Ron Lucas at Halstock, generally suggest continuity of settlement from the Iron Age and gradual Romanisation throughout the Roman Conquest period.

The apparent difference of treatment by the Romans between the peoples of Dorset and Somerset may be between an enemy that was pacified and an ally that revolted. The continuing separateness of the two areas is supported by the inscriptions from Hadrian's Wall, set up by the Durotriges of Ilchester (*Durotrigum Lendiniesis*), this leading to the supposition that there was a separate *civitas* in this area.

9

CENTRAL DORSET

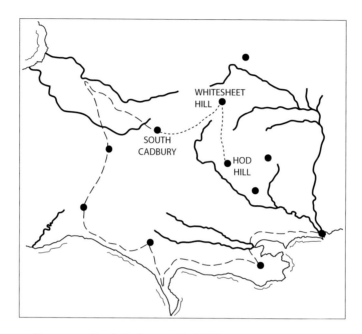

35 Tour map 5: South Cadbury to Hod Hill.

THE CENTRAL DORSET CHALKLAND

The survey has skirted the area of chalk downland north of the River Piddle and south of the Blackmore Vale. Comparatively little excavation has taken place here. RCHM staff carried out earthwork surveys of the enclosed farmsteads and extensive field systems of this undulating landscape. Many have since been levelled by ploughing. The farmsteads typically consisted of one or two round houses within or around a larger ovoid or rectilinear enclosure containing evidence for storage pits surrounded by trackways and rectilinear fields. The variety of forms can be seen around Cerne Abbas, at Giant Hill, Black Hill, Smacam Down and Dickley Hill. The evidence suggests that the area was intensively farmed from the Early Bronze Age until the Romano-British period.

The settlements on and around the high central chalk downlands typically remained as native style farmsteads; the Romanised settlements and villas generally developed from settlements beside tributaries of the rivers Frome and Piddle closer to Dorchester. This can be seen beside the Devil's Brook at Dewlish, where the Roman villa complex was constructed near a Late Iron Age settlement.

The hillforts of this area have not been archaeologically excavated and lie to the south above the Piddle valley at Weatherby Castle, Milborne St Andrew; Woodbury Bere Regis; Woolsbarrow in Bloxworth parish; and Bulbury, Lytchett Minster. Another group lies to the north along the chalk escarpment overlooking the Blackmore Vale at Dungeon Hill in the parish of Minterne Magna, Nettlecombe Tout in the parish of Melcombe Horsey, and Rawlsbury in the parish of Stoke Wake.

THE BLACKMORE VALE

Within the Blackmore Vale, only a few Iron Age sites have been recorded and these tend to be concentrated along the valley of the upper Stour (see below). This is an area of predominantly pasture fields where aerial photography is a less successful tool for identifying sites than on the chalk. With fewer opportunities for fieldwalking across ploughed land, discoveries tend to be made during building development, quarrying or when service trenches are excavated.

Prominent within Blackmore is Duncliffe Hill which lies between Shaftesbury and Gillingham. The hill has archaeological potential as it is of the same size and prominence as South Cadbury hillfort, 20km to the west, but the only record of a possible Iron Age find here is a bronze boar associated with a Roman figurine.

STOURHEAD

On the north side of Blackmore, beyond Bourton and Mere, on ridge tops and escarpments are three hillforts. These fortifications surround the source of the River Stour, a key north-south routeway across central and south-eastern Dorset. Castle Wood is univallate and lies on the Somerset border. Park Hill Camp is bivallate and the third is Whitesheet Hill (*36*), which is protected by three ramparts and ditches where it faces the downland plateau to the north. The natural defence of the steep escarpment meant that only a single rampart needed to be constructed on the hillfort's south side. A few surface finds of Early Iron Age pottery have been recovered from the site. Whitesheet was already significant in the Neolithic period as two causewayed enclosures can be seen near the hillfort.

None of these hillforts have been excavated although remains of an Early to Middle Iron Age settlement were found near the foot of the slope on the west side of Whitesheet Down beside a chalk quarry. The pottery found here dated to the fifth to fourth centuries BC.

Cold Kitchen Hill is 4km north of Whitesheet and the numerous finds from this site range from the Early Iron Age to the Romano-British period and include south-western series/Durotrigan staters. The finds indicate that a sacred site existed here throughout the Iron Age, with a Romano-Celtic temple subsequently erected on the hill. Roman coins and pottery from the site indicate that it was in use from the first to fifth centuries AD. This place was carefully chosen it seems. It occupies a hilltop, close to the sources of the rivers Brue, Wylye and Stour and near the escarpment that forms the northern edge of the Durotrigan zone.

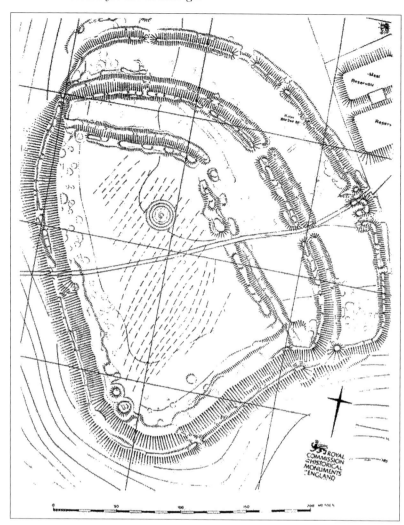

36 Earthwork plan of Whitsheet Hill hillfort, Stourhead Estate. (RCHME 1988) *Crown Copyright*

The survey now turns south back into Dorset and the Blackmoor Vale. On the west side of the Stour at Gillingham, Late Iron Age artefacts have been found associated with Romano-British settlement remains. Finds from this site at Common Mead Lane included a sherd of South Western Decorated Ware and fragments of Durotrigan pottery.

MARNHULL

The best recorded Iron Age settlement within the Blackmoor Vale is located another 6km down the River Stour in Marnhull parish. At Great Down Quarry, west of Todber, quarrying in the nineteenth century disturbed a Romano-British cemetery and occupation debris. The Iron Age origin of the site was found during excavations at Allard's Quarry about 200m to the south. This was excavated in 1932-39 and 1942-45. The large assemblage of distinctive late Middle Iron Age pottery from this site enabled a

Dorset typology of forms to be established for this period, known as the Maiden Castle-Marnhull classification.

Further south are two Roman villas that may have developed from Iron Age sites although they have never been excavated below their late Roman levels. These are Hinton St Mary, famous for its mosaic floors, and Fifehead Neville.

Only 2km to the east is the small univallate hillfort of Banbury Camp (*colour plate 21*), Okeford Fitzpaine. It was constructed on the summit of a low flat-topped hill on the south-west side of the Stour. In the late eighteenth century, a hoard of over 70 Durotrigan coins was found near this site. South-east of Banbury are the great hillforts of Hod and Hambledon.

STUDY AREA 5: CENTRAL DORSET, HOD AND HAMBLEDON HILLS

Topographic Description

The meandering River Stour cuts the 10km by 8km study area diagonally in half, entering at its north-west corner beside Sturminster Newton and leaving from the south-east where it flows through Blandford Forum. Between these two towns it passes through the villages and hamlets of Hammoon, Fontmell Parva, Child Okeford, Shillingstone, Hanford, Durweston and Stourpaine.

Near the centre of the study area, the Stour crosses from the Blackmoor Vale into the chalkland of central Dorset, cutting its path into the chalk escarpment and forming a natural gateway. The chalk escarpment is an irregular steep edge, consisting of a series of coombes and spurs generally following a north-east to south-west alignment.

At the centre of the study area are two hills of chalk, separated from the main escarpment by the valley of the River Iwerne. This tributary flows into the Stour from the north, passing through the villages of Iwerne Minster, Iwerne Courtney and Iwerne Steepleton.

The southern hill is occupied by the ramparts of Hod Hill which has the Iwerne against its east side and the Stour flowing at the foot of its steep western slope. The two rivers converge at Stourpaine 1km south of Hod.

Beyond a dry valley on the north side of Hod is Hambledon. The central summit of the hill is occupied by a Neolithic causewayed enclosure and three fingers of chalk radiate from it, pointing south towards Hod, east towards the village of Iwerne Courtney and north towards the settlements of Fontmell Parva and Child Okeford. Hambledon hillfort lies on this northern spur.

Hod and Hambledon are 1.5km apart but are not intervisible. Both hillforts can only be viewed from the Neolithic causewayed enclosure on the central summit of Hambledon Hill.

To the north-west and south-east of the Stour valley, other farms and settlements lie beside streams that feed the river. The largest of these are Pimperne to the east and Okeford Fitzpaine to the west. However, settlement is clearly concentrated along the river valleys of the Iwerne and Stour; only a scattering of farms and barns occupy the coombes and spurs of the chalkland to the north-east and south-west.

Chronological Development

Hambledon Hill

For the Neolithic and Bronze Age periods the available evidence clearly indicates that Hambledon Hill (*colour plate 20*) was a significant place. Few Neolithic sites are known elsewhere in the study area. But for Hambledon, the central summit causewayed enclosure, the Shroton, Stepleton and Hanford enclosures, and that presumed to lie beneath the hillfort, suggest an Early Neolithic complex more extensive than Whitesheet Hill 20km to the north.

Associated with the enclosures are two long barrows, one on the summit of the hillfort and one on the south edge of the main causewayed enclosure. Polished stone axes, found on the site, indicate the trade links of the population. In addition to a jade axe from central Europe, others were made from Cornish, Devonian, Welsh and Cumbrian stone. Radiocarbon analysis provided dates of 3800-3200 BC for the main period of occupation.

Later occupation of the central causewayed enclosure was found during the 1951 excavations. Finds included Peterborough and Beaker pottery of Late Neolithic to Early Bronze Age date.

Compared with Cranborne Chase to the east, there are very few Bronze Age burial mounds within the study area. Two lie on Shillingstone Hill, on the chalkland south-west of the Stour, but otherwise they are sited on Hod or Hambledon.

There is evidence for a single round barrow at Hod Hill but it was levelled to build the Roman fort. Fragments of pottery found in Roman features around the site may derive from this possible burial mound. Six round barrows have been recorded on Hambledon, five within the hillfort and one within the central causewayed enclosure.

Some settlement on Hambledon Hill is likely throughout the Bronze and Iron Age periods. A socketed bronze spearhead and a socketed bronze axe of Late Bronze Age date have been found. A univallate hillfort may have been built at this time and the earthwork analysis carried out by Royal Commission surveyors clearly demonstrates that there were several phases of expansion and remodelling of the site (*37*).

The 1959 survey interpreted the northern hillfort spur as the earliest phase of the hillfort. However, Roger Mercer reinterpreted the site following his excavation and suggested that the northern and central thirds comprised the original hillfort enclosure of 7ha. The circuit of this enclosure is irregular and may have included earlier features including a Neolithic enclosure. The steepness of the hill slopes meant that a large rampart (now 22m wide and 4.5m high) and ditch were only necessary where the defensive circuit crossed the spur where the ground slopes up from the southern third of the fort.

This early rampart was later modified to accommodate three hut platforms, including one 15m in diameter (Site J), the largest of *c.*365 round houses now identified within the hillfort. On the east side of Site J was the entrance to the early hillfort. Another entrance probably lay at the north end of the spur but the gap in the ramparts has been mutilated by quarrying.

Nearly all the dating evidence derives from the middle and northern thirds of the hillfort. Most of this comprises casual finds collected from erosion scars or rabbit scrapes. The Iron Age pottery found in the late nineteenth and early twentieth century is described in various ways but not illustrated. From Edward Cunnington's unlocated late nineteenth-

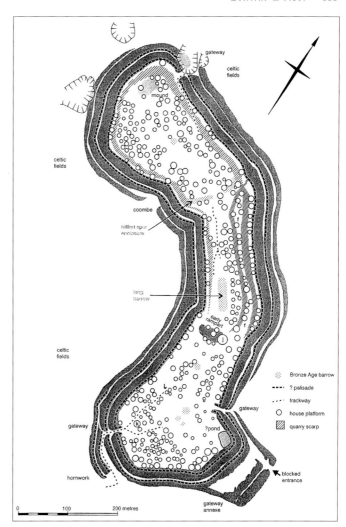

37 Plan of the earthworks of round house sites observed within Hambledon hillfort. (RCHME 1996, 36) *Crown Copyright*

century excavation on the summit, it is recorded as 'badly burnt soft pottery' and in the 1920s Eric Gardner classified his finds as 'All Cannings Cross ware that can be assigned to the Early Iron Age'. In 1959, Charles Bean described the pottery he found in the north-west hillfort ditches as 'Early Iron Age A'.

Roger Mercer's excavation of the ditch crossing the northern hillfort spur enclosure took in an Iron Age house platform terraced into the upper silts of the earlier ditch. The house was circular in plan and 6.5m in diameter. Finds included a fragment of a bone weaving comb, glass beads similar to those found at All Cannings Cross, and an iron 'swan's neck' pin suggesting a sixth- or early fifth-century BC date (RCHME 1996, 15). The house does not seem to have been rebuilt although there was a single sherd of Late Iron Age or Romano-British Black Burnished Ware included in the topsoil.

Although the ceramic evidence indicates an Early Iron Age date for the hillfort, the Royal Commission survey established a relative chronological framework for the development of the ramparts and ditches. These include enclosing the southern third of the hillfort, the building of an outer rampart around the entire hillfort, the building of the east and west gateways, the addition to them of hornworks and, in the case of the east entrance, the later addition of a barbican. However, because of the lack of excavated evidence it is unclear whether these changes took place during a short period of time or over several centuries. It is possible, as indicated at Poundbury, that the hillfort was maintained, upgraded but not widely occupied in the Late Iron Age.

Pimperne

Five kilometres south-east of Hambledon, the 2.5ha enclosure near the summit of Pimperne Down reveals that despite the concentration of house sites at Hambledon, settlement was not restricted to the hillfort in the Early Iron Age. Only one house was identified within the enclosure and pottery associated with this and pits and post-holes at the south and east entrances dated the site to the sixth to fifth centuries BC. Barry Cunliffe compared the 15m diameter Pimperne round house to that at Cow Down, Longbridge Deverill near Warminster. He suggested that the size of the enclosure at Pimperne may not reflect the size of a settlement but rather the status of the occupants. Large round houses like those at Cow Down, Pimperne and perhaps Site J at Hambledon are generally of Early Iron Age date. At the south entrance were found semi-articulated remains of a horse and ox. At the east entrance the ditch terminal contained a human femur and half a skull.

Hod Hill

Hod Hill is the largest hillfort in Dorset and its ramparts enclose a roughly rectangular, gently domed area of 22ha (*colour plates 17 & 18*). There is a counterscarp bank and two ramparts and ditches on all sides except the west. The steepness of the ground on this side meant that only a single rampart was necessary. Hod is particularly distinctive because a first-century Roman fort was built within the highest north-west corner of the hillfort. The ramparts have been breached in five places. The Iron Age entrances were built near the north-east and south-west corners. The Romans cut a gate in the north-west corner and perhaps near the centre of the eastern ramparts. The cut through the south-east corner is a medieval drove-way leading down to the village of Stourpaine.

Sir Ian Richmond's excavations of 1951-58 have provided most information to enable dating and phasing of the site.

There is some pottery from Hod Hill attributed to the Latest Bronze Age or Earliest Iron Age. Four of the five illustrated sherds were found near the round barrow within the Roman fort. As this is the highest point of the hill, the finds may indicate an early focus of occupation here although all were redeposited in Roman features. The fifth sherd was also redeposited and was found in the filling of the annex ditch to hut 56 in the south-east quadrant of the hillfort. The pottery was decorated with finger impressions typical of the Deverel-Rimbury style. Only one sherd was identified as All Cannings Cross pottery, in contrast to the finds from Hambledon.

The pottery from Hod Hill is predominantly of Middle and Late Iron Age date. As with Hambledon, although the pottery indicates a short period of occupation, the development of the hillfort takes place in several phases. These phases, if compared with the evidence from Maiden Castle and South Cadbury, would be expected to have taken place over several centuries.

Ian Richmond excavated sections through the ramparts. One was excavated on the north side of the north-east gateway and the other midway along the north side of the hillfort. Richmond's Stage I was a box rampart which he compared to Maiden Castle and 'typical of Iron Age A date'. His section drawing shows the forward post of the box rampart cutting a layer that overlies a scooped hollow in the chalk 2m wide and 0.3m deep. This earlier phase is not mentioned in the stratigraphic description and may be evidence for pre-hillfort occupation.

The ditch for the box rampart was altered in subsequent phases. The original dimensions survived where it was buried by the causeways for the Late Iron Age north-east ('Steepleton') and south-west ('Water') gates. The original Iron Age entrances for the Stage I hillfort are therefore unknown.

In Stage II, the rampart was altered to a 'glacis' style rampart of dump construction with a continuous slope from the bottom of the ditch to the top of the rampart where a stone wall was constructed. Stage IIA retained the back post of the box rampart and had an additional timber palisade in front of the ditch and in Stage IIB this palisade was removed and a rampart was constructed on the site and the ditch between the ramparts was deepened.

In Stage II at the north-east entrance, a twin portal gateway was erected. To this phase belongs a pit burial of a young woman interpreted as a 'foundation' burial within the extension of the gateway. Similar burials, but of young men, were found beneath ramparts at Maiden Castle and South Cadbury.

In Stage III the inner rampart was heightened and the stone summit wall rebuilt and a flint paved walk constructed behind it. A small outer ditch was constructed with an outer counterscarp bank. Richmond argued that this outer ditch and additional 'hornwork' defences at the two Iron Age gateways were incomplete when the Roman army occupied the site. This suggests that the Hod Hill people were working to improve their defences as the Roman army approached their fortified settlement.

Stage IV was the Roman demolition of the gate and rampart wall and the erosion of a hollow-way through the gate which was subsequently covered with a Roman roadway of flint.

Settlement Layout

The most visible settlement earthworks lie in a wedge of unploughed land in the south-east corner. The north-east quadrant was only ploughed for a few years and following John Brailsford and Ian Richmond's work, the then owners were persuaded to return the land to pasture. Over the last 50 years the old ploughsoil has settled to reveal lines of round houses and although Royal Commission archaeological surveyors had plotted the earthworks of the unploughed south-east triangle, the emerging north-east earthworks remain unsurveyed. However, in 2005 David Stewart offered to test the suitability of the site for geophysical survey. His results were remarkable and using Bournemouth University and National Trust geophysical equipment he has surveyed the whole interior and created a detailed plan. The results are considered here with reference to grid coordinates on figures *38-41* (see also *colour plate 19*).

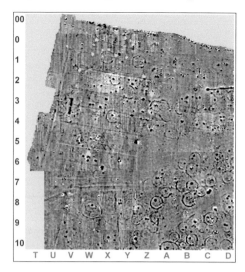

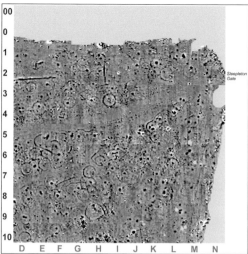

38 Fluxgate gradiometer survey Hod Hill, north-west quarter (Stewart 2006, 52)

39 Fluxgate gradiometer survey Hod Hill, north-east quarter (Stewart 2006, 54)

The fluxgate gradiometer survey of Hod Hill, demonstrates the density of occupation within the hillfort. Over 200 ring ditches are visible and there are traces of others, indicated by part circles and concentrations of pits and post-holes. The street system fanning out from the north-east gateway is clear. Few geophysical anomalies cross the line of the tracks indicating that the main routes tended to follow the same alignment during the occupation of the hillfort. The main east to west route is prominent and measures over 10m wide, broadening out to 50m (Y6) as it approaches the Roman fort gateway (V3). This broad area, which is about 60m long, has very few anomalies within it. Other tracks branch south, south-west and one continues west to the south side of the Roman fort gate. It is likely that the Roman soldiers utilised this track to the north-east gate as there is no geophysical evidence for another track crossing the central concentration of round houses towards the east gate.

The open area broadening out from the main track appears to be a focal point, a route centre, and perhaps an assembly point and possible site of a market. A similar open area within a crowded settlement can be seen on the geophysical survey plot for the Iron Age/Romano-British settlement at Crab Farm, Shapwick (*58*, see Chapter Eleven).

Near the north-east gate, a track diverges south from the main track and between the two are groups of post-holes that appear to be a line of four post structures (K4). Many of the hut circles have groups of four posts in close proximity, particularly those closest to the gateway. These are probably granaries but alternatively they may have been built or reused as mortuary platforms for excarnation. Many of the huts on the plot contain pits. These may originally have been for grain storage but a high proportion of the excavated examples had later been backfilled with structured 'ritual' deposits, including part or complete human burials (see below).

Of the five huts excavated by Ian Richmond, hut 36A lay in the north corner of the roughly square ditched enclosure 36, with sides 22m long and an entrance on the south-west

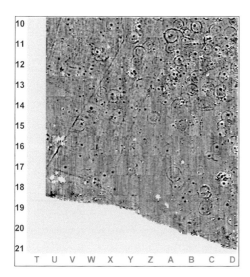

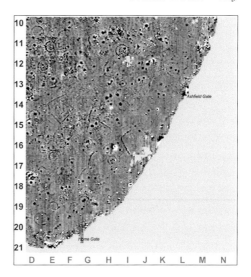

40 Fluxgate gradiometer survey Hod Hill, south-west quarter. (Stewart 2006, 53)

41 Fluxgate gradiometer survey Hod Hill, south-east quarter. (Stewart 2006, 55)

side. The hut had a central hearth and a spearhead was found beside the south-east facing entrance. Hut 37 is immediately north-east of 36A, its ring ditch cut into the edge of the enclosure ditch of 36. These three features 36, 36A and 37 had Roman ballista bolts embedded in them all similarly aligned. A single bolt was found in nearby hut 43 but none in 56 or 60 and Richmond concluded that 36 was a significant target (perhaps a chief's residence) chosen by the Romans to demonstrate the deadly accuracy of their artillery. The lack of other signs of conflict within the hillfort indicated that the inhabitants capitulated without a fight.

Huts 43 and 56 had small ditched annexes on their north sides and, from a pattern of post-holes and area of trampling, each was interpreted as a stable. Hut 60 was D-shaped in plan with a palisade trench along its west side. Beside the entrance of this unusual building were a horse terret and a knife, and two currency bars lay on the hut floor. All the huts had south-east entrances and all but 37 had finds on the south-west side of the entrance passage. In hut 56, 117 sling stones were found at the entrance, with a further 218 found in hut 43, as though they were placed there in readiness. These finds within the huts give an impression of sudden departure with no opportunity to return to retrieve valuable items.

The square enclosure (Richmond's 36) is clearly visible, E14 on the geophysical survey plot, with a minor track leading past its north-west side. However, three other enclosures stand out. One other rectilinear enclosure containing a hut circle lies beside a track in the north-east quadrant (H6). Its sides are 15m long as opposed to 22m for enclosure 36. An ovoid enclosure 20m long (H9) is 40m south of the smaller square enclosure H6 and contains a hut circle 6m in diameter. A similar ovoid enclosure lies 200m west of the last (W8) and measures 22m long, containing a 10m-diameter hut circle. These variations in size of hut circles and enclosures imply differences of social status for the occupants. Ian Richmond was sure that the finds within enclosure 36 and hut 36a were associated with an important leader within the settlement. In addition to the size of the enclosure, the find in the doorway of hut 36 was a spearhead rather than a store of sling stones and in neighbouring hut 37 was a rare and complete *tazza* jar, of Durotrigan fabric but continental style.

The geophysical survey has confirmed that none of the other enclosures are quite as large as 36, although the three listed above have their own private compounds apparently in contrast to the others which have no discernible property boundaries. As the survey plot is studied, more huts with attached annexes are apparent and compounds and stable areas attached to round houses may be more frequent (e.g. A3 & C7). The grouping of buildings probably reflects relationships, with household/extended family units occupying discrete areas within the settlement.

An area of strong magnetic responses was found beside the track leading to and 60m north-east of Richmond's enclosure 36. David Stewart recovered slag from mole hills on this site and also took soil samples for magnetic resonance testing. The samples proved to contain very high levels of iron and the slag was a typical product of iron smelting. The high magnetic readings cover an area 60m by 30m and indicate an industrial zone for iron production and smithing within the hillfort.

Burials

Compared with other Iron Age sites, Hod Hill has a high ratio of recorded human pit burials in relation to the number of pits excavated. In addition to the crouched 'foundation burial' from the north-east (Steepleton) gate and another burial found in 1953 eroding from the counter-scarp bank at the south-east breech in the ramparts (Home gate), remains of another twelve individuals have been found in pits. Four were complete adult crouched burials, two were infants and only fragments of skeletons represented the others. Both Professor Boyd-Dawkins in 1897 and Sir Ian Richmond excavated enclosures that may have been round house sites or mortuary enclosures. Each contained three pits.

Boyd-Dawkins' enclosure 6 was 13.7m in diameter, defined by a bank with no visible ditch. His pit A had human leg bones in one layer and part of a spine in another. The floor of pit B contained a 'hearth of flints covered in wood ashes' and pit C contained the burials of a crouched inhumation and the bones of a child and old man which were fragmented and therefore assumed to have been disturbed by the crouched inhumation.

Richmond's enclosure 15 was a horseshoe shaped scoop measuring 8m by 10m surrounded by a low bank. Pit 15a was small and contained Middle Iron Age pottery and an unusual number of metal objects, a bone weaving comb and chalk loom weight. Pit 15b contained a left tibia and foot, interpreted as all that remained of a primary burial dug away by the insertion of a secondary burial. This crouched skeleton of a woman was accompanied by a lock ring, bucket, latch lifter, a bobbin and two loom weights. The accompanying pottery was dated to the Late Middle to Late Iron Age. Pit 15c had a primary filling containing an unusual collection of objects, including a sickle or knife, spearhead, part of a shale bracelet, lower jaws of horses and bones of ox, sheep and pig. This deposit was cut into by another pit in which the crouched inhumation of a woman was found. Both deposits contained similar pottery of Middle or Late Middle Iron Age date. Richmond suggested that the female crouched burials in pit 15b and 15c were related because of similarity of the skull sutures.

It is interesting to note the similarities between the burials within enclosures Boyd-Dawkins 6 and Richmond 15 in the south-east quadrant of the hillfort. The earlier phases of two pits were represented by parts of skeletons and the later burials as complete inhumations. The female burial in pit 15b with an infant child between her legs, accompanied by objects associated with the home and joints of meat, led Richmond to believe that these were grave goods for the afterlife. Therefore, this Late Iron Age pit burial has similarities with the south Dorset burial tradition.

Currency

Derek Allen reviewed the evidence for sword-shaped 'currency bars' within the hillfort. He listed 27 items found on four separate occasions between 1856 and 1958. The two found within hut 60 were associated with Iron Age B pottery, leading Allen to suggest that the bars were currency immediately before the introduction of coinage. Julius Caesar mentioned that some of the British tribes used bars of iron as currency.

Allen's survey of all Iron Age coins recorded from the hillfort revealed that they were mainly later bronze Durotrigan issues but there was one rare silver issue with the word CRAB inscribed on it. Other coins of this type have been found beside the Solent but particularly on the Isle of Wight. There were also Dobunnic coins and two Icenian coins and two tin coins of Kentish origin. From Gaul, there were two coins of the Coriosolites and one identified as of the Lemovices. This concentration of coins from beyond the Durotrigan zone demonstrates that Hod drew people from a distance and that it probably acted as a market centre.

The Iwerne Valley Settlement

Other Iron Age coins have since been found on the land either side of the River Iwerne. These are predominantly silver or bronze Durotrigan issues but the finds include at least one silver Dobunnic coin and two others described as quarter silver staters of geometric type of the 'Sussex Group'.

Melinda Mays has reviewed the coins from the area and placed Hod Hill near the northwest boundary of the earlier period Phase I of Durotrigan coinage.

When the finds are plotted, the coins are clustered in three groups along the Iwerne, spaced at 1km intervals below the eastern ramparts of the hillfort (*42*). Each site has Roman artefacts and coins found in close proximity suggesting continuity of occupation. That to the north, near Iwerne Steepeleton, has a spread of building debris on its east side that crosses the Child Okeford road and the finds indicate that the site may have developed into a Roman building of status, perhaps a villa. Further south near Lazerton Farm, Iron Age, Roman and also Saxon coins have been recovered mixed with building debris.

We carried out a gradiometer survey in 2002 and this showed a cluster of small contiguous rectilinear enclosures underlying the Roman and Iron Age occupation debris in the field north-west of Stourpaine village. Following his work on Hod Hill, Dave Stewart has surveyed this area and demonstrated that these enclosures continue along the west bank of the Iwerne. They indicate a concentration of occupation features flanking a trackway that follows the contour of the hill. In 2009, his excavations to investigate some of these geophysical anomalies have revealed Middle and Late Iron Age storage pits and boundary ditches overlain by remains of Romano-British buildings and structures.

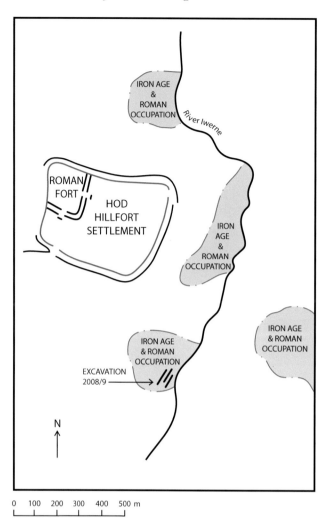

42 Areas of Iron Age and Romano-British occupation debris along the Iwerne valley.

The extent of the finds combined with evidence from geophysical survey and excavation indicates that this place developed into a major settlement in the Roman period. Two fifth-century brooches, Saxon *sceattas* dating from the seventh to eighth centuries, together with a tenth-century Viking coin, indicate that this continued to be a significant place. The land had been divided into a series of manors and farms by 1086 and the present Stourpaine village may represent settlement shift but continuity of occupation in this area from the Iron Age.

WIDER LANDSCAPE

Beyond the hillforts, occupation evidence is divided between the upland and river valley sites (*44*). From the available evidence, it seems that the upland sites continue to be occupied from the Late Iron Age into the Romano-British period, but continuity from the

Early to Late Iron Age is less certain. The one excavated site on Pimperne Down was abandoned by the fourth century BC although there may have been a shift south into a nearby smaller enclosure in the Late Iron Age. This has not been dated by excavation.

The ovoid Pimperne enclosures, as with others sited on the crests of downland spurs, lie within field systems, for example, Ringmoor, Turnworth (*43*), South Down, Ibberton, Shillingstone Hill and Meriden Down, Winterborne Houghton. Pottery found after ploughing on the South Down, Shillingstone Hill and the southern Ringmoor enclosures indicates that they were occupied in the Romano-British period. South Down and Meriden Down contain house platforms. Meriden Down, like Ringmoor, lies at a junction of trackways, although it is a larger 2ha-ovoid enclosure with earthwork evidence of later expansion south across former 'Celtic' fields.

The available evidence for these sites does not suggest that their occupants were wealthy. Finds of Iron Age and Roman coins tend to be concentrated on lower hill slopes or valleys. In addition to the Iwerne valley finds, Iron Age and Roman coins have been found at Green Line Farm, Okeford Fitzpaine and Park House Farm, Iwerne Minster, north-east of Hambledon. The valley sites of Shillingstone, west of Hambledon, and Bryanston School, south of Hod, represent 'green field' Romano-British settlement beside the Stour as no Iron Age material has been found associated with them. However, General Pitt Rivers' excavations demonstrate that Park House Farm is a good example of a valley site continuously occupied from the Late Iron Age through to the fourth century AD. He considered that the earlier occupation of the site lay north-west of the excavated area. The various Late Iron Age storage pits underlying the Roman building footings contained Durotrigan silver coins. By the fourth century, the inhabitants were living in a substantial rectangular stone house 40m long and 8m wide, decorated with painted plaster.

Places like Dorchester and Ilchester demonstrate their local economic importance by having a ring of villas in the countryside around them. Hod Hill has villas around it and

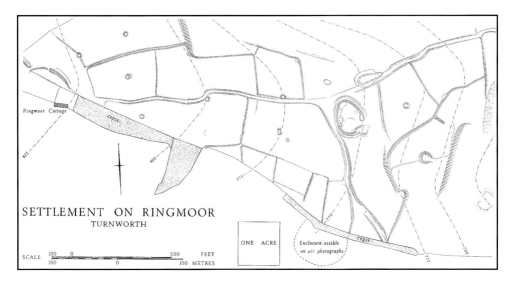

43 Earthwork plan of Ringmoor, Turnworth 7. (RCHM 1970b, 291) *Crown Copyright*

these include Shillingstone, Hinton St Mary and Fifehead Neville to the west, Park House Farm to the north and Barton Farm, Tarrant Hinton, to the east. They provide further evidence for the significance of the Iwerne valley settlement in the Roman period.

CONCLUDING REMARKS

Some time has been spent in weighing up the combined evidence from Hod and Hambledon hills in an attempt to understand why two such large hillforts lie in close proximity.

The simple answer seems to be that the earlier site was Hambledon and from the Early Neolithic period it developed as a key occupation focus with Late Neolithic, Bronze Age and Early Iron Age material all found there despite the minimal amount of excavation within the hillfort itself.

In contrast, Hod seems to have developed later as it only seems to have one Early Bronze Age barrow, no Late Bronze Age metalwork and a few scraps of Earliest Iron Age pottery. However, Charles Warne's assertion that round house earthworks were cut by the construction of the hillfort's ramparts and ditches suggests Early Iron Age occupation. Ian Richmond's construction phases for the ramparts demonstrate development over several centuries.

Similarly, it is difficult to use the sparse finds of Early Iron Age pottery from Hambledon to suggest that the hillfort was abandoned by the Late Iron Age in preference for the more spacious hilltop location of Hod. This is because much of the pottery comes from beneath or within the rampart material and, like Hod, the hillfort earthworks demonstrate defensive development over a long period of time. The more sheltered southern third of the hillfort has never been excavated and there is earthwork evidence for hundreds of round houses there. The development of the elaborate east and west gateways, similar to those at Hod, indicate later as well as Early Iron Age people lived in this area.

However, the combined evidence suggests a gradual shift of prominence from Hambledon to Hod during the Later Iron Age. The recent geophysical survey shows the interior of Hod packed with round houses and other features. The lines of trackways are generally clear of anomalies and this implies a shorter period of concentrated occupation, suggesting a settlement conforming to a plan that has not altered greatly during its lifetime. This is in contrast to elements of the Crab Farm settlement, Shapwick, where tracks and roads can be seen superimposed on earlier features (see 58). This process of settlement change between the Early and Late Iron Age may be reflected at Pimperne, where the occupation ceases in the Early Iron Age but local settlement may have shifted to the smaller enclosure to the south.

Hod and Hambledon are not intervisible and they command different vantage points. If they worked co-operatively then a signalling site would be required on the central summit of Hambledon, above the causewayed enclosure. One could argue that Hambledon was largely abandoned as a settlement but the earthwork defences continued to be modified in case of attack or as a symbol of prestige. This seems to have been the case at Poundbury, Dorchester, where the main settlement lay outside the ramparts beside the river but the hillfort earthworks were maintained and enhanced. The references to Roman material found at Hambledon by John Aubrey in the seventeenth century and Edward Cunnington in 1894 provides some evidence for later occupation of the site.

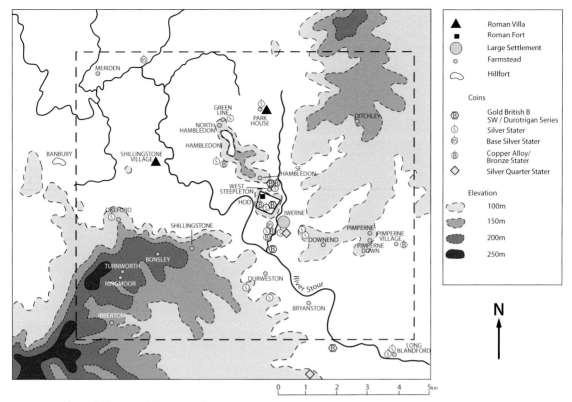

44 Sites within central Dorset study area.

The evidence from the land beside the Iwerne River, below the eastern ramparts of Hod, highlights the importance of looking at the immediate environs of hillforts rather than concentrating investigation within the ramparts. A significant settlement lay within the hillfort but also a string of households or farmsteads occupied the river valley. Another Late Iron Age site lies on the north side of Hambledon. The close proximity of these hillforts to the river made occupation beside the water convenient.

The secure cultural focus of the hillfort, as well as the political and economic status and perhaps its sacred importance, were retained. In the Late Iron Age, valley residence was becoming increasingly desirable and settlement was expanding there. Nevertheless, despite the presumed attraction of the valley, settlement drift that might cause gradual abandonment of the hillfort is not implied in Ian Richmond's excavation report. This is in contrast to the evidence from Maiden Castle and South Cadbury. Perhaps this was because the river lay too close to significantly decrease the population in the Latest Iron Age and the occupation along the river and within the hillfort may all be part of one large Hod/Iwerne settlement. This combination of the benefits of the economic route centre of the Stour/Iwerne confluence and the grand defended settlement icon of Hod is likely to have acted as a magnet drawing people from the surrounding countryside rather than from the hillfort to the valley. One might suggest that Hod was reoccupied in the Latest Iron Age as a response to the Roman military threat. However, this is not confirmed by the excavated evidence which demonstrates long periods of occupation for each of the excavated round house sites and a sudden departure when the hilltop was requisitioned by the Roman army.

Unlike many other sites, there is evidence that Iron Age status dwellings occupied the hillfort interiors. The Hod Hill geophysical survey shows several round houses within enclosures, particularly Richmond's enclosure 36. At Hambledon there are large 15m diameter round house platforms and size suggests status, particularly platform J which occupies a commanding position beside the rampart dividing the southern and middle thirds of the hillfort. However, the large Hambledon round houses may be early. The 15m diameter round house as at Pimperne was dated to the Early Iron Age, in contrast to Hod where the Late Iron Age round houses are smaller. Nevertheless, Hod's enclosed round houses indicate status for their residents. They may represent an early definition of increased private social space for the occupier, a developing trend for the wealthy throughout the Romano-British period. Another Late Iron Age example of a separate space for a round house is the Phase 3 circular enclosure at Gussage All Saints (see Chapter Eleven).

The coinage from the area includes occasional gold British B coins and some Durotrigan staters with high silver content. This study area lies on the west edge of the Cranborne Chase coin concentration and falls just within Melinda Mays' earlier phase of south-western series/Durotrigan issues. The reported locations of exotic coins within the study area lie exclusively within the Hod/Iwerne settlement and this supports the hypothesis that trade with neighbouring communities was concentrated there.

The Hod/Iwerne settlement is a strong candidate for a Late Iron Age *oppidum* or proto-town with trade links to the Gallic communities to the south and Dobunni to the north along the Stour. Hod is thought to be the location of Ptolemy's *Dunium*, the principal place of the Durotriges, and in the Roman period may have been the site of *Ibernio* of the *Antonine Itinerary*. The geophysical survey creates an impression of order and industry and the open area near the centre may be interpreted as a gathering point for meetings and perhaps a market.

Hod and Hambledon are clearly key locations within their environs and it is difficult not to refer to them other than as central places surrounded by smaller settlements and farmsteads like those at Turnworth, Shillingstone Hill and Meriden Down. The idea that Hod was just another type of settlement and of no great significance compared to others in this study area cannot be supported. In contrast, the surrounding area contains typical upland enclosures for farmsteads or hamlets. It is interesting to note that none of these can be categorised as 'banjo' enclosures or farmsteads with antenna entrances, despite the proximity of such sites on Cranborne Chase a few kilometres to the east.

More sophisticated sites lie in the valleys and certainly at Park Farm, Iwerne Minster, the Roman settlement developed from a Late Iron Age site which eventually included rectangular stone buildings decorated with plaster.

The survey now backtracks along the Stour and returns to Cold Kitchen Hill near the source of the Wylye River.

10

SOUTH WILTSHIRE
AND CRANBORNE CHASE

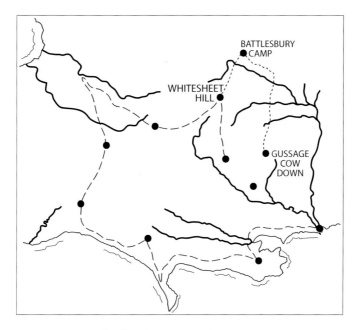

45 Tour map 6: Hod Hill to Gussage Cow Down.

This area east of Stourhead as far as Salisbury and south across the Wylye, Nadder and Ebble rivers, contains a variety of significant Iron Age sites. These will be summarised in brief descriptions linked to past research. The Cranborne Chase study box will then be examined.

THE WYLYE VALLEY

The sacred site of Cold Kitchen occupies a chalk ridge near the sources of the Stour and Wylye rivers. Wiltshire derives its names from the Wylye and for the first 12km it is known as the Deverill and flows north-east, flanked by downland hills. The river emerges into a lowland landscape at my home town of Warminster and then turns east back into the chalkland.

At this important gateway, a group of four hillforts cluster around the valley entrance. The 7ha Cley Hill (*colour plate 22*) is a dramatic landscape feature 2km west of the town and escarpment. It is a chalk outlier rising from the gently undulating Greensand, crowned by

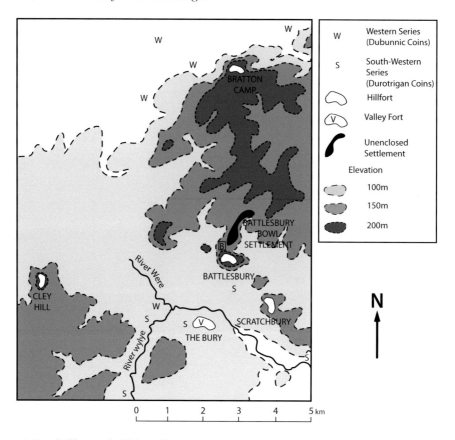

	Western Series (Dubunnic Coins)
W	
S	South-Western Series (Durotrigan Coins)
◯	Hillfort
Ⓥ	Valley Fort
❚	Unenclosed Settlement

Elevation

◌	100m
◌	150m
◌	200m

46 Four hillforts at the Wylye valley entrance at Warminster.

the prominent profile of a round barrow. Bratton Castle, 6km to the north, near Westbury, encloses 12ha and lies on the crest of the escarpment with clear views north and west towards Trowbridge, Bradford on Avon and Frome. Two kilometres into the valley, on its north side, is the 10ha Battlesbury and 2km further south-east is Scratchbury hillfort enclosing 17ha. All of these sites have two ramparts and ditches except Cley Hill which is enclosed by a single low rampart. Only Battlesbury has excavation records. In the 1920s, a local school teacher, Victor Manley, recorded Later Iron Age material here during the construction of a reservoir.

Battlesbury and Scratchbury lie either side of Middle Hill and the gaps between these landscape features give access from the Wylye to a dry valley known as the Battlesbury Bowl where an extensive Earliest Iron Age settlement has been recorded (*colour plate 23*).

Each morning I drive to work along the valley with the earthworks of these last two hillforts on the skyline. At Eastleigh Court, Bishopstrow, is a fifth significant Iron Age feature. This is known as the Bury and was built at a bend in the river on a low ridge of land. From the office window I can see the bank and ditch that forms its boundary. Geophysical survey has revealed ditches and traces of building footings within it. In the early nineteenth century, Richard Colt–Hoare of Stourhead had this 22ha univallate enclosure surveyed and drawn (*47*). This is the best illustration for the site which has been badly damaged over the last 200 years. Finds from this valley settlement indicate that it was occupied from the first to fourth centuries AD.

This local concentration of significant sites from the Battlesbury Bowl to the Bury represents 1500 years of a shifting focus of settlement from the high ground to the valley floor. This is clearly an important centre and will be considered further in Chapter Twelve.

Along the valley, many earthworks have been recorded. Five kilometres east of Scratchbury, on the north side of the Wylye, lies the small 1.7ha plateau fort of Knook Camp and 5km south-east of this is the 5ha circular bank and ditch known as Codford Circle. Neither has been dated. The 13ha hillfort of Yarnbury Castle lies 5km east of Codford Circle and has three ramparts and ditches with an elaborate east entrance.

Other hillforts and enclosures further east were built beside the various rivers to the north of the Salisbury confluence but these are thought to be outside the Durotrigan zone. They are the Stapleford Down univallate enclosure on the east side of the River Till; 5km to the east, the univallate Ogbury Camp beside the Avon; and 6km to the south, also on the east bank of the Avon, the great univallate hillfort of Old Sarum. Old Sarum's pre-conquest importance is implied by the large Romano-British settlement that developed beside the river at Stratford south of the hillfort, associated with *Sorbiodunum* of the *Antonine Itinerary*. Five kilometres further east, beyond the River Bourne, is the circular univallate hillfort of Figsbury Rings. Other circular defended enclosures lie 6km north of Salisbury along the Bourne at Boscombe Down West and 3km south-west at Cockey Down.

The survey now continues south and crosses three rivers and two ridges before entering Cranborne Chase.

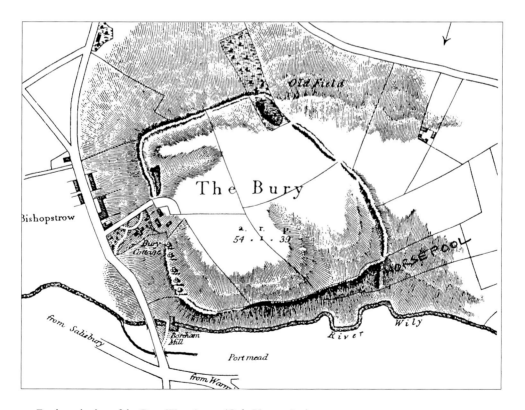

47 Earthwork plan of the Bury, Warminster. (Colt-Hoare 1821)

The Nadder–Wylye Ridge

The wedge of land between the rivers Wylye and the Nadder extends about 20km west of their confluence at Wilton. A series of remarkable Iron Age sites are spaced along the crest of the ridge.

In 2004, Ian Powlesland plotted the aerial photographic evidence along the Wylye valley and this demonstrates that enclosed settlements and farmsteads occupied many of the numerous chalk spurs along the south side of the Wylye valley.

Stockton, Hanging Langford, Hamshill Ditches and Ebsbury Hill

Along the eastern half of the ridge between the rivers, there are a very distinctive group of large Iron Age sites. They differ from the settlements around Warminster and will be compared with them in Chapter Twelve.

Mark Corney has surveyed and described four major nucleated settlements here which have their origins in the Late Iron Age but continued to be occupied throughout the Roman period, each defined by multiple and single ditch systems. These are, from west to east, Stockton, Hanging Langford, Hamshill Ditches (*48*) and Ebsbury Hill above Wilton. North of these sites, on spurs overlooking the Wylye, are two small hillforts, Bilbury Rings and Grovely Castle. On a spur between these two is an enclosed farmstead known as East Castle. Bilbury was dated to the Late Iron Age from excavations directed by Rev. Steele from 1959-65 and a few stray finds of Late Iron Age pottery have been found at Grovely. On the other side of the ridge overlooking the Nadder at Dinton, is a similar small hillfort known as Wick Ball Camp. This lies 4km south of Bilbury but there are no datable finds from this site. These three hillforts are 3-4ha in area.

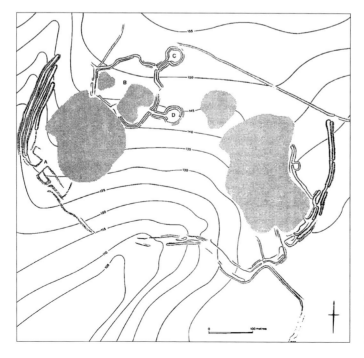

48 Earthwork plan of the Hamshill Ditches settlement. (Corney 1989, 115) *Crown Copyright*

THE EBBLE-NADDER RIDGE

Less is known of the ridge between the Nadder and Ebble rivers, an area about 6km wide and 25km long extending from the Avon in the east to the Blackmore Vale.

Castle Ditches

The most impressive monument of the Ebble-Nadder Ridge area is Castle Ditches, a developed hillfort built on a spur of Upper Greensand on the south side of the Nadder opposite the village of Tisbury. Strong double ramparts enclose a flat hilltop area of 10ha. The fort has opposing Iron Age entrances on the east and west sides. Middle, Late Iron Age and Romano-British pottery has been found on this site and geophysical survey has revealed a number of round houses within the ramparts (Payne, Corney & Cunliffe 2006, 104).

Castle Ditches commands a position overlooking the Nadder and the Vale of Waldour. This area was the subject of a fieldwalking project from 1976-78 which was noteable for its lack of Iron Age and Romano-British finds.

Castle Rings and Chiselbury Camp

On the chalk escarpment above the Nadder, 7km south-west of Castle Ditches, lies Castle Rings. It is sited 5km south of the Late Iron Age East Knoyle settlement near Shaftesbury overlooking the Blackmore Vale. In 1913, Heywood Sumner drew a plan of the univallate Castle Rings which shows four entrances. It is undated apart from a hoard of Durotrigan coins that has been found nearby.

Four kilometres to the east of Castle Ditches is the smaller hillfort of Chiselbury Camp, Fovant. This is about 4ha in area and also overlooks the Nadder lying above a steep escarpment (Crawford & Keiller 1928, 76).

Swallowcliffe and Fifield Bavant

In the 1920s, R.C. Clay excavated two enclosures on Swallowcliffe Down and they were dated from pottery finds to *c.*550-400 BC. In contrast, two settlement sites excavated at Fifield Bavant 4km to the east were found to have been occupied *c.*600-100 BC.

In 1965, Peter Fowler published a survey of the west part of the Ebble-Nadder Ridge and examined in detail the available aerial photographic and earthwork evidence. In addition to the settlements mentioned above, he identified a 5ha polygonal enclosure at Precombe Down in a similar position overlooking the Ebble and 1km west of the Fifield Bavant sites. One of the prehistoric field systems along the ridge clearly respects this enclosure. On Buxbury spur above the Nadder, 2km north-east of Swallowcliffe and 4km south-west of Chiselbury, lies a cross-ridge dyke which isolates the spur, perhaps indicating the site of a defended settlement but it may only have functioned as secure penning for livestock.

Little Woodbury

At the east end of the ridge where the Nadder and Ebble join the Avon are three sites. The best known are the Woodburys, Little Woodbury and 0.5km to the west Great Woodbury.

In 1939, on Harnham Hill, 0.5km north-west of Great Woodbury, an Iron Age site was recorded during road construction. It was thought to be very similar to Little Woodbury and was dated to 500-200 BC.

Apart from Castle Ditches there is little evidence for Late Iron Age occupation on the Ebble-Nadder Ridge and therefore the settlement evidence here contrasts with the discoveries along the Nadder/Wylye and Oxdrove ridges.

THE OXDROVE RIDGE

Running along the south side of the River Ebble is another ridge of chalk known as the Oxdrove Ridge. This area is about 25km long and 4-5km wide and extends from the Avon in the east to Melbury and Fontmell Downs in the west overlooking the Blackmore Vale.

Winkelbury Camp is a 5ha hillfort, 6km east of Fontmell and 4km south of the Swallowcliffe Down enclosure. During the 1880s, excavations by General Pitt Rivers revealed that the Late Iron Age hillfort had been built on an Early Iron Age settlement.

Cross-Ridge Dyke System

In 1959, the ridge east of Winkelbury was the subject of a detailed survey by Royal Commission staff. Paul Rahtz combined this work with targeted excavation and produced a report which provided a significant insight into the Late Iron Age character of the Oxdrove Ridge. Six cross-ridge dykes were found to divide an area measuring 6km east to west by 3km. All evidence for prehistoric settlement, burial, boundaries and field systems was mapped. Two of the Oxdrove Ridge dykes (dyke A 'Great Ditch Banks' and dyke C 'Middle Chase Ditch') were dated to the Late Iron Age by excavation.

Mark Corney studied the Royal Commission plan of the area. He thought that it demonstrated the complexity and extent of land division with many prehistoric field blocks being associated with enclosed and open settlements. These settlements include Chickengrove Bottom and Marleycombe Hill east of dyke A and Woodminton Down East at the south end of dyke F.

On the east side of Knighton Hill, 3km along the ridge from Bower Chalke, there is a settlement known as 'Wudu-Burh'. The site consists of a group of enclosures above a coombe associated with Iron Age and Roman pottery.

Clearbury Ring

At the east end of the ridge on a spur above the Avon is Clearbury Ring, a 2ha univallate enclosure. It is rectilinear in plan with an entrance in the west side. On the next spur 1km north-west and within Odstock Copse lie the remains of a circular univallate hillfort, the north part ploughed down and two banks added to the east side. Neither of these sites has been dated by excavation.

The land south of Clearbury slopes down from the Oxdrove Ridge into the western incursion of Hampshire. The county boundary here extends west of the Avon, driving a wedge between Dorset and Wiltshire.

HAMPSHIRE WEST OF THE AVON, NORTH-EAST OF BOKERLEY DYKE

Whitsbury Castle Ditches is 4km south-west of Clearbury and is a trivallate hillfort enclosing 7ha with the original entrance probably to the west, now occupied by Castle Farm buildings. In 1960, an excavation by Philip Rahtz on the site of a new farm building uncovered the plan of a D-shaped Iron Age hut with a rammed chalk floor associated with pottery of the Yarnbury-Highfield group of 'saucepan-pot' style (Bowen 1990, 77).

Collin Bowen examined the settlement remains either side of Bokerley Dyke, the massive linear earthwork that forms the Dorset-Hampshire border. He concluded that there were significant differences and that Bokerley was a territorial boundary in the Iron Age.

Two sites, Soldiers Ring and Rockbourne Down, Bowen termed large polygons and are an enclosure type only found on the Hampshire side of the boundary. Soldiers Ring, Damerham, is 11ha in area and five-sided, with an entrance between the two parallel enclosure banks on the east side. The Rockbourne Down site is also five sided and the rampart and flanking ditches enclose 36ha.

The Romano-British Woodyates settlement lies against the north side of Bokerley Dyke but the Iron Age settlement enclosures are immediately south of the Bokerley gateway. General Pitt Rivers and Philip Rahtz excavated part of the Roman settlement and found some first-century AD material but most of the occupation dated from *c.*AD 275-400. Collin Bowen described the details of the Iron Age settlement that had been revealed by aerial photography. The photograph shows two conjoined oval enclosures each of 0.7ha containing numerous pits. This could be interpreted as a gateway site behind the entrance through the Bokerley Dyke.

A line of 1.5-2ha ovoid enclosures about 0.5km from the south-west side of Bokerley have been plotted from aerial photos. A further 0.5km behind these are the 'unfinished' univallate hillforts of Penbury Knoll and Mistleberry Wood which will be considered in the next study area.

STUDY AREA 6: CRANBORNE CHASE, GUSSAGE HILL

This 10km by 8km area occupies the centre of Cranborne Chase and contains a range of distinctive, well-researched Iron Age settlements.

Topographic Description

The land varies in height from 200m OD in the north-west to 50m in the south-east. It is chalkland terrain that consists of a series of coombes and spurs.

The study area includes the south-east side of the Oxdrove Ridge and from this high point; the trend of slope is downwards towards Knowlton in the valley of the Allen where the river clips the south-east corner of the study area.

Three valleys aligned north-west to south-east contain streams which drain into the Allen. That to the south-west is the Crichel with the villages of Chettle at its source and Long Crichel 3km to the south-east. The central valley contains the Gussage stream which has the village of Farnham at its source and meanders through a string of hamlets and villages spaced at 1-2km intervals along the valley. These are Minchington, Gussage St Andrew, Cashmoor, Gussage St Michael and Gussage All Saints. The north-east valley is the source of the Wimborne or Allen which flows through the villages of Monkton up Wimborne and Wimborne St Giles before turning south-west and, after crossing the study area, eventually joins the River Stour at Wimborne Minster 14km to the south.

At the south-west corner of the area is the Tarrant valley and just beyond the north-east boundary lies the valley of the Crane. Therefore the area is characterised by a succession of near parallel ridges and troughs.

The village of Tollard Royal, beside Rushmore Park, is on the spring-line below the Oxdrove Ridge escarpment in the north-west corner of the study area. The B3081 links Tollard with the village of Sixpenny Handley 6km to the east. Other hamlets along the escarpment foot are Woodcuts, Deanland, Deanend and West Woodyates.

The area is cut diagonally in half from north-east to south-west by the main Salisbury to Blandford Road (A354). This diverges from the line of the Roman road to Badbury Rings, after crossing Bokerley Dyke just east of the study area. The minor roads to the villages branch from the A354 and follow the valleys and ridges north-west towards the escarpment or south-east towards the Allen.

Apart from the large block of woodland on the escarpment near Tollard Royal and Rushmore, the area has been heavily ploughed. This has enabled many of the prehistoric sites to be identified through aerial photography.

Chronological Development

It might be argued that the multiple ditch systems and enclosures extending from Berwick Down to Gussage All Saints were once part of one or two large integrated settlement areas similar to those on the Nadder-Wylye Ridge. However, with the exception of the double 'banjo' enclosures on Gussage Cow Down, each farmstead or household enclosure seems to be a discrete site.

The early prehistory of the area has been described in detail by Martin Green (2000), John Barrett and Richard Bradley (1991).

From the Neolithic until the Middle Bronze Age, the local population built extraordinary monuments to create one of the most outstanding designed landscapes of prehistoric earthworks. The earliest features are the earthen long barrows which are closely associated with the Dorset Cursus. This is an unparalleled earthwork measuring 90m wide and 10km long, built across the upper Gussage and Allen valleys. Downslope, on the valley floor of the Allen, in the south-east corner of the study area, are the Knowlton henge monuments surrounded by a concentration of round barrows.

In the Middle Bronze Age, ditches and banks defined the locations of some settlements. Three sites of this date have been excavated in the study area. Angle Ditch on Handley Hill was excavated by General Pitt Rivers in the 1890s. South Lodge near Rushmore and Down Farm near Gussage Hill were excavated 1977-84. South Lodge was completely enclosed by a bank and ditch, rectilinear in plan with an entrance to the south-west. The other two sites were only enclosed by a ditch on two sides, their enclosures probably completed by fencing. At Down Farm, other post-holes suggested at least five round houses with entrances to the south-east, two pre-dating the construction of the enclosure. In the latest phase a long rectangular building was constructed against the east bank. At South Lodge two round houses were identified.

Both settlements lie near Late Bronze Age, Deverel-Rimbury barrow cemeteries. The radiocarbon dates for the South Lodge and Down Farm enclosures indicate that they were occupied from *c.*1200-950 BC.

A Late Bronze Age settlement enclosure, areas of burnt flint, finds of bronze artefacts and linear ranch boundaries have been plotted along the Gussage valley and these indicate the division of the land into farms or territories by that time.

Within Cranborne Chase, as elsewhere, there appears to have been significant social change between the Middle and the Latest Bronze Age. During this period, cremation cemeteries cease to be used and settlements move to new locations where storage pits begin to be excavated.

At Down Farm, the recent excavations directed by David Northcott have demonstrated that settlement moved from the Late Bronze Age farmstead to a 'tombstone' or D-shaped enclosure 200m to the west. The Late Bronze Age hiatus is demonstrated here, as there is a gap of 200-250 years in the current understanding of the ceramic sequences from both sites. The Down Farm enclosure is thought to have been occupied from 700-200 BC although only the interim report is available at this stage.

The Hillforts

This part of Cranborne Chase is distinctive because of its lack of developed hillforts but there are four, possibly five, univallate hillforts located in and around the study area (see *53*). Winkelbury on the Oxdrove Ridge 1km north of Rushmore has already been described. Mistlebury Wood is on a spur 4km south-east of Winkelbury on the Oxdrove Ridge escarpment. Penbury Knoll hillfort, 4km to the south-east of Mistlebury, lies on a hill overlooking Bokerley Dyke. All three of these sites are between 1.5 and 3ha in area and described as 'unfinished'. Dating evidence is lacking apart from at Winkelbury where some Late Iron Age sherds were excavated from the rampart.

The fourth site is known as Bussey Stool Farm. It is of similar size to the other three, 6km south-west of Winkelbury and 1km west of the study area. This has opposing entrances on the south-east and north-west sides and is a complete enclosure. Once again there is no excavated evidence from the site. It lies above the Tarrant valley.

Martin Busby of English Heritage has recently identified another possible hillfort from aerial photographs. This occupies a knoll north-west of Mycen Farm and is of similar size to the other hillfort sites with traces of a bank and external ditch, the location enabling clear views in all directions.

In contrast to the abundant Late Iron Age remains within the study area, Earlier Iron Age evidence is generally lacking. However, there is evidence from excavated settlement enclosures at Oakley Down, in the north-east part of the study area, and from Gussage All Saints to the south-east.

Oakley Down Enclosure

From 1947-51, five trenches were excavated within the 3.7ha rectangular enclosure on Oakley Down (Brown, Corney & Woodward 1995, 67-79). Aerial photographs show dense settlement evidence across the main enclosure and a 1ha annexe on its north side which may be contemporary. The site is associated with up to five trackways. One track crosses the main enclosure through entrances in its north-west and south-east sides and links the enclosure to the Roman road to Badbury. The prehistoric field system that surrounds the site appears to be aligned with it, suggesting that it was laid out after the enclosure's construction.

The excavation of the 3m wide and 1.5m deep enclosure ditch recovered Early Iron Age pottery of *c.*550-450 BC from the primary silts. The bank of the enclosure overlay post-holes which contained pottery of similar date, suggesting that the site was initially unenclosed. A single sherd of Middle Iron Age pottery from the ploughed down remains of the bank may date the enclosure to this period. However, this is uncertain and there may have been a gap between the construction of the enclosure and the Middle Iron Age occupation. Trenches I and V certainly show that the enclosure ditch was allowed to silt up during the Middle Iron Age. The shape of the enclosure is unparalleled in the area and the types of pottery and fibulae found here indicate that this was a higher status site in the Early Iron Age than the settlement at Gussage All Saints (20) (see below).

Nine hundred and eighty-seven sherds of pottery were present in the excavation archive although the high percentage of rims and bases indicated that the original excavators had been selective in what they retained.

The form of the Phase 1 Oakley Down sherds compared well with those from Phase 1 of Gussage (20). However, in contrast to Gussage, only two body sherds decorated with finger-tip impressions and one haematite-coated sherd were found at Oakley Down. The Early Iron Age pottery fabrics indicated manufacture in the Jurassic Ridge, Upper Greensand and Poole Harbour areas as well as local production. This was a greater Early Iron Age diversity of sources than at Gussage (20). The pottery forms and fabrics suggest that the inhabitants had contacts with the Dorset coast, Wiltshire, Somerset and Hampshire.

The Middle Iron Age fabrics also indicate products from various locations but predominantly from Poole Harbour and forms such as ovoid jars, proto-saucepan pots and developed saucepan pots are typical of the Maiden Castle-Marnhull style. Lisa Brown noted that the assemblage correlates with Phase 2 at Gussage, Phase 2 & 3 Rope Lake Hole, Purbeck and Phase 6 at Maiden Castle.

Most of the pottery from the site came from the Late Iron Age-Early Romano-British period; all the excavated pits in the enclosure were of this date. Poole Harbour pottery dominated the assemblage and all the usual developed Durotrigan forms were present. The site continued to be occupied throughout the Roman period.

Gussage All Saints

The best site sequence from the area was found in the Gussage All Saints excavation, which produced over 76,000 sherds of pottery mainly derived from the 477 pits (*49*). The nine radiocarbon dates and a range of other evidence led Dr Wainwright (1979) to estimate that the site was occupied 'from a time prior to the middle of the first millennium BC to the latter part of the first century AD'. The occupation evidence was divided into three phases.

One hundred and twenty-eight of the pits (27 per cent) were assigned to Phase 1 or Early Iron Age *c.*550-300 BC; 69 pits (14 per cent) were assigned to Phase 2 or Middle Iron

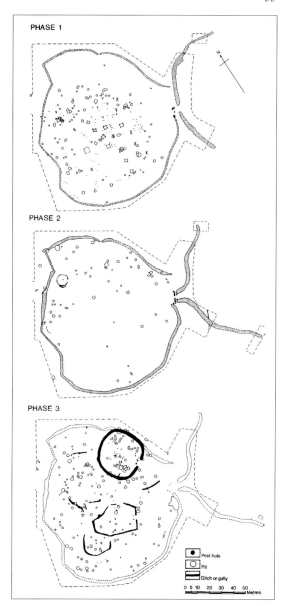

49 Plan of archaeological features at
Gussage All Saints settlement, Phases 1–3.
(Wainwright 1979, 185) *Crown Copyright*

Age *c.*300–100 BC; 184 pits (39 per cent) were assigned to Phase 3 or Late Iron Age (100 BC–AD 50). The remaining 96 pits (20 per cent) could not be dated.

In Phase 1, the settlement consisted of a 1.4ha area surrounded by a shallow ditch with an external bank. A main entrance on the east side of the enclosure had a timber gate flanked by antennae ditches. The pits, post-holes and working hollows for this phase occurred some distance from the main enclosure ditch. Seventeen groups of four post-holes, interpreted as 'granaries', were concentrated near the centre of the enclosure. Some of these structures had been rebuilt on more than one occasion. No round houses were identified.

In Phase 2, continuity is implied. The enclosure ditch was made larger but on the same alignment. The east entrance was retained, although reconstructed, and ceramic forms continued but new types appeared. The Phase 2 pits were less numerous but larger than Phase 1 and therefore total storage capacity was similar. There were less barrel-shaped pits and more cylindrical and 'beehive' pits. One, perhaps two, round houses were identified from the arrangement of excavated post-holes. One hut was 9m in diameter with a south-east entrance. The evidence for other houses had probably been removed by modern ploughing.

In Phase 3, continuity is assumed because the positions of the enclosure boundary and east gate were retained. However, the Durotrigan ceramic forms dominate but once again some of the forms such as counter-sunk handles overlap from Phase 2. Many new storage pits were created and three subsidiary enclosures were constructed within the settlement. Of these, a six-sided enclosure with an east facing timber gate was interpreted as a stock enclosure. A near circular 35m diameter ditch, which incorporated part of the main enclosure, presumably contained the principal domestic buildings. Geoffrey Wainwright considered this enclosure to have been created late in the life of the settlement and only maintained for a short period of time. A timber gate was constructed across its south-east entrance.

A petrological study of the pottery was undertaken and from this it was concluded that in the earliest phase, nearly all the pottery was made with local clay, unlike Oakley Down at this time. This included all of the haematite-coated vessels apart from two which were made of clay that probably came from the Jurassic Ridge area. The nearest outcrop of the clays used to make these vessels was around Milborne Port, Somerset. In the middle phase, the pottery is made increasingly of fabrics typical of the Poole Harbour area and in Phase 3 virtually all the pottery is from this source.

In Phases 1 and 2 there were 157 vessels categorised as 'saucepan' pots. Of these, 132 were likely to be made of a local type of clay and the other 13 vessels were made with shell temper typical of the Jurassic Ridge area. The 'saucepan' pots were found in Phase 1 (20 per cent) and Phase 2 (76 per cent) contexts. The remaining 4 per cent from Phase 3 were thought to be residual.

The three-phase pattern of ceramic influence, that is, Early Iron Age local production, Middle Iron Age local and other sources, followed by Late Iron Age Poole Harbour dominance (already suggested for the Ham Hill, South Cadbury and Maiden Castle ceramics) seems to work here but to a lesser degree.

There is very little decorated pottery from the middle phase. Yarnbury-Highfield and South Western Decorated styles are not illustrated or described in the pottery report.

The Hengistbury Class B bowl describes a type of burnished bowl with a hollow neck, rounded shoulder and foot ring or pedestal base considered to be a Gallo-Belgic import. However, petrological analysis showed the Gussage examples to be British copies. Of the 38 examples excavated from Phase 3, 20 were made of the Poole Harbour type fabric and 18 may have been made of the local type of clay.

Thirteen amphorae fragments were recovered, including Dressel 1 and Spanish Globular type. Gallo-Belgic imports include a few sherds from *Terra Rubra* butt beakers and a platter. An Arretine sherd and six fragments of Samian Ware were also found. However, there were no Iron Age coins found on the site despite its total excavation. This range of finds may be an indicator of the status of the settlement.

This site, Gussage All Saints (20), lies near five enclosures of similar 1-2ha area mapped by Collin Bowen (1990) and identified by site numbers within parishes (50). All except

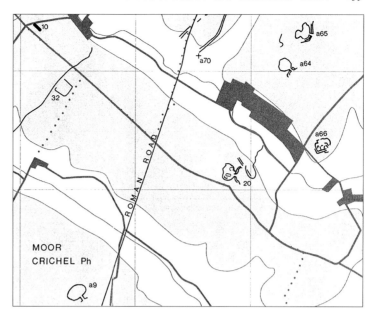

50 Plan of a group of farmstead enclosures near Gussage All Saints. (Bowen 1990, fig. 1) *Crown Copyright*

Long Crichel (32) are ovoid or sub-circular in plan with evidence of an entrance on the south-east side. Long Crichel lies 1.5km west along the Gussage valley and is a rectangular enclosure. The site is immediately east of a linear feature and may be of Late Bronze Age or Early Iron Age date from finds made in the vicinity by Martin Green.

The other sites are closely comparable. Moor Crichel (a9) is on the south-west side of the Crichel brook in a similar topographic position and 1.5km south-west of All Saints. It seems to be a hybrid 'banjo'/'antennae' entrance with short splayed entrance ditches leading to a short 40m-long parallel ditched entrance passage. Gussage All Saints (a66) is the closest to 20, only 0.5km east and on the opposite side of the Gussage stream. Its irregular ovoid plan has a parallel additional ditch on the south-west side. The south-east entrance has an L-shaped external extension and two small ovoid enclosures with a short linear in the interior attached to the gateway. There is also a gap in the north-west side suggesting that the main enclosure had opposing entrances. Gussage All Saints (a64) is 1km north-west of a66 and 1km north-east of 20, with which it compares very closely. It is the same size, has a south-east 'antennae' entrance and aerial photographs show numerous storage pits within it. A south-western series/Durotrigan 'starfish' coin has recently been found on the site. This farmstead differs from 20 in having a ditched track and small rectangular enclosures overlying and crossing in front of its south-east side. This may be evidence of occupation continuing through the Roman period unlike 20. On the summit of the spur 0.5km north-east of a64 lies an irregular enclosure (a65) but with a very regular south-east entrance. This consists of two sets of three parallel ditches linked at right angles to converging ditches forming a short entrance passage into the enclosure. The arrangement would not look out of place on a Roman fort but the aerial photographs show that within the kidney-shaped enclosure lie numerous dots indicating storage pits typical of the Iron Age.

This group of settlement enclosures is described here to indicate the pattern of closely spaced discrete settlement units, which are a key feature of this study area. All but Long

Crichel (32) are of comparable size and form and are likely to possess a similar chrono-logical development to All Saints (20). They appear to be households/farmsteads of similar rank yet each is idiosyncratic. Their occupiers have left their own mark on their place and in looking at their settlement plans, particularly the entrances, one is reminded of modern instances of neighbourly competition and expressions of status.

Berwick Down and Rushmore

Moving from the south-east to the north-west corner of the study area, the survey will now compare Dr Wainwright's Berwick Down excavation results (1968, 102-147) with those from Gussage All Saints (20).

The kite-shaped enclosure bank with external ditch surrounded an area about half the size of 20. It had a single entrance on the south side. A bank and ditch surrounded the south, east and west sides about 40m from the main enclosure but there was no occupa-tion evidence recorded between the two banks. Apart from a crouched inhumation on the north-west side, all the pits, post-holes and working hollows lay within the kite-shaped enclosure. The excavation revealed the plan of a round house, 4 'granaries' (four- or six-post structures), 35 storage pits, 4 working hollows and an area empty of features interpreted as a stock-holding area. The site was considered to be a typical Durotrigan farmstead (see Chapter Four).

The pottery report records 2928 sherds representing 225 pots, nearly all of which were Poole Harbour-type fabric. There were a few 'Hengistbury Class B derivative' bowls which had a finer fabric, but from the petrological analysis of such vessels at Gussage they may have been made in the Poole Harbour kilns. A single sherd of a storage jar was of a 'soft gritless orange fabric'. The report indicated no recognisable Roman influence in the pot-tery forms and it seemed likely that the farm had been abandoned just before or after the conquest. The finds from the site include no Gallo-Belgic imports and, like Gussage (20), no Iron Age coins.

In the first century AD, the population of this short-lived, single-phase farmstead may have only moved 100m to the north-west. The 1965 RCHM plan shows a 120m diam-eter ovoid enclosure containing rectilinear banks and structures. East and north of this are remains of a co-axial field system, the hollows of pits and a *c.*15m diameter ring bank with an east entrance that appears to be the remains of a round house. Therefore, on Berwick Down, the excavated enclosure probably represents the middle phase of occu-pation, with the Early Iron Age unenclosed occupation and the Roman farmstead lying north of the site.

Rotherley

Berwick Down is only 0.5km from Rotherley, the nearest of Pitt Rivers' Rushmore Park sites. Rotherley lies on the next spur east from Berwick Down. The main ovoid enclosure ditch was 50m in diameter with a south-east entrance. Another 25m diameter enclosure is 30m to the north-east but General Pitt Rivers' plan shows a series of trackways south and east of the site and various pits and hollows within and between these ditches and enclo-sures. The site covers an area of about 170m in diameter and is probably part of a larger settlement grouping.

The 1885 excavation revealed a greater diversity of pottery than that found at Gussage or Berwick. Most of it is Durotrigan, including counter-sunk handles and bead rim bowls but there are also examples of Black Burnished tankards, jars, 'dog bowls' and decorated Samian indicating Roman period settlement. There were at least two *tazzae* (a cordoned type of beaker with a pedestal base) and in the report there are illustrated decorated sherds suggesting Late Iron Age imports. Two Durotrigan coins were found: a silver stater and struck bronze stater.

Fifteen adult skeletons were found, most buried in the local Iron Age style, crouched within pits and enclosure ditches but two were extended in separate graves and were presumably of later Roman date. One pit over 2m in diameter and 3.5m deep contained a structured deposit with the skull of an ox near the bottom and four crouched inhumations near the top.

Woodcutts

The settlement on Woodcutts Common lies just within the Dorset border 2km south-east of Rotherley. The site included Late Iron Age items that suggested a higher status than Rotherley. The near circular main enclosure was about 90m in diameter, approached from the south-east by a 10m-wide trackway flanked by banks which merge with the main enclosure bank. Collin Bowen described it as a necked or 'banjo' enclosure. The settlement was occupied until the end of the fourth century AD and included a building with painted plaster, corn-drying ovens and a well. These were constructed within enclosures that both incorporated and overlay the Phase 1 enclosure.

Burials of 13 adults and 22 infants were found in pits, ditches and in one of the corn-drying ovens. The usual scatter of separate human bones found in various pits was also noted.

Four Durotrigan coins were found, three silver staters and one struck bronze stater. The illustrated pottery includes Late Iron Age pottery predominantly of Durotrigan form and decoration but the punched zig-zag decoration on one sherd is similar to the decorated pottery characteristic of the Highfield-Yarnbury style. Two other pots appear to be Gallo-Belgic Black Cordoned Ware presumably imported through Hengistbury Head, where the nearest other examples have been recorded. A third example was found by Pitt Rivers 1km north-west of Woodcutts, near Park House, and he remarked on the similarity and distinctiveness of these three items of hard black pottery. Analysis would determine whether or not these are Poole Harbour copies (*52*).

The discoveries near Park House included a ditch and bank and four Iron Age pits containing pottery of 'superior quality'. One of the estate workers discovered this site while planting an avenue of trees and Pitt Rivers believed it to be more extensive. The *Victoria County History for Wiltshire* (1957, 39) noted defensive linear earthworks and settlement evidence from Carrion Tree Rack to Shiftway Coppice a distance of 1km. When plotted on a map, the known enclosures and excavated sites from Berwick to Woodcutts cover a 2km by 1km area occupying the slopes and spurs ringing the coombe above Tollard Royal. The finds indicate a higher status site, perhaps Woodcutts, surrounded by lesser households.

51 Cordoned Ware pottery (top left and bottom right) excavated in Rushmore Park. (Pitt Rivers 1888, Plate LXXII)

'Banjo' Enclosures

Woodcutts was the only banjo-like enclosure that had been excavated within the Durotrigan zone until 2009, when Miles Russell of Bournemouth University excavated a site at Winterbourne Kingston. Single and double 'banjos' in this study area and at the east end of the Nadder-Wylye Ridge seem to be associated with high-status objects (Corney 1989, 122). However, apart from Woodcutts and Winterbourne Kingston, these finds have not been recovered from stratified deposits but from ploughed fields by metal detection and fieldwalking.

Bowen (1990, 90) described them as typically small enclosures 50-90m in diameter, sometimes appearing in pairs and integral with ditch systems. The necked approach he suggested was functional, perhaps for processing stock.

Peter Fasham excavated an example in Micheldever Wood, Hampshire, and using radiocarbon dating, concluded that its main period of occupation was in the last two centuries BC although it continued to be used into the first century AD. He thought that the site was lived in and associated with the normal farming practices relating to animal and crop husbandry. He summarised the evidence from the other excavated site in Hampshire, at Bramdean, and thought that the occupants were also a mixed farming community. He also thought that the necked approach was for stock management. The finds from these sites did not suggest that the occupants were of above average status.

A double 'banjo' enclosure was the subject of geophysical survey and excavation in 2001. The site was at Beach's Barn, 2km south-west of Everleigh, Wiltshire, and on the east edge of Salisbury Plain. The site was dated to the Middle to Late Iron Age and trenches across one enclosure revealed intercutting storage pits and other occupation evidence. The other enclosure may have been for stock although further excavation would be needed to confirm this. The entrances faced south-east towards the hillfort of Sidbury. The site developed into a villa in the Roman period continuing in use into the fourth century.

Mark Corney considered the possibility that twin 'banjos' may reflect the duality of late Celtic society but perhaps there was a practical division of stock and domestic space. In 2005, a functional division of this kind was demonstrated when the grand twin villas were excavated at St Lawrence School, Bradford on Avon. Their outlines were almost identical but one building proved to be the domestic accommodation of the villa owner and the other building contained the working and service rooms of the complex.

The Gussage Hill Complex

Moving south-east from Rushmore, enclosures revealed by aerial photography are encountered every 0.5-1.5km. These are of various types and most are thought to be of Iron Age date, many with numerous storage pits visible within them (Bowen 1990, 84-94). The variety is demonstrated if a transect is followed across the landscape from Chettle Down to Humby's Stock Coppice, a distance of about 5km (*53*).

The Chettle Down site (Chettle, a20) consists of two ovoid enclosures linked by a ditch, a settlement type known as a 'spectacles' site. The next enclosure, 1km north-east (Farnham, a13), is ovoid in plan but has a 100m wide gap on the south-west side of its ditched perimeter. Another enclosure 0.5km to the north-east consists of three concentric ditches with an east entrance (Farnham, a14). Lying 0.7km north-east of this is a larger 5ha ovoid enclosure with a north-west entrance (Sixpenny Handley, 24) where Durotrigan pottery has been found and a further 2km north-east lies the 'banjo' enclosure near Humby's Stock Coppice (Sixpenny Handley, a20).

At this site, the entrance passage faces south-east and ditches fan out in 'antennae' style but in extended and irregular courses. That to the north-east curves to accommodate another circular enclosure which, like the 'banjo', seems to contain storage pits. Continuity of occupation into the Romano-British period is indicated here as immediately north-east of this site is an area of occupation debris dating from the second to fourth centuries AD.

Another 'banjo' site is found on Chapel Down, 0.5km to the south-east (Sixpenny Handley, a65). Here, finds dating from the Late Iron Age include two Durotrigan coins and the only Gallic *Coriosolite* coin known from Cranborne Chase. The numerous objects recovered from the ploughsoil indicate occupation until the fourth century. The 'banjo' entrance faces south-east and is attached to linears similar to a20.

A further 2km south-east of Chapel Down lies Gussage Cow Down with its two sets of double 'banjo' enclosures and attendant square and ovoid enclosures associated with extensive multiple ditch systems. This site has been described by Collin Bowen and also Mark Corney, who compared Gussage with the Nadder-Wylye Ridge sites.

The multiple ditches and banks on Cow Down form an enclosure of over 100ha and although there are gaps, the ditch system can be traced west for 5km crossing the north-west ends of the Gussage and Crichel valleys via Thickthorn Down towards Launceston Down.

On Launceston Down, an array of linear dykes can be seen on the high ground above the Crichel Brook that appear to form another large enclosure although this is smaller enclosing about 90ha.

Within the Cow Down enclosure there is a prehistoric field system and further east and north there are other traces of fields. However, on Launceston and Thickthorn Downs and down the Gussage and Crichel valleys as far as the five household enclosures described above (i.e. Moor Crichel, a9; Gussage All Saints, 20, a64, a65, a66) field systems are absent. Mark Corney (1991, 233) suggested this area was used for stock management. Multiple banks and ditches extending west from the end of the Cursus on Thickthorn Down may indicate that the Neolithic earthwork was reused to aid this function but excavations here in 1958 failed to date these features. Pottery finds from the buried soil beneath the banks and the upper silting of the ditches provided only a broad date range, indicating that they were constructed between the Early Bronze Age and the medieval period.

Standing back and looking at the arrangement of linears on Collin Bowen's distribution map and bearing in mind duality of function, then Cow Down and Launceston Down may present related contemporary land uses. Cow Down served as the occupation area balanced by Launceston's great enclosure which, on current understanding, is devoid of settlement features. Therefore it could be interpreted as a large stock holding area. Perhaps the Badbury and High Wood enclosures in Chapter Eleven might be considered in the same way.

Pit 209, excavated in Gussage All Saints (20), contained thousands of mould fragments for three-link horse bits, terrets and linchpin terminals. This find confirms the value of horses within the Durotrigan zone, particularly in the Late Iron Age. If the Launceston area, defined by linear earthworks and apparently without field systems, was for livestock, then a likely key function would be for raising horses. One could imagine this ranch land being used for training chariot teams, but it would be difficult to prove such a hypothesis.

The Gussage Cow Down group of enclosures (52) has yielded finds indicating that some of the residents were of a higher status compared with the people who once lived within Gussage All Saints (20). Mark Corney listed five Durotrigan coins from the north double 'banjo' enclosure (7a, 7b) and two from the south (7c, 7d). At that time 13 coins had been found across the site with much Durotrigan pottery and fibulae of various types. Finds continue to be made and Martin Green reported that two more Durotrigan coins have recently been recovered here.

The southern double 'banjo' may be a triple-enclosure as immediately south of 7d is 7e, another ovoid enclosure visible on aerial photographs. This site is joined to the bank and ditch that forms the west side of the Gussage Cow Down multiple ditch system that runs along the top of the slope above the Gussage valley.

Other settlement enclosures on Gussage Hill include the ovoid Drive Plantation site 8, where Late Iron Age pottery including a sherd of Dressel 1 amphora has been found. Occupation here continued to the end of the Roman period and similar continuity is demonstrated from finds from around the north and south double 'banjos'. Another enclosure, with a necked entrance on its west side, lies 200m east of 7e (Gussage All Saints, a63) and also contains abundant occupation debris of the Late Iron Age.

In addition to this unique Dorset grouping of multiple ditches and 'banjo' enclosures, is another exotic feature excavated 300m north-west of the northern double 'banjo' 7a and 7b. This site is a barrow surrounded by a square ditch with sides 16m long (Sixpenny Handley, 30). When excavated (White 1970, 26-36), it was found to have been robbed in antiquity but covered the remains of a Late Iron Age cremation pyre. This cremation within a square barrow is unique for Iron Age Dorset; indeed, Romano-British cremations are rare in the county, yet they have been found at Woodcutts and Oakley Down within the study area. Four Romano-British cremations were found in the ditch of the Iron Age settlement during the 1947-51 excavations; others were found in the nearby Oakley Down barrow group.

Small square enclosures that may be burial sites have been identified from aerial photographs in the area. One, perhaps two, lie immediately north of 7c on Cow Down;

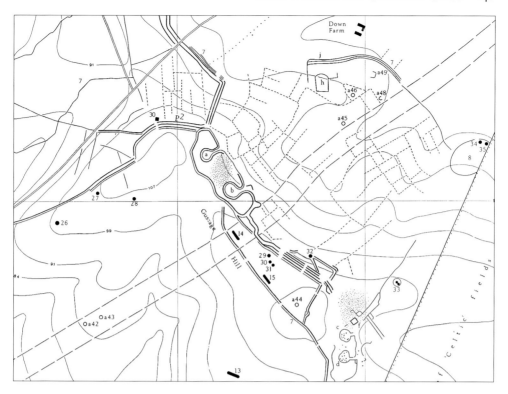

52 Detail of the Gussage Hill group of archaeological features. (Bowen 1990, area plan 2) *Crown Copyright*

another was excavated by Martin Green in the Gussage valley but contained late Roman burials.

Finds of ballista heads have been made at Rotherley, Woodcutts and Gussage Hill. Mark Corney suggested that these objects indicate that the area was significant during the Roman Conquest and may have witnessed military engagement.

Concluding Remarks

The study area includes nearly all the 'banjo' enclosures in Dorset although Collin Bowen identified another three to the south-west in the neighbouring Tarrant valley, and in the last two years others have been identified from aerial photographs around Winterborne Kingston. There are none known in the Hod Hill and Badbury study areas.

This type of enclosure is a settlement feature of the land further north and east. Mark Corney has plotted their distribution across Hampshire and east Wiltshire. It seems unlikely that they developed independently as a settlement form in Dorset and more likely that the 'banjo' was introduced into Cranborne Chase from the east in the same way coinage became adopted first in this area. It is not possible to say whether the earliest coinage arrived with the fashion for 'banjo' building or whether the 'banjos' represent a migration or conquest by people from the east.

The sharp contrast between the Cranborne Chase and Stour valley settlement patterns will be commented on here even though there is unlikely to be an archaeological consensus on any particular explanation of the available evidence.

A useful test would be to find whether eastern styles of pottery or other material evidence were associated with the Dorset 'banjos' at an early phase and replaced by the Durotrigan ceramics later on. Only the Woodcutts enclosure has been excavated and although the pottery should be examined again, the available drawings do not seem to hold out much hope of proving that an eastern ceramic influence was present in the earliest phase.

Surface finds from 'banjos' across the study area seem to be, without exception, Late Iron Age and Durotrigan. One might suggest that the people who first constructed the 'banjos' in Dorset brought in a distinctive settlement type but had no ceramic identity. If, for example, the people of Pilsdon Pen had moved east and occupied the land around Eggardon or Maiden Castle they would be archaeologically invisible.

One could argue that there is evidence for settlement shift and disruption across the Durotrigan area where 'banjo' enclosures are known. Within the study area, using the limited information available, the general rule is for rectilinear enclosures to be earlier and ovoid enclosures to be later. Therefore, the rectilinear sites excavated on Down Farm and South Lodge proved to be earlier and similar rectilinear sites at a distance from ovoid enclosures may demonstrate settlement shift.

An example of this would be the 'tombstone' enclosure, Gussage St Michael (7h), excavated at Down Farm which was abandoned in the Middle Iron Age and lies 0.5km from double 'banjo' (7a-7b). A similar settlement shift may be visible in Sixpenny Handley parish, where another one of Bowen's 'tombstone' enclosures (a64) is 0.5km from the Chapel Down and Humby's Stock Coppice 'banjos'. However, Sixpenny Handley (36) on Oakley Down is an excavated example of a rectilinear Early Iron Age enclosure which continued to be occupied into the Romano-British period. But this site is not typical as it is larger and squarer in plan than the 'tombstone' sites.

The change in the settlement pattern seems to date from the Early Iron Age. This is indicated from the latest finds in the abandoned sites and from the absence of developed hillforts. Only four univallate hillforts are known in the vicinity and only the western example, Bussey Stool Park, is a well-finished enclosure.

Gussage All Saints (20) should demonstrate disruption, if this can be defined in this area in the Middle and Late Iron Age, but it does not. In fact it is very similar in form to Little Woodbury which lies in the west Hampshire and Salisbury area. Collin Bowen believed that this region had a different settlement morphology than Dorset south-west of Bokerley Dyke. The similarities between Little Woodbury and Gussage seem to disprove this hypothesis although Little Woodbury was abandoned in the later Middle Iron Age whereas Gussage continued to be occupied until the first century AD.

Looking across the south Wiltshire and north-east Dorset area, there are more Iron Age abandoned and shifted settlements than are known further south and west. Examples of this are the Battlesbury bowl extensive settlement that withdraws to the hillfort, Longbridge Deverill Cow Down, East Knoyle and the Swallowcliffe and Fifield Bavant settlements on the Ebble-Nadder Ridge. In contrast, a settlement like Marnhull is an example of Stour valley continuity, a large, apparently open settlement occupied from the Early Iron Age through to the Roman period. This sort of long-term occupation on extensive settlement sites will be considered again in the Badbury study area below.

With the exception of Gussage (20), elsewhere in the Cranborne study area the settlement evidence suggests increasing numbers of Late Iron Age farmsteads being newly established in the landscape. Pitt Rivers' excavations at Rushmore indicate that the storage pits and settlement features found at Woodcutts, Rotherley and Park House begin to be constructed in the Late Iron Age. In addition, although there are other earthworks in the vicinity, the Berwick Down farmstead was a Late Iron Age creation.

There is also a strong argument for settlement hierarchy within the study area with the settlement remains and ceramic evidence from Berwick placed at the lower end of the scale.

The pottery analysis from Gussage All Saints (20) reveals Durotrigan copies of imports but very little exotic material and no coinage. Presumably they were a middle-ranking extended family group on a par with the similar-sized neighbouring four households (a64-66 and Moor Crichel a9) who presumably divided or were allotted the arable, pasture and meadow land to create similar-sized farms.

Above them on Gussage Hill lie the double 'banjo' enclosures (7a-7d) and multiple ditch systems. Here, at Rushmore and on Chapel Down (a65) the coins and pottery, the elaborate earthworks and the continuity into the Roman period suggest a higher level of significance and wealth amongst the inhabitants. The *Coriosolite* coin from Chapel Down and also the three examples of probable Black Cordoned Ware from Woodcutts and Park House suggest trade with Armorican merchants. If these sherds are imports and not Poole Harbour copies then they are rare inland examples of this type of pottery. Black Cordoned Ware is not known from Maiden Castle and Hod Hill.

The finds from the study area seem to confirm those from the Stockton, Hamshill, Hanging Langford, Ebsbury group of sites, having a cluster of higher status objects noted by Mark Corney. It could be argued that the 'banjo' occupants were incomers from the east who had the power and wealth. Most of the population seems to have continued with the 'normal' funerary practices of placing crouched inhumations and parts of human skeletons in pits and ditches. However, at least one Late Iron Age burial mound within a square ditch existed on Gussage Hill and the interred body or bodies were cremated. This was an alien form of burial in comparison with all that is known for the rest of the Durotrigan zone.

The Thickthorn multiple bank and ditch system that continues the line of the Cursus seems to suggest that the Gussage Hill site was chosen partly because of its extraordinary Neolithic and Bronze Age earthworks. Perhaps the Cursus was seen as a valuable legacy from the past. There is a sense of the sacred in the way long and round barrows are usually left undisturbed within the hillforts of the Durotrigan zone and one would expect a sense of awe in the magnitude of the ditches and banks of the Cursus. It crosses the headwaters of the Allen and Gussage and it appears that in the Late Iron Age the earthwork was extended across the Crichel Brook and up to Launceston Down. Another system of banks and ditches 0.5km north-west lie either side of the source of the Gussage. If Christopher Sparey-Green's suspicions are confirmed, the Mycen Farm Roman buildings mark a sacred site which can be traced back to the Iron Age. His evidence for this is the rectilinear ditch system near a spring site seen on aerial photographs and partly excavated. The use of the linear earthworks to control livestock was probably part of their function but they seem

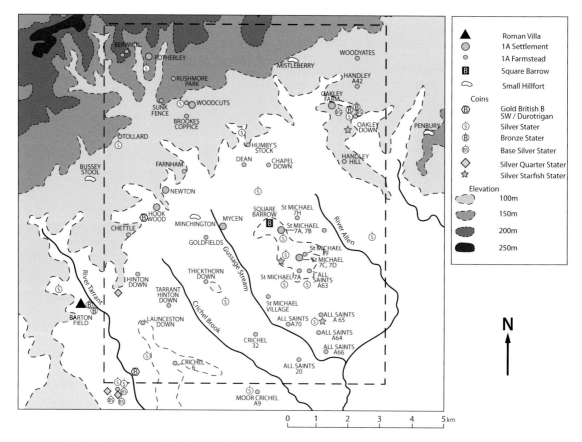

53 Map showing sites within the Cranborne study area.

too monumental and intricate to be solely functional boundaries and there is likely to be a sacred as well as a secular element to their construction.

Taking the enclosure and ditch systems, the imported objects and the cremation burial, also the evidence for settlement shift, there is a case to be made for the idea of an immigrant elite controlling the established population. Perhaps not quite like the establishment of a Norman motte and bailey beside a Saxon village, but the 'banjos' do seem to represent a new order. It is the impression given on the Oxdrove Ridge where the land is parcelled up by a series of Late Iron Age cross-ridge dykes.

Looking across the whole area examined in this section there are blocks of land with different settlement characteristics suggesting the evolution of different types of community. These will be considered in Chapter Twelve but it is clear that the Cranborne study area is a distinctive element in a landscape full of settlement diversity. To the west lies Hod and Hambledon and to the south is the confluence of the Stour and Allen near Badbury. This will be the last study area in the survey of the Durotrigan zone.

11

EAST DORSET

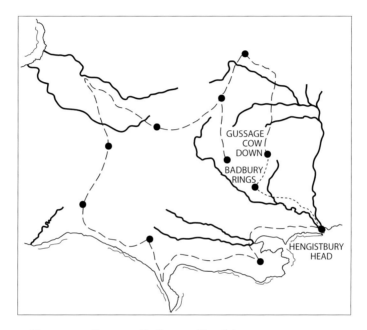

54 Tour map 7: Gussage to Badbury to Hengistbury.

The Tarrant and Allen valleys link the Cranborne and Badbury study areas. Only 3km separate them but a marked settlement change takes place. Some of the Cranborne settlement types appear in the upper Tarrant valley but despite excellent aerial photographic cover they are not currently known within 6km of its confluence with the Stour.

A distribution map of south-western series/Durotrigan coins located by the Stour Valley Detector Group demonstrates that the Tarrant valley has an unusually high number of finds. There are scattered groups of coins from the chalk spurs above both sides of the river at Tarrant Hinton, Tarrant Monkton, Hogstock, Tarrant Rushton, Tarrant Rawston and Tarrant Crawford (55).

There is one notable piece of research that has taken place between the Cranborne and Badbury study areas. From 1968-84 excavations in Barton Field, Tarrant Hinton found evidence of a Roman villa overlying an Iron Age settlement dating from about 500 BC. Aerial photographs show that the settlement was extensive and the pottery assemblage from the site includes Early, Middle and Late Iron Age forms increasingly derived from Poole Harbour. As with the Marnhull site, a few sherds of South Western Decorated Ware were found. This place can be compared with Bradford Down (see page 150) as an extensive Stour valley settlement that had become a courtyard villa by the fourth century. At Barton Field, two flexed Middle Iron Age inhumations and one crouched Late Iron Age burial in a shallow oval grave were excavated (Graham 2006).

Two silver Durotrigan staters, a quarter stater and a bronze stater were found during the excavations. One of the silver staters was excavated from the upper filling of the 1.5m-deep southern boundary ditch of the settlement which ran under the courtyard villa. North of this ditch, Iron Age buildings were excavated, as well as storage pits of Early, Middle and Late Iron Age date. An Early Iron Age 15m diameter round house was found beneath the villa bath house which lay about 100m north-east of the main villa. Six other hut circles were found during the investigations.

STUDY AREA 7: BADBURY ENVIRONS

The land around Badbury was my pilot study area and I have carried out much of the fieldwork and excavation here or commissioned and supervised others to undertake finds analysis and survey work. Twenty years of archaeological research has enabled me to accumulate a considerable body of additional evidence which, when added to the existing data, has improved the understanding of this landscape.

Topographic Description

The geology of the study box is predominantly chalk, apart from where tertiary sands, clays and gravels are found on the tops of the higher hills and to the south-east. The flood plains of the valleys are composed of river alluvium.

The twin peaks of Badbury/High Wood hill are the watershed for the three rivers that surround it. The rivers form a roughly triangular area with sides about 7km long. The River Allen lies east of Badbury, the River Tarrant lies to the north-west and these drain into the River Stour to the south.

The Allen meanders along the east side of the study area flowing through the village of Witchhampton and the hamlets of Hinton Parva, Stanbridge and Clapgate before joining the Stour at the market town of Wimborne Minster at the south-east corner of the study box. The Tarrant flows through the villages of Tarrant Rawston, Tarrant Rushton, Tarrant Keyneston and joins the Stour south-west of the hamlet of Tarrant Crawford.

The larger villages occupy the banks of the River Stour. These, from north-west to south-east, are Chalton Marshall, Spetisbury, Shapwick and Sturminster Marshall.

Most of the chalkland settlements are beside the rivers, but on the tertiary beds the occupation is more dispersed with a cluster of hamlets lying between Kingston Lacy Park and Wimborne, including Hillbutts, Cowgrove, Tadden, Chilbridge and Pamphill.

The chalkland consists of undulating spurs and coombes draining into the river valleys and radiating out from the high points of Buzbury, north-west of the Tarrant, High Lea, north-east of the Allen, and Badbury. Each of these vantage points is occupied by an Iron

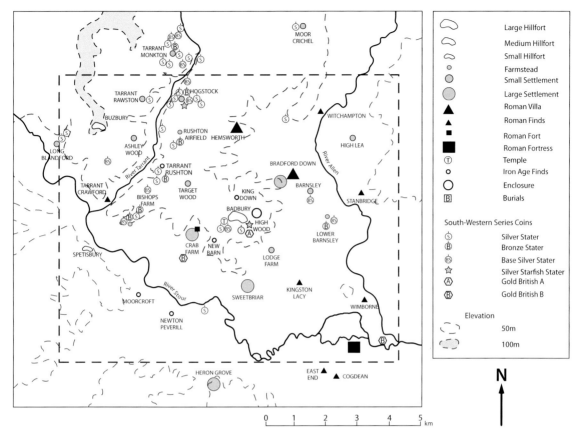

55 Map of sites within east Dorset study area.

Age site. Spetisbury also occupies a high strategic position above a ford south-west of the Stour. Here, the river flows directly below the hillfort.

The spacing of the known sites is between 1.5km and 2km and most spur crests or hilltops were occupied. The pattern is so consistent that it seems likely that fieldwork will eventually reveal Iron Age occupation at key locations where sites are still unknown. Two of these sites, on spur crests above the Stour and Tarrant, west of Tarrant Keyneston, and between Tarrant Rushton and Hogstock, had no recorded occupation evidence until recently. Metal detectorists have now plotted scatters of south-western/Durotrigan coins across both sites.

Chronological Development

Neolithic flints have been found on the summits of Badbury/High Wood and there are numerous Bronze Age sites within the study area including over 120 round barrows mainly grouped on the chalk spurs around Badbury.

Linear boundaries of the Bronze Age can be seen on aerial photographs. Collin Bowen considered the Badbury group to be the second largest concentration of such features in Dorset. We excavated along the line of the Blandford Road before the second Kingston Lacy beech avenue was planted in 1989. This work revealed various ditches and it became clear that the linears sometimes cut across Early Bronze Age field ditches. This was seen when a D-shaped enclosure (Shapwick, a86) south-west of Badbury was excavated in 1988. The bank of the enclosure lay above the burial of a sheep which was cut into one of the typical Early Bronze Age V-shaped ditches. Radiocarbon samples from this sheep burial and an ox skeleton from the inner ditch of the enclosure, date the site to the Late Bronze Age 1200-950 BC. The date range is similar to that of the South Lodge and Down Farm enclosures on Cranborne Chase.

This creation of a system of linear boundaries took place in an extensively farmed and occupied landscape. The banks and ditches often took account of existing features and this can be demonstrated using aerial photographic evidence. Some linears used barrows as boundary markers and others can be seen kinking around existing field systems and enclosures.

One massive linear bank and ditch (Shapwick, 35) can be traced for 3km across the landscape. It was built in three phases. Phase I was constructed in the Middle Bronze Age and was less than 1m deep. By Phase III, the V-shaped ditch had been enlarged to make a formidable obstacle 5m wide and 4m deep with a bank 10m wide. The excavators, H. and M.L. Vatcher, found first- to second-century Romano-British pottery in the upper filling of the ditch and an iron projectile head, possibly a ballista bolt, in the eroded edge of the bank. From this they believed that the Phase III earthwork dated to the Late Iron Age.

This particular linear can be traced as an earthwork or on aerial photographs from Badbury Rings south-west as far as the Crab Farm settlement at Shapwick, where it turns west to meet an ancient track known as the Swan Way. The scale of this feature, compared with the other linears, indicates that it may have been a defensive earthwork. Its association with the Badbury and Crab Farm Iron Age settlements will be considered below.

It seems likely that Badbury Hill was already significant by the Late Bronze Age as the only bronze metalwork from the area has been found here. In the nineteenth century, a bronze rapier was ploughed up on the west side of Badbury and in 1987, National Trust warden David Smith found a palstave axe while clearing a drainage pit south of the hillfort.

Sweetbriar Drove

The Southampton to Purbeck BP pipeline crossed the Kingston Lacy Estate in 1988 and great care was taken to conserve the archaeology by avoiding all known sites. Nevertheless, south-west of Kingston Lacy Park, at Sweetbriar Drove, the pipe trench cut through a large, previously unrecognised, Iron Age settlement. This lay 1.9km south-east of Badbury Rings and included numerous pits, post-holes and ditches. Thirty were excavated and radiocarbon samples were taken from three pits.

Pits 31 and 57 were backfilled between 800-400 BC and pit 91 from 360-50 BC. The pottery report stated that 1345 sherds were examined from two large ditches, twelve storage pits, nine other pits, six post-holes and two smaller linear gullies.

Thirty-nine per cent of the pottery was dated to the Early Iron Age and included All Cannings Cross-style vessels. Typical pottery from this phase included angular vessels and forms with upright rims and gently sloping shoulders. Sixty-eight per cent of this pottery was burnished with 34 per cent haematite coated. Jars were the most popular form of vessel followed by bowls. Some jars had finger-tip decoration on the shoulder, rim top or just below the rim.

The Middle Iron Age pots of Phase 2 made up 58 per cent of the pottery and typically consisted of plain, coil-built globular jars in coarse sandy fabrics and included examples of counter-sunk handles. A storage pit (51) was cut by the ring gulley of a Middle Iron Age round house (35) this in turn was cut by a rectilinear enclosure ditch containing Late Iron Age Poole Harbour pottery.

The 20m-wide pipeline easement was aligned north to south and crossed 50m of set-tlement features. The geophysical survey of the area demonstrated that the axis of the settlement was north-west to south-east and pits, rectilinear enclosures and ring gullies continued beyond the 160m-long survey area.

Ann Garvey analysed the Early Iron Age petrology and concluded that nearly all the pot-tery was locally produced, although 5 per cent of the sherds contained glauconitic fabric found in Upper Greensand deposits. The nearest useable source of Greensand is 22km away at Chaldon Herring in south Dorset. Alternatively, the pottery may have been produced in the environs of Castle Ditches hillfort, Vale of Wardour, which lies 26km to the north.

Heron Grove

The pottery from Sweetbriar is similar to that from the Earliest Iron Age phase of Heron Grove. This site is on a spur top above the south bank of the River Stour 3km from the Sweetbriar settlement but on tertiary gravel rather than chalk.

The area was excavated by John Valentin and Peter Cox in advance of gravel extraction in the early 1990s and at least 15 ring gullies for round houses, numerous post-holes and pits and intercutting enclosure ditches and gullies were found. A few Early Neolithic and Early Bronze Age features were excavated but most of the occupation evidence dated to the Earliest Iron Age. Many of the occupation features and six of the round house sites contained exclusively Early Iron Age pottery.

Of the 5273 sherds from the site, 4108 were dated to the period *c.*800-600 BC. The pot-tery forms are similar to those found on the Purbeck sites of Eldon Seat and Kimmeridge, with finger-tip decoration predominantly found on the jars and stabbed decoration on the furrowed bowls and long-necked carinated bowls. The fabric analysis indicated that 15-20 per cent of the sherds came from non-local sources. About 12 per cent had fabric typical of the Purbeck area and 2 per cent had glauconitic inclusions typical of a production area close to Upper Greensand geology.

Frances Raymond thought the ceramics indicated that the excavated area was abandoned in the Early Iron Age and reoccupied in the Middle Iron Age. Four hundred and fifty-three sherds were dated to the period 350-50 BC. The high percentage of Poole Harbour-type fabics (65 per cent), the high-shouldered jars and ovoid jars, indicated that the reoccupation of the site took place in the late Middle Iron Age, perhaps in the second century BC.

Six hundred and twelve sherds from the site were dated to the Late Iron Age. The iden-tifiable forms tended to be bead rimmed jars of typical Durotrigan style. A local copy of a Gallo-Belgic wheel-turned Black Cordoned Ware jar was identified. The fabric of 98 per cent of the sherds came from Poole Harbour. The other 11 sherds from Late Iron Age fea-tures contained flint temper and were thought to be residual Middle Iron Age sherds. This last phase of the site, therefore, is like other settlements in Dorset in the period 50 BC-AD 43, where local pottery production disappears in favour of Poole Harbour Ware. Most of the pottery from this phase was found in the rectilinear ditch that was dug across the site and this is similar to that excavated at Sweetbriar. There is no evidence that Sweetbriar and Heron Grove continued to be occupied into the Roman period.

Bradford Down

Bradford Down is about 1.5km north-east of Badbury Rings on a spur of land west of the River Allen. Badbury Hill is clearly visible and the bedrock is chalk overlain in places by brown clay mixed with round pebbles. The triangular 18ha field is framed on the east and south-west by farm roads and on the north-west by an ancient hedge which forms the boundary of the Kingston Lacy Estate.

The land was downland when the earthworks of a settlement were discovered and drawn in the 1930s, but the land was ploughed up in the war. During the 1960s, it was noticed that each ploughing threw up many flints with occasional Roman roof tiles. One of several archaeological test pits, dug in 1967, located the floor of a Roman building. Local archaeologist, Norman Field, excavated three areas within the ditched area known as the 'Twisted Thorn' mound. Four Romano-British buildings were identified and they were found to cover pits and ditches of Iron Age date (Field 1982).

The trenches were spaced 10m apart and excavated in the area defined by the Iron Age boundary ditch that followed the north, west and south sides of the 'Twisted Thorn' earthwork. The largest trench (A) was positioned over a scatter of building debris. Trench B, to

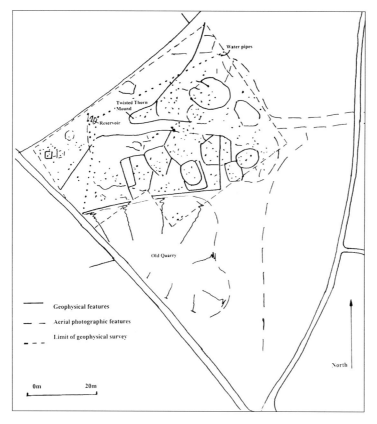

Geophysical features
Aerial photographic features
Limit of geophysical survey

0m   20m

North

56 Geophysical survey plot of anomalies at Bradford Down. (Papworth)

the north-east, was located over another discrete rubble scatter and C, south-west of A, was dug into the top of the mound.

In trench A the footings of three Roman buildings were found dating from the second to fourth century AD. These overlay 14 pits: two were dated to the Early Iron Age, seven to the Late Iron Age, two were early Romano-British and three were undated. In section, the pits were generally of 'beehive' type.

In trench B the footings of a small building were found. These probably dated to the second century and overlay a deposit containing a coin of Claudius. A cluster of three intercutting pits were excavated. The central pit (B28) contained Early Iron Age pottery, B27 contained Late Iron Age finds and B29 was undated.

In the east corner of the trench were two intercutting ditches. The earlier, B32, was traced for 30m aligned south to north before it turned north-east. B33 seems to have been excavated soon afterwards and followed a similar course along the east side of B32. Both were 2m wide and 1m deep and were deliberately backfilled rather than allowed to silt up gradually. The sherds of Durotrigan pottery and early Roman flagons from B33 indicated a mid to late first-century AD date.

The smallest trench, 'C', revealed a group of seven post-holes scattered around a circular hollow 8m in diameter. The filling of the hollow contained no dateable finds but some of the post-holes contained pottery, including an Early Iron Age sherd with finger-tip decoration. The burial of a headless sheep was found on the south side of the hollow mixed with other animal bones. This was interpreted as a possible ritual deposit.

This trench was extended to the south to section the boundary ditch of the mound. It had two phases: the earlier ditch measured 1.5m wide and 0.9m deep; the later ditch converged on the earlier and cut through it from the east. It measured 3m wide and 1.8m deep and three sherds of Late Iron Age pottery were found in its primary filling. The ditch silted gradually and was still a clear earthwork with a counterscarp bank when it was surveyed in the 1930s.

Aerial photographs indicated that Norman Field's trenches had sampled part of a much larger site. Therefore in 2002, we divided the field into 20m grids. Geoffrey Brown carried out a fluxgate gradiometer survey of the north-west part of the field covering 6ha. Where the survey crossed the old excavation trenches we used the same grids to carry out a resistivity survey and collect finds across an area measuring 60m by 40m.

The fieldwalking recovered mainly worked flint and Roman building debris. No Iron Age pottery was found. The Roman debris lay across the areas 'A' and 'B', where Norman Field excavated the Roman buildings, and continued down the slope to the east where the resistivity survey revealed a U-shaped area of high resistance 40m wide surrounding a low resistance area. This evidence may represent building foundations around a courtyard.

On the top of the down, in the grids immediately west of the 'Twisted Thorn' mound, there was a concentration of struck flints. Many of these showed secondary working, typical of a Late Bronze Age flint technology.

The geophysical survey showed that 'Twisted Thorn' mound lay at a junction of two main trackways in the Late Iron Age, one approached from the north-east and the other from the east (56). To the east and south of this junction, extending for about 200m, is the main occupation area consisting of about 12 rectilinear and curvilinear enclosures averaging about

30-40m wide and containing pit-like anomalies. The enclosures are defined by boundary ditches, sometimes with traces of minor trackways between them.

Norman Field's excavations dated the boundary ditches to the Late Iron Age and compared these ditches to the Late Iron Age inner enclosure at Gussage 20, excavated by Geoffrey Wainwright. The Bradford enclosures are contemporary with those excavated at Cleavel Point and East of Corfe River in Purbeck.

Some of the linear features are probably earlier than the main rectilinear enclosure phase. It is apparent that many of the clusters of pit-like anomalies do not seem to be related to the ditched enclosures. Field's three excavation trenches demonstrate a long period of occupation on the site throughout the Iron Age.

The main 10m-wide track through the settlement can be seen on aerial photographs continuing east. At the centre of the settlement, the track is obscured by an area containing many anomalies corresponding with the zone of the high resistivity readings. This suggests that the later Romano-British buildings ignored the Iron Age track-side boundaries and that this section went out of use at some time in the Roman period.

On the west edge of the survey area, is a clear 12m-wide square enclosure with traces of another on its east side. These features lie beyond the clusters of enclosures and most of the pit-like anomalies. It has an entrance to the north that would enable access from the central track. There are pit-like anomalies within and around the square enclosure and these may indicate the sites of Iron Age or perhaps Roman burials associated with the settlement. Similar square mortuary enclosures have been mentioned above, for example at Allards Quarry, Marnhull.

The combined archaeological evidence indicates that the summit and south slope of Bradford Down were occupied by a settlement that originated in the Bronze Age and by the end of the Iron Age had grown to become a cluster of households each within a rectilinear enclosure.

Lodge Farm

In 1986, I excavated the remains of an Iron Age settlement in advance of underpinning work at Lodge Farm at the north-west corner of Kingston Lacy Park. This medieval hunting lodge lies 1km south-east of Badbury and 2km south of Bradford Down. There was evidence for two phases of prehistoric occupation. In the earlier phase, a 2m-wide and 0.3m-deep ditch aligned east to west terminated at a 1m diameter post-pit at its west end. In Phase 2, the ditch was recut and continued across the post-pit. To the north of this boundary were post-holes and a yard surface. The yard was constructed of flint gravel including numerous burnt flints. This had been constructed over one of the post-holes. These features contained fragments of thin-walled coarse black pottery with a flint temper which Ann Garvey has dated to the early Middle Iron Age. The Iron Age features were recorded where they were exposed within the foundation trenches of Lodge Farm but the settlement was more extensive. Contemporary boundary ditches have been recorded during excavations in the garden and adjacent field.

Compared to other settlements in the area, this was a shortlived site occupied for about 50-100 years *c.*350 BC. The site was then abandoned until the medieval deer park ditch was cut through it in the fourteenth century.

Barnsley

On similar sites to Bradford Down, on spurs above the west side of the Allen River, lie the settlements of Barnsley and Lower Barnsley. Barnsley is 1km south-east of Bradford and 1km north-west of Lower Barnsley.

Barnsley occupies the crest of a spur above the 40m contour. Norman Field walked this area after ploughing in 1966 and found the lower half of a Greensand rotary quern and fragments of Roman pottery and tiles. Aerial photographs show two parallel ditches 300m long and 10m apart curving from the south towards the west side of an ovoid enclosure 250m in diameter with the darker marks indicating pits within it. This suggests that the Roman pottery represents a later phase of a settlement overlying an Iron Age enclosure.

The Lower Barnsley settlement was sited below the 30m contour south-east of Barnsley and was found by David and Michael Burleigh after deep ploughing in 1991. Using a metal detector they found many Roman coins and the pottery from the site included Durotrigan and Black Burnished Ware. A large Greensand rotary quern was found in the hedge beside the field and earlier occupation on the site is indicated by worked flints, including an Early Bronze Age barbed and tanged arrowhead. The site is lower down the valley slope and more deeply buried; therefore the survey of the aerial photographic evidence has not revealed any more detail. Durotrigan coins have been found on both of these Barnsley sites, including bronze and silver staters and a silver quarter stater.

High Lea Farm

On the opposite side of the valley, on a west facing slope above the 40m contour lie the remains of a settlement which is clear on aerial photographs. Badbury hill is visible from the site. It resembles one of Collin Bowen's concentric enclosures covering about 1.5ha. Trial trenches in 2003 revealed the footings of walls associated with pottery and fibulae dating to the first to third centuries AD. John Gale of Bournemouth University found no indication for an Iron Age origin for the site but subsequent geophysical survey has detected ring ditches within the settlement, probably round house gullies.

A curvilinear trackway can be seen on the aerial photographs leading from this site to the river at Hinton Mill. It may link up with the track that continues through the Bradford Down settlement on the west side of the Allen.

Buzbury Rings

Collin Bowen classified Buzbury not as a hillfort but a concentric enclosure settlement similar to High Lea but larger, enclosing about 3ha. The site occupies a strong position on the ridge top above the Tarrant and Stour valleys, with Badbury visible 4.5km to the south-east. Like High Lea, the inner enclosure is not central to the outer but lies against its south side.

The outer enclosure is kidney shaped and about 250m across. There are traces of a middle enclosure on the south and west sides of the 120m diameter ovoid inner enclosure. A modern road crosses the site and parts of the settlement have been affected by ploughing and the construction of a golf course on the east side.

The RCHM earthwork survey shows that the site is associated with contemporary trackways and a field system. The original entrance probably lay on the south-east side facing Badbury. At least eight hollows within the inner enclosure, visible on aerial photographs, are interpreted as hut circles.

Before 1914 and the construction of the golf course, O.G.S. Crawford (1928) mentioned finding hundreds of sherds of reddish flint gritted pottery in molehills dating to the Early Iron Age. He also found perforated lugs or handles, which may be a reference to countersunk handles typical of the Late Iron Age. Since then, many other fragments of pottery have been recovered, mainly from the inner enclosure. The assemblage indicates that the site was occupied from the Early Iron Age to the end of the Roman period.

Spetisbury Rings

The 2ha hillfort of Spetisbury Rings (*colour plate 29*) is located 4km south of Buzbury. It was strategically placed on the summit and north-east slope of a 75m high hill. The entrance through the single rampart and ditch is on the north-west side.

The movement of the Stour in its flood plain has cut into the hill slope here creating a steep drop from the hillfort rampart to the river. Poundbury Camp occupies a similar position in relation to the Frome.

From Spetisbury there are clear views to Badbury 5km to the east and along the Stour valley to Hod Hill 11km to the north-west. The river is fordable as it flows past the hillfort and the medieval Crawford Bridge now takes advantage of this position.

The narrow gap between the river and the hillfort meant that in 1857, when the Somerset and Dorset railway was built between Wimborne and Blandford, a cutting was needed in the hillslope to create a level bed for the track. The cutting removed the east edge of the hillfort and exposed a pit containing 80-90 skeletons 'laid irregularly'. Later, at least another 40 skeletons were unearthed. The local antiquarians, Mr Durden and Mr Akerman, recorded the first exposure but were not given access to this second discovery.

In 1939, Colin Gresham looked at the notebooks and accounts of Durden and Akerman and compared them with the objects that were donated to the British Museum from the site. He thought that the burial pit was the hillfort ditch and that the burials represented a mass grave following a battle. Fragments of scabbard and shield binding and four 'javelin-heads' were thought to be Roman. A long sword with part of its scabbard, fragments of five sword shaped currency bars, two brooches, a bronze cauldron and nine spearheads among other objects were thought to be Iron Age. There was evidence of violence. One skull had been cut with a sword, another had a spear lodged in it.

It is generally believed that these objects are from a battle at the river crossing between the Romans and the local Iron Age people *c.*AD 43-44. However, Gresham classified the brooches as Late La Téne II and this dates them to *c.*150 BC. He also thought two sword chapes from the site were early. The currency bars also suggest a pre-conquest date. No coins were recovered from the site and only one pottery fragment of unusual form is included in the collection.

In 1994, Bruce Eagles looked at the spearheads again and suggested that four of them were post-Roman and that the shield binding could also be fifth to seventh century. Therefore, the jumble of bodies in the mass grave or graves may represent more than one conflict at the river crossing. The earlier material may have been disturbed by the later burials. Whatever the explanation, the evidence does not suggest a mass grave dating to the mid-first century AD. Perhaps the bodies were interred at various times over several generations and represent a local burial tradition.

The univallate fort may have been abandoned in the later Middle Iron Age in favour of the developed hillfort of Badbury or, like Poundbury, may have been regularly repaired by a local population living outside the ramparts. This, like Battlesbury, is a place where modern scientific excavation is needed to determine the date for a massacre site often linked with the Roman Conquest.

Badbury Rings

The twin peaks of Badbury Hill can be seen from all the settlements described above. The hillfort occupies the west summit and the High Wood enclosure the east. To the north-west, beyond Buzbury, Blandford Down interrupts Badbury's sight line to Hod. Any signal would need to be relayed via a location like Spetisbury.

The domed 7ha interior of Badbury Rings (*colour plates 24 & 25*) is covered in earthworks which only became apparent when the site was cleared of scrub in the 1980s. Later uses of the hilltop, such as the eighteenth-century tree-ring enclosures, the pine plantation and the 1940s concrete installations, have disturbed or hidden some of the prehistoric features.

RCHME staff carried out an earthwork survey in 1998 and recorded 28 potential hut sites beside the inner rampart. Other hollows and terraces can be seen in the 30-40m-wide ring of land between the inner rampart and a pronounced scarp that defines the geological change from chalk to the clay and gravel capping on the hilltop. Excavations have shaped this scarp and many of the hollows cut into it are probably round house sites (*57*).

At the top of this slope are traces of a bank and the RCHME surveyors suggested that an earlier hillfort may have been built on this upper part of the hill and later levelled when the present inner rampart was constructed. A process like that was revealed by excavation at Yarnbury in Wiltshire in 1933.

Rectilinear as well as circular earthworks are apparent and some of these may be Romano-British or later. Geoffrey Brown has carried out a geophysical survey across the interior and this has revealed many pit-like anomalies and some linears. In the south-east quadrant, a group of regularly spaced pits form a rectangular plan measuring 30m by 15m, indicating a substantial structure. Other notable anomalies are the concentrations of ferrous material spaced around the inner rampart every 100m or so. These indicate dumps of metal or areas of metalworking but it is unclear whether they represent modern debris or something more archaeologically significant.

In 2004, using this survey information, we excavated three small trenches within the hillfort to establish a basic chronology for the site. Trench 1 was located 20m south of the west entrance against the east side of the inner rampart. At this point there was an oval hollow 12m across and a 6m square trench was excavated to sample its northern half (*colour plate 26*).

At first we were surprised because after carefully removing layers representing 1500 years of collapsed rampart; a chalk surface was found covered in late Roman material. Fortunately, this proved not to be the natural chalk, as underneath it was the Iron Age occupation evidence. This included a yard surface, two shallow pits and the ring gulley for a round house with an east facing entrance. The finds from the site were Late Iron Age and included large pieces of Poole Harbour pottery, cattle and sheep bones and an ovoid clay sling shot (*colour plates 27 & 28*).

Trenches II and III were aligned north-west to south-east and located either side of a path between the pine trees planted on the summit. Trench II, on the south-west side of the path, was 43m long and 1.0m wide and extended from the hilltop to the plantation edge.

Tree roots and modern disturbance had damaged the archaeology here. Post-medieval and predominantly 1940s debris lay directly on a layer of early prehistoric flint flakes, cores and burnt Heath stone. The subsoil consisted of compact pebble stones overlying a fine, plastic clay. Cutting into this was a pit and a ditch that contained Late Mesolithic to Early Neolithic flint debitage.

The Iron Age occupation evidence was confined to the lower, north-west end of the trench where the clay overlay compact yellow brown sand. Here, a terrace had been cut through the flint debris into the hill slope and the floor and lower slope of this feature were covered in burnt flint and pebbles mixed with numerous fragments of black pottery and red daub. Three fragments of iron were found and two of these were part of a curved object consisting of two strands twisted together, probably a torc or armlet. A similar iron object was found at Spetisbury Rings.

Trench III on the north-east side of the path also located this terrace but there were fewer pottery finds from its floor. Trench III demonstrated the same lack of Iron Age stratigraphy on the gravel and clay geology on the summit of the hill. From this area came a bar-shaped whet stone which may be Iron Age.

We had expected to find far more Iron Age material at the top of the hill but perhaps the compacted gravel and plastic clays together with the exposed position made this part of the hillfort undesirable as an occupation site. The clay layer makes the upper slope of the hill very wet in winter. The small areas sampled by excavation suggest that the place was not densely occupied but the trenches were on the west side of the hillfort and like Hod Hill, the principal entrance and concentration of buildings may have been to the east. However, the earthwork and geophysical evidence indicates that the settlement covered the whole interior. The pottery assemblage is also surprising as nearly everything from the site is Late Iron Age. The current evidence cannot be used to claim that the place was the principal settlement from the Earliest Iron Age.

In 2006, Ann Garvey looked at the petrology of the pottery from Badbury and found that all the rim sherds were of quartz fabric and that 55 per cent were of Q4, the coarse Poole Harbour Ware. Fabrics Q7 and Q11 amounted to another 18 per cent of the assemblage and were coarser and finer equivalents of Q4. Therefore over two-thirds of the Badbury pottery was of Durotrigan type produced around Poole Harbour. The Badbury ceramic forms correspond with phases 6G and 6H at Maiden Castle, which had about 80 per cent Poole Harbour pottery by this time. Lisa Brown dated these phases to the middle to late first century BC.

Other fabrics were present in the Badbury assemblage indicating that grog, shelly, calcareous, flint and sandy tempered pottery were still in use in the Late Iron Age. However, the absence of the Latest Iron Age Poole Harbour forms such as bead rim bowls and jars in finer fabrics (Phase 7A at Maiden Castle) suggests movement away from the hillfort in the first century AD.

The Badbury earthwork evidence indicates that an early hilltop enclosure was later replaced by the present inner rampart, with its Iron Age east gateway including characteristic

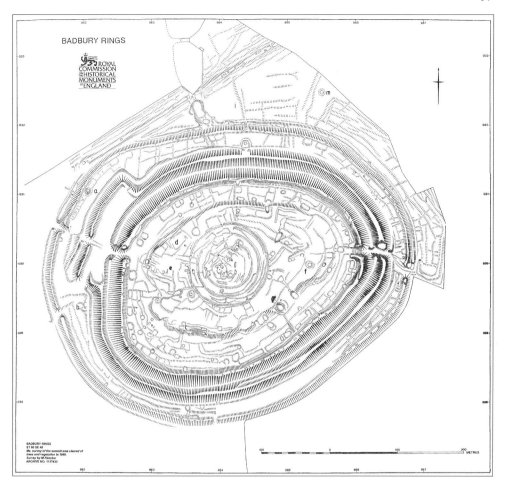

57 Earthwork survey of Badbury Rings hillfort. (RCHME 1998) *Crown Copyright*

inturned entrance banks. The west entrance could be contemporary as there is a slight inturned bank on its south side. The middle rampart may be an addition, or part of the original design, as it exhibits a similar form and is tightly concentric with the inner rampart, except on the west. It may originally have continued close to the west entrance and was later diverted 50m to the west to create a barbican. This is a 150m-long rectilinear enclosure defined by the middle rampart and the inner rampart. The barbican may have been created as a separate stock or stabling enclosure. The two breaches in the barbican are probably later, particularly that in its south-west side. In 1774, William Woodward surveyed Badbury as part of his estate survey of Kingston Lacy and he does not show a gap in the rampart there although he clearly shows the others. The causeways across the western breaches, both in the barbican and outer rampart, have settled into the ditches, which were backfilled when the entrances were made. This demonstrates that they post-date the original design.

It has been suggested that this outer defence line was built in response to imminent Roman attack and its low humped profile indicates that the work was never completed. Perhaps there was not enough time to finish the work before the enemy crossed the

Stour. The late Roman finds allow for an alternative interpretation as they show that Badbury was occupied and defended again and therefore the rampart could date to the sub-Roman period.

High Wood Enclosure

The east summit of Badbury Hill is occupied by a 90m in diameter D-shaped enclosure consisting of a bank with an internal ditch. This earthwork within High Wood has been damaged by gravel pits. We dug a trench across the enclosure in May 2008 to date the site. This revealed that the earthwork was constructed in the Late Iron Age and was built on a Middle Iron Age occupation site. Pottery dated the gravel pits to the Roman period. Earlier prehistoric flint debitage was found in all contexts (*colour plates 31 & 32*).

High Wood, like Badbury Rings, was valued as a key vantage point and was occupied at the same time as the hillfort. The ditch within the bank indicates that it was built to contain something rather than defend against attack. Perhaps this was a corral or stock enclosure.

The Badbury/Shapwick Hoard

Early in 1983, a hoard of over 800 Durotrigan coins was found near Badbury. Ian Darke and Clive Gibb of the Dorset Detector Group spoke of seeing about 900 coins arranged in drawers by type soon after their discovery and before the hoard was broken up and sold through various dealers.

Robert Van Arsdell and Melinda Mays have examined the available information on the metal-detected finds from the area.

Melinda Mays had obtained information on up to 600 coins but could list in detail only 242 found in the study area between 1983-84. She divided them into twelve groups using the available information.

The descriptions show that the hoard had been broken up by the time she began her study. The titles for the listed groups range from 'Badbury Rings', 'Badbury Rings fields', 'Shapwick' and 'Shapwick Crab Farm'.

Van Arsdell estimated 850 coins in the hoard and from his research suggested that it was found somewhere south-east of Crab Farmhouse. Ian Darke was told that the coins were found in the point-to-point course field west of Badbury. The farmer and National Trust countryside staff had reported signs of metal detector activity in the same field during the 1980s near the Shapwick parish boundary. This information led to a metal detector survey of the area in 2004 combined with a gradiometer survey but both provided no significant information. However, notes made by David Thackray in March to April 1984 recorded 'considerable digging' in ploughed fields either side of High Wood north-east of Badbury.

Since 1900, excavation and chance discovery have recovered 25 Durotrigan coins from the temple site immediately west of Badbury Rings. This has led Melinda Mays to tentatively suggest that the hoard came from this site because deposits of Iron Age coins are frequently associated with sacred sites. However, references to Crab Farm in some of the coin group descriptions may indicate that the find spot lay 1km further south-west.

Despite the frustration of not knowing the location of the discovery or series of discoveries, it clearly marks out Badbury, Crab Farm and the land between as significant in the Late Iron Age. Van Arsdell believed that the coins he saw were from a single hoard because they had the same appearance within metal types and seemed to have been cleaned in one lot. He believed that Badbury-Shapwick had parallels with the Le Catillon hoard from Jersey as both bridged the transition from gold to silver coinage. He dated the hoard to around 35 BC but Mays and Haselgrove would consider this too precise a date. Melinda Mays would agree that the hoard represents the earlier phase of Durotrigan coinage likely to date to the first century BC, particularly because of the presence of gold staters and over 25 starfish design pieces, which were thought to be rare before the Badbury hoard was discovered.

In Melinda Mays' lists of coins attributed to Badbury/Shapwick there are examples of non-Durotrigan coins. In a list of coins found 'near Badbury' there is one British A and one coin attributed to Verica, a leader of the Atrebates *c.*AD 40 (therefore too late for the hoard). In the list of coins reportedly found in 'Badbury Rings fields' was a coin of East Midlands type. In the list for the 'Shapwick/Badbury Rings' group were four British B and one attributed to Cunobelin, who ruled the Catuvellauni in the first century AD (also too late for the hoard). Other lists are of possible coins attributed to the area including a Dobunnic coin and a coin of the Armorican Baiocasses type. The Gallic link to Badbury is strengthened by a coin of the Veneti found at Badbury before 1940.

All of these coins may not be from the hoard but they demonstrate contact with other coin producing communities in Armorica. There seem to be stronger links with eastern British groups here based on the records of British B Atrebatic and Catuvellaunian coins, if indeed each of these finds was actually from Badbury.

Recent metal detector surveys by the Stour Valley Detector Group have revealed clusters of south-western series/Durotrigan coin finds in the surrounding area, particularly to the north-west, for example at Tarrant Rushton, Tarrant Rawston and Tarrant Crawford. The surveyors were able to give eight-figure grid references for each find, and this accuracy, with the incidence of silver, base silver and bronze issues, indicates scatters of coins across settlements rather than hoards of coins spread by ploughing.

Badbury Romano-Celtic Temple

This site lies immediately west of Badbury Rings and consists of a 60m diameter eight-sided boundary bank with an east entrance surrounding a mound.

Earthwork, resistivity and gradiometer surveys have revealed the plan of a 15m square stone temple building surrounded by a covered walkway. Across a gravel courtyard was a small rectangular building built against the temple precinct (*temenos*) boundary wall.

In September 2000, we camped beside the temple earthwork and excavated an evaluation trench measuring 40m long and 1.2m wide. At the south edge of the site, beneath the Roman *temenos* wall, was a ditch backfilled with early Roman material where the gradiometry plot shows a ditched, barrel-shaped enclosure with a small rectangular annexe attached to the east side. This may be Iron Age although most of the Durotrigan coins were found in the triangular area between the hillfort, Dorchester Roman road and the temple. Therefore the original Iron Age site may lie just north of the Roman buildings. Coin finds from sealed deposits beneath successive floors of the temple building indicated that it was in use from the first to fifth century AD. Only one Durotrigan coin was found in our excavation but three have been found in mole hills on the site, six from an excavation by E. Wallace in 1900 and 15 from an excavation in 1952 by Chris Rudd.

It could be argued that the site was sacred before the Iron Age because a Bronze Age barrow lies immediately to the west and other ring ditches were detected around and under the site during the geophysical survey.

The latest coins from the temple were early fifth century and therefore it seems that the heath stone walls had been robbed after this date. This building material may have been taken and used to strengthen the ramparts of Badbury as heath stone with mortar attached was found in the rampart collapse above the late Roman or sub-Roman levels within the hillfort.

Crab Farm Settlement

Although the Roman fortification at Crab Farm was known from John Boyden's aerial photographs of 1976, it was not until 1990 that the extent of the site began to be understood. A chance conversation with a local builder drew my attention to the arable fields south-west of Crab Farmhouse.

The farmer told me to look in the Ash Tree Field north of Shapwick village. This field had just been ploughed and the bright autumn sunlight picked out areas of debris which on closer examination were the remains of Roman buildings. Subsequent fieldwalking, geophysical survey and excavation revealed evidence for roads and property boundaries defining rectilinear plots containing building footings and pits. Painted plaster, tesserae and box flue tiles indicated that some of the Romano-British residents were wealthy enough to have decorated homes with mosaics and underfloor heating. In 1991, we excavated two evaluation trenches (A & B) which revealed features dating from the second to fourth century AD (58).

Further geophysical survey was carried out in Long Field, east of the Shapwick road. This field is crossed by the Badbury-Dorchester Roman road and includes 60 per cent of the 2.4ha fortification. The fluxgate gradiometer survey indicated that the site had been occupied before its construction. In 1995, two trenches were excavated, one to date the features underlying the fort (trench C) and one to discover the relative dates of the Dorchester Roman road and fortification (trench D).

Trench C, at the north-east end of the field, confirmed that the Roman occupation overlay numerous pits and ditches dating from the Middle and Late Iron Age. Two 1.7m-deep parallel ditches (165 and 167), set 4.5m apart, had steep V-shaped profiles. Their primary fillings contained Middle Iron Age pottery. One fragment from a bowl had a shell temper and was possibly of Early Iron Age date but no other finds were this age.

A vertical sided pit, 2.6m in diameter and 1.7m deep, was half-sectioned and contained a structured deposit. In the bottom layer was the skeleton of a newborn puppy and above it the skeleton of a lamb. Overlying this was the skeleton of a mature dog and above this a deposit of carbonised grain and burnt wood mixed with large sherds of pottery. Radiocarbon analysis of the charcoal from this layer produced a date of about 300-200 BC. Also in this layer and the one above were found the remains of two frogs, a finch and a piglet. The upper layers contained Late Iron Age and Roman finds indicating subsidence and gradual silting.

58 Total plan of geophysical survey anomalies at Crab Farm, Shapwick. (Papworth)

Ann Garvey examined the pottery from the pit (109). There were 11 jars, 4 saucepan pots and 1 bowl. All the pottery was undecorated and 81 per cent was made from fabrics that could be obtained locally. The shelly fabric of 6 per cent of the pottery was thought to come from the coast and the fabric of the other 13 per cent was Q4, typical of pottery produced around Poole Harbour.

The other Iron Age pits excavated in trench C underlay two second-century smithing hearths. They contained pottery typical of the Latest Iron Age or earliest Roman period. Pit 158 contained 100 sherds of Poole Harbour Ware with the normal range of late Durotrigan forms, including bead rim bowls and jars with counter-sunk handles. Only nine of the sherds were of the coarse Q4 fabric, indicating that by this time the pottery was generally made of a finer fabric. The pit contained part of a Gallo-Belgic Terra Nigra platter and two sherds of a Dressel 20 amphora. Pit 139 contained a similar range of Poole Harbour Ware, most commonly the bead rim bowl. Therefore, by this stage, local manufacture of pottery had apparently ceased. The only pottery other than Poole Harbour Ware were rare imports from the continent.

The geophysical survey of the Crab Farm settlement revealed that the site covers over 25ha. However, many of the storage pits seem to lie within the ditch of a large enclosure, ovoid in plan, and interpreted as the boundary of the principal Iron Age settlement. This was located at the top of a north-east facing slope in view of Badbury Rings. The boundary ditch encloses about 2ha and has an inturned east entrance.

The north side of the enclosure is 40m south of the Late Bronze Age linear Shapwick 35/a89 at a point where this significant bank and ditch, after heading up hill from Badbury, turns through 90 degrees and runs north-west, following the contour of the north-east facing slope. The geophysical survey shows that two parallel ditches 5m apart have been dug from the ovoid enclosure towards this corner of the linear, presumably to control access. Another interesting feature lies 50m north-west of the right-angled turn where a causeway is clearly visible crossing the bank and ditch. This gateway through the linear is protected by a short length of ditch on its south-west side apparently preventing direct access. This suggests that security was important and the Bronze Age linear was still a significant feature in the Late Iron Age.

The geophysical survey plot indicates two circular enclosures about 30m in diameter. One lies within the ovoid enclosure, the other is about 300m to the south-west and has been cut by the modern Shapwick road. Both sites contain many pits and may be Iron Age enclosures for significant households. Other circular enclosures 15-20m in diameter may be Iron Age round houses and enclosure sites or Bronze Age ring ditches underlying the later prehistoric and Roman occupation.

Another Late Iron Age to Early Roman occupation site may lie beneath Shapwick village, as the finds made by Oliver Leighton during building work in 1954 included a Claudian coin and early Roman and possible Gallic imports.

To the south and west of the ovoid enclosure are numerous contiguous rectilinear enclosures, each 0.2-0.5ha in area. It was originally assumed that this layout originated in the Roman period but following the surveys at Bradford Down and Sweetbriar Drove it became more probable that the settlement pattern originated in the Late Iron Age. The main Roman road to Dorchester ignores this ditch system completely.

Before the excavation, the analysis of the Shapwick aerial photographs led Norman Field to suggest that Crab Farm was a first-century Roman fort, located to oversee and control the hillfort populations of Spetisbury and Badbury. This military establishment had attracted settlement and provided the economic stimulus for growth. A road was built from the fort to Dorchester and after about 20 years the fort was abandoned but the road enhanced. The settlement developed along the line of the main road, particularly as it lay near a ford across the Stour and only 2km south-west of the Badbury Roman cross-roads. This was a reasonable hypothesis supported by the development histories of other Romano-British settlements.

However, the 1995 excavations had shown that the Crab Farm settlement pre-dated the fortification and road, which were not built until the later Roman period. Therefore the rectilinear ditch system that formed the framework of the town was likely to have an early origin.

In 2004, we excavated trench E near the south-west end of Long Field, where the Dorchester Roman road crossed one of the significant ditches of the boundary system (*colour plate 30*). The excavation showed that the original ditch (428) had been cut, backfilled, then recut (440) and allowed to silt up. Both cuts were V-shaped and 1.4m wide and 0.5m deep.

The later ditch filling contained an early hinged brooch of Bagendon type dated to the mid-late first century AD. The fillings of both ditches contained consistently early first century pottery, including a Samian platter and Poole Harbour Ware. The lower filling of ditch 428 contained only Late Iron Age forms and therefore seems to have been excavated before the Roman Conquest. Given the evidence for similarly dated enclosures at Sweetbriar, Bradford Down and Heron Grove, many of the Crab Farm enclosures may be pre-Roman and hint at a step towards urbanisation in the Latest Iron Age. The difference at Crab Farm is that this ditch system continued to be used during the early Roman period (Papworth 2004, 181-186).

At the west edge of the settlement is an isolated square enclosure with sides about 12m long. David Stewart carried out a geophysical survey here in 2007 and this showed that there was an entrance through its east side. The form is similar to the enclosure found to the west of the Bradford Down settlement and is interpreted as a possible mortuary enclosure.

The main road of the settlement is aligned roughly east to west and is flanked by enclosures and building sites. At its east end, near the centre of the settlement, is an open area with few geophysical anomalies. This area measures 80m by 60m and may once have functioned as a market or meeting place. The same interpretation has been suggested for the open space shown in the geophysical survey for Hod Hill.

The Lake Farm, Fortress

The Crab Farm fortification was first thought to date to the first century AD, but in 1995 trench D demonstrated that the Roman road to Dorchester was built across the backfilled fortification ditches which contained fourth-century material. Therefore the fort went out of use at the end of the Roman period not the beginning. However, an early Roman military site has been confirmed by excavation in the south-east corner of the study area.

In 1959, Norman Field dug an exploratory trench at Lake Farm to test whether an earthwork ridge was a length of Roman road. The excavation recovered first-century Roman pottery from beneath the earthwork. Further excavations from 1960-81 and geophysical survey 1976-83 revealed the site of a legionary fortress.

The site has not been published but in 2005 Keith Jarvis, Poole Museum's archaeologist and one of the site directors, kindly sent me copies of his manuscript and the available specialist reports.

The fortress was located on a low gravel terrace on the south side of the Stour. It was a rectilinear enclosure of 13.4ha consisting of two parallel ditches with rounded corners fronting a rampart surrounding barrack blocks and other military buildings (59).

The excavated archaeological features have been divided into three phases. Phase 1 was the preliminary construction camp within the fortress. Phase 2 was the occupation period after the barrack blocks had been completed. Phase 3 was the demolition phase when the timbers were deliberately dismantled. The rampart and ditches of the fortress were also deliberately levelled at this time.

Finds from the south-west side of the fort indicated that there had been a military bath house there. Industrial activity, such as gravel extraction and iron working, was recorded.

There is also evidence of a military cemetery 0.9km south of the site. In 1865, at Cogdean Elms, Corfe Mullen, a cremation in a Durotrigan bowl was found with two glass

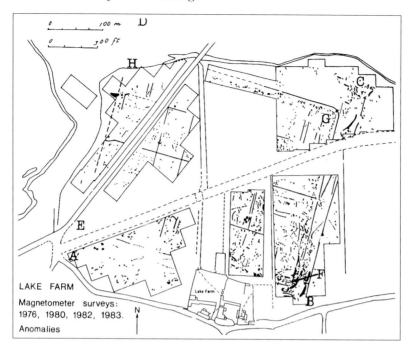

59 Geophysical survey plan of Lake Farm Roman fortress. (Field 1992, 44) *Surveyed and drawn by the Ancient Monuments Laboratory. Crown Copyright*

phials and a Claudian coin. Other cremations in pots had been found in the same gravel pit in 1847.

These burials were found about 300m east of the settlement at East End, which contained an early Roman pottery kiln and settlement evidence from the Late Iron Age to the fourth century. The distinctive products of the kiln have become known as Corfe Mullen Ware and have not been found in pre-Roman deposits within the study area. This settlement's early link with the fortress is indicated by the establishment of this kiln, the presence of first-century imports, such as Belgic platters, amphorae and south Gaulish Samian Ware, and the find of a first-century donkey-mill indicating that flour was being produced on a commercial or military scale. This millstone is made from alkali basalt lava from Chaine des Puyes, central France and is a rare import. This is a fascinating site but it has only been recorded as a series of chance discoveries during quarrying, gardening and building work, mainly in the early twentieth century.

The early products of the Corfe Mullen kiln are interesting because they were oxidised, thin-walled Roman versions of Durotrigan cooking jars. The early adoption of Poole Harbour products by the Roman army has already been noted at the Waddon and Hod hillforts and considerable quantities of this pottery together with sherds of Corfe Mullen Ware were found in the fortress.

There are 34 coins from the fortress site. All were thought to be early Claudian and dated to AD 41-54. Norman Sheil, who examined the coins, concluded that there was a total lack of post-Claudian coins (i.e. later than AD 64). The Samian report by G.B. Dannell also concluded that the site was abandoned *c*.AD 65, although vessels pre-dating AD 55 were not identified. Francis Grew examined the metalwork from the site which included fragments of Roman military armour and belt and sword fittings typical of the mid-first century AD.

The Roman road to Hamworthy links Lake Farm to the coast, where Peter Bellamy has confirmed the location of a first-century Poole Harbour-side military enclosure. This is thought to be the base from which military supplies, brought by ship, were unloaded and carted the 6.5km to the vexillation fortress beside the Stour.

It has generally been thought that the Lake fortress was the base for the conquest of the Durotrigan zone and that the soldiers within the fort belonged to Legio II Augusta, commanded by the future emperor Vespasian. However, no finds bearing an inscription to this legion have been found in Dorset. Keith Jarvis compared Lake Gates with similar sized 13-15ha fortifications found in the Midlands at Longthorpe and Newton on Trent. These were not full legionary fortresses of about 22ha but bases for vexillations or substantial parts of a legion.

In 1976, Norman Field described a 0.19ha enclosure on Keyneston Down. The site was discovered by aerial photography and was almost square in plan and had been constructed on high ground 0.7km south-east of Buzbury Rings. He argued that this was a Roman fortlet beside his suggested road from Badbury to Hod Hill and functioned as a first-century military outpost guarding the route between the fortress at Lake and the fort within Hod Hill. However, no first-century finds have been recovered from the site.

Setting aside the mass burial at Spetisbury Rings, the evidence for first century AD conflict in the area is sparse. It amounts to a possible ballista bolt from the linear 'Shapwick 35' and a javelin head from the north side of the Badbury Romano-Celtic temple.

THE ROMAN PERIOD

Following the Roman Conquest, some sites ceased to be occupied, some continued as settlements and others were newly established.

People were increasingly choosing to live near water in the first century AD. At Langton Long Blandford, a scatter of Roman occupation debris has been found beside the Stour and a find of four silver Durotrigan coins along the valley to the south-east indicates that the trend had already begun in the Late Iron Age. This trend has been seen along the Iwerne below Hod Hill and beside the Frome near Dorchester. Further along the Stour valley, Roman pottery was found at Tarrant Crawford church and probable Roman burials have been found at Newton Peverill.

A similar pattern can be seen along the Allen. Roman building footings have been found at Witchampton and Stanbridge. Roman pottery has been recovered from the cemetery at Wimborne Minster and tesserae have been reported beneath the minster church near the confluence of the Stour and Allen.

Farmsteads continued to be occupied throughout the Roman period on spurs and valley slopes. The scatter of pottery at New Barn Farm shows that people lived at this exposed location from the Late Iron Age until the fourth century. The site overlooks the Crab Farm settlement and a cluster of linked stock enclosures to the east may be evidence for livestock farming on the downs.

Other sites on spurs and valley slopes above the Allen at Lower Barnsley, Barnsley and High Lea continued as farmsteads, but Bradford Down (Pamphill 70) condensed from an extensive group of linked households to a villa site. Hemsworth, 1.5km to the north-west, was a villa with mosaic pavements and underfloor heating but the excavation records of 1905 are poor and it is not known whether an Iron Age site previously existed there.

The largest settlement in the area was at Crab Farm, arguably a small town rank-ing second in importance to Dorchester within Dorset. This site developed during the Romano-British period and included buildings with mosaics, painted plaster and under-floor heating. Coins and pottery have been recovered from the site which have shown that it was occupied until at least the fifth century.

A track linking Crab Farm with Badbury and further north-east to Bradford Down and across the Allen to High Lea is implied. Sections of this trackway are visible on aerial pho-tographs. It is probable that this meandering Iron Age route crossed the Stour at Shapwick and continued a further 9km south-west to the next large settlement at Bagwood, Bere Regis and from Bagwood on to Dorchester. However, the main route to Dorchester in the early Roman period was probably from the Lake Farm fortress and the excavated evidence and geophysical survey at Crab Farm has demonstrated that the main road was only con-structed through Shapwick in the later Roman period.

The later Roman success of the Crab Farm settlement is implied by the construction of a 2.4ha fortification with a large building complex occupying its southern quadrant. This may be the site of an inn for imperial officials (*mansio*). If this were so, it would increase the likelihood that Shapwick was once *Vindocladia* – a place significant enough to be listed in Iter XV of the third-century *Antonine Itinerary* as the only named place between Old Sarum (*Sorbiodunum*) and Dorchester (*Durnovaria*).

The present village of Shapwick is recorded in Domesday Book and it seems likely that the site has been continuously occupied. But the main road across the river to Dorchester has been abandoned and the settlement has declined to become a few streets beside the River Stour.

Concluding Remarks

The settlement pattern of the Badbury environs differs substantially from the Gussage and Hod Hill study areas. In the Latest Iron Age, Badbury hillfort does not appear to draw set-tlement towards it as at Hod. The Badbury area also lacks the range of distinctive, discrete enclosure types that are seen around Gussage hill.

Within the Badbury study area there are many settlements occupying spurs and valley slopes. They are comparable with types seen along the Stour valley or further south in Purbeck but there are also influences from the north and east.

The range of settlement types includes hillforts, concentric enclosures, ovoid enclosures and rectilinear enclosures, either single examples or conjoined in clusters. The elaborate entrances to farmsteads and settlements found at Gussage are not present at Badbury with the excep-tion of Barnsley and Tarrant Rawston. However, each of these enclosures is over 200m in diameter and approached from the south-west by a parallel-ditched avenue several hundred metres long. This type of avenue entrance has not been recorded in the Gussage study area.

The excavations carried out around Badbury have been small incisions into large sites and therefore any conclusions that can be drawn from these sample areas must be treated with caution. To compensate for this, aerial photography and geophysical survey have provided settlement plans to back up the excavated material.

A feature of this area is the presence of Early, Middle and Late Iron Age evidence occurring on the same sites and many of these settlements continue to be occupied into the Roman period. For the sites around Badbury, there is less evidence of settlement shift over time in comparison with Gussage. Settlements like Heron Grove and Sweetbriar adapt and change over time but they stay on the same site. It is difficult to say whether they are continually occupied or reoccupied several times over the centuries. However, a ceramic range from a single site, 800 BC-AD 50, is not found in the Gussage study area. There is a sense of long-term establishment from the sites around Badbury. Pottery collected from Bradford Down, Buzbury and Lower Barnsley also include Early, Middle and Late Iron Age examples. The settlement evidence found below Lodge Farm is an exception to this rule as it was occupied and abandoned in the Middle Iron Age.

Bradford Down, Sweetbriar Drove and Heron Grove are also large sprawling sites, communities of linked households rather than discrete farmsteads. These are not the small ovoid downland enclosures amongst the Celtic fields that are found surrounding Hod Hill. These smaller sites do exist within the Badbury study area but they are spaced at 1-2km intervals around the larger sites.

Ann Garvey has demonstrated the growing influence of the Poole Harbour potteries within the study area. But it is less surprising here because Poole Harbour only lies 10km south of Badbury. Nevertheless, the Early Iron Age assemblage from Sweetbriar had only 5 per cent of its pottery that could be attributed to the Poole Harbour area. The Middle Iron Age assemblage from Crab Farm had 13 per cent Poole Harbour material, Late Iron Age Badbury 77 per cent and Latest Iron Age Crab Farm 98 per cent.

In the earlier phases, pottery containing Upper Greensand fabric elements may come from outcrops around Shaftesbury and the Vale of Wardour to the north. In the Latest Iron Age Greensand querns were imported from this area.

Badbury's evidence for product exchange with the people in the surrounding districts can be compared with similar contacts between medieval communities in the same area. A useful historical analogy can be found in the archive for the Kingston Lacy and Corfe Castle Estates. In the fourteenth-century manor court rolls for Kingston Lacy, repairs to the prestigious manorial buildings were carefully itemised. Timber came from the oaks of Holt Forest east of Wimborne and chalk and clay were dug locally for lime, daub and cob walling. Hazel rods were cut within Badbury Park for wattles. The Greensand building stone was transported from quarries near Shaftesbury and Simon the Hellier took regular trips to Purbeck to cart back thousands of limestone roofing tiles. Iron Age carters bringing products from a similar distance should be expected. It also seems likely that the annual labour services exacted from the customary tenants of Kingston Lacy are a reflection of what would have been demanded from Badbury's farmers 1500 years earlier. This work for their lord would enable them to plough the same land as their medieval equivalents. Their work was needed to repair and enhance the palisades, ramparts and ditches of Badbury Rings. The thirteenth-century account rolls of Corfe Castle give a week-by-week description of repair works needed to maintain this medieval hilltop fortress and the ramparts, gates and palisades of Badbury Rings would also have required regular repairs.

South-western series/Durotrigan coinage is well represented in the records from the area although the only excavated examples are from the temple site west of Badbury and these coins were found in disturbed levels. The range of coins from around Badbury shows they were reaching this area in the first century BC. The Shapwick/Badbury hoard includes examples of British A and B coins from the east and north. Early silver south-western series/Durotrigan issues have also been found here, including 'starfish' coins. A few coin finds indicate the contact the Badbury area had with the Dobunnic communities to the north, and the Armorican communities to the south.

By the Middle Iron Age, Crab Farm had become established and the development of this settlement appears to cause the decline of Badbury. The two places are linked by the Late Bronze Age linear Shapwick 35/a89, which, long after its original construction, became incorporated into the enclosure system at Crab Farm, apparently as a security measure.

The ditch of 35/a89 lies on the north side of the bank and therefore when this 4m-wide and 3m-deep ditch was first excavated it was to divide the north from the south. Perhaps the population pressure continued to be from the north during the Iron Age and the Cranborne Chase communities posed a threat to the local people. The evidence for differing communities is seen in the change in settlement types from Gussage to Badbury. The evidence for conflict is limited to this large bank and ditch, the bodies thrown into the Spetisbury Rings hillfort ditch and perhaps the Badbury/Shapwick coin hoard (if this represents wealth buried for safe keeping before conflict). However, these conflict indicators are spread over a broad date range. Shapwick 35 was first excavated in the Middle Bronze Age; the brooches and sword chapes from Spetisbury are dated 200-100 BC and the coin hoard dates from around 50 BC.

When the trenches were excavated at Badbury Rings it was expected that there would be a 'Danebury-like' deep stratigraphic build-up of occupation debris, particularly against the rampart. This was not the case, and the evidence from the excavation indicated that much of the occupation within the hillfort may be pre-Iron Age or late Roman. Curiously, nearly all the Iron Age ceramic evidence that is currently available is Late Middle or Late Iron Age. There is a distinct lack of Early Iron Age material.

Therefore, it seems that Badbury was not like Hod Hill or Maiden Castle in containing the principal local population centre, but lay on a high point in the landscape surrounded by settlements. It is more likely to have been a secure place and a place of status when hillforts were in vogue, but became depopulated towards the end of the Iron Age. The trench across the bank and ditch of the High Wood enclosure has indicated the significance of the eastern hilltop of Badbury. This may have been a site paired with the hillfort, the internal ditch of the enclosure dug to corral horses or stock, in contrast to the fortification ditches of the hillfort built for defence on the west summit.

Ann Garvey has analysed the pottery from Badbury and concluded that Q4 Poole Harbour fabrics dominate the assemblage. None of the classic latest Poole Harbour ceramic forms and fabrics were found there. At Crab Farm, the Latest Iron Age pits contain late Poole Harbour pottery, predominantly BB1 fabric. Therefore, it is suggested that, as the Crab Farm settlement developed and increased its influence, so Badbury declined as a settlement. Badbury may have been maintained as a defensive work but an excavated section through the ramparts would be needed to prove this.

The continuing value placed on Badbury Rings is indicated by the site of the Romano-Celtic temple on its west side. The Late Iron Age origin of the site is shown by 25 south-western series/Durotrigan coins, found at various times there, together with Late Iron Age pottery including bead rim bowls and jars with counter-sunk handles. The range of finds from the site shows that the temple continued to be visited and refurbished up to the fifth century AD. At this time, Badbury was occupied again, the sub-Roman chalk floor in trench I was constructed directly above the Late Iron Age deposits.

Therefore, by the time of the Roman Conquest, Crab Farm had become the population centre of the area but value was still attributed to the hillfort. However, new influences were becoming accepted. It is in the Latest Iron Age that rectilinear contiguous boundary systems become conspicuous in this area. In Purbeck they have been detected at Cleavel Point and Corfe River East and the geophysical survey of Bradford Down produced a settlement plan very similar to Cleavel. This type of enclosure system has been found at Sweetbriar and Heron Grove and in both cases they have been proved by excavation to be the latest phase of the site. Barton Field, Tarrant Hinton and Crab Farm are other examples where Latest Iron Age material has been found in the backfilled ditches.

The geophysical survey of the Crab Farm settlement produced a plan of an extensive recti-linear ditch system and a small excavation across one of these ditches produced a first-century AD date. This excavated evidence, although across a very small part of the total site, creates the possibility that much of the ditch system is Latest Iron Age rather than Roman and deliberately laid out on the south-west side of the 2ha ovoid settlement enclosure. The excavated ditch is an integral part of the settlement pattern and therefore it is likely that many of the other ditches are of similar date. Michael Fulford has proved that the settlement plan of Silchester pre-dates the Roman Conquest and perhaps further work at Crab Farm might establish an early first-century proto-urban origin for the settlement. Further geophysical survey by David Stewart in the fields beside Shapwick High Street has demonstrated that elements of the Iron Age settlement continued to the Stour and the objects recovered from this area in 1954 provide additional evidence for this. The present extent of the survey demonstrates a complex pattern of features including circular and rectilinear enclosures flanking trackways.

The growth of Crab Farm was probably at the expense of other nearby settlements like that at Heron Grove and Sweetbriar as both were abandoned at this time. Other sites like Bradford Down shrank to become villa sites. They may have become depopulated as a result of the presence of the Roman army at Lake Farm, which became the headquarters of upwards of 3000 troops from c.AD 43-65. It is curious to note that the ditch systems here, at Tarrant Hinton and in Purbeck are backfilled at this time. The reason for the Latest Iron Age adoption and subsequent rejection of this settlement element is not known. The geophysical survey of Bradford Down illustrates how these communities of people lived together. The pattern of anomalies can be interpreted as a series of living areas defined by rectangular ditched enclosures linked by paths flanking a central track with each (family/household?) enclosure containing numerous grain storage pits.

The establishment of the fort, with the Stour on its north side, implies expected conflict from that direction. The Corfe Mullen cremation burials and the settlement with numerous imported goods lying near to the fortress, suggest an element of the local population that co-operated and took early advantage of the presence of the soldiers. The establishment of the Corfe Mullen kilns using a clay different from the Poole Harbour clay but producing pots similar to the distinctive Durotrigan forms may be significant; also perhaps, the use of a Durotrigan bowl for a Roman style cremation burial. The early adoption of the Poole Harbour and Purbeck industries by the Romans has already been noted. It seems likely that the supply route from Hamworthy to the Lake Farm fortress was secure and this part of the Durotrigan zone had already accepted the new regime.

The significance of the Badbury study area is its position on the southern edge of the highly populated chalk geology at the confluence of the Stour and Allen. It lies in close proximity to both Christchurch and Poole harbours. The Stour valley gives access to the important nodal centre at Hod Hill and the Allen and Tarrant valleys lead towards the Gussage study area and Cranborne Chase. To the east lies the heathland, the Avon and the New Forest. A route implied by a line of Iron Age settlements, indicates a pre-Roman track towards the west and the Maiden Castle/Dorchester area. This apparent crossroads of various influences would explain the range of pottery, coins and settlement types found in the area. The decision to build the legionary vexillation fortress here supports the suggestion that this was a strategic location.

The Heathland South and East of Badbury

South of the Stour and east of the Allen are the parishes of Corfe Mullen, Lytchett Minster, Lytchett Matravers, Poole, Colehill and Holt. This is a heathland area and few Iron Age settlements have been recorded here. Two sites can be noted.

The Colebarrow, probably a univallate hillfort, has only recently been discovered on a seventeenth-century map within the Kingston Lacy archive. The site lies in Holt Forest 10km east of Badbury. It is difficult to see the earthwork now as forestry and agriculture have levelled the site but the map shows that the rampart enclosed about 3ha and had opposing entrances on its east and west sides.

A similar site is located 10km south-west of Badbury near Lytchett Minster. This is Bulbury, a univallate hillfort which had four entrances, the original entrances are probably those on the east and west sides. The rampart encloses about 3ha and it is sited on a small but strategic hill, with views towards Lytchett Bay in Poole Harbour, 3km to the south-east. In 1882, Edward Cunnington read a paper to the Society of Antiquaries concerning the discovery of a group of unusual Late Iron Age objects dug up within the camp. These included chariot fittings, glass beads, a tankard handle, figures of bronze bulls and an anchor. They are on display in Dorset County Museum.

The anchor indicates that this survey has completed the circuit of the Durotrigan zone and has returned to the coast near Hengistbury.

The concluding part of this book will bring together the diverse evidence from the seven study areas and compare the various Late Iron Age communities represented there.

12

CONCLUSION:
THE FADING OF
THE DUROTRIGES

INTRODUCTION

Two inscriptions and a second-century document provide the basis for a Durotrigan culture that has generally been accepted by historians and archaeologists. This book has set out
to critically examine Durotrigan group identity. It has demonstrated differences between
the Iron Age communities of the Dorset environs and brought them into sharper focus.

Seven 10km by 8km study areas were chosen, usually with a key group of monuments in
mind. Each area had the advantage of containing sites where a significant amount of previous research had been carried out. Different researchers had used various definitions and
divisions of the Iron Age over time and this had sometimes made direct comparisons difficult. The amount of available archaeological information also varied within and between
each study area. Nevertheless, compared to other regions within the British Isles, the level
of archaeological investigation of Dorset and surrounding land is high and provides an
opportunity for a level of analysis that would not be possible elsewhere.

THE OTHER COMMUNITIES

Significant differences in the origin of communities and the way they lived have been
demonstrated, and looking beyond the seven specific study areas it can be seen that this
diversity existed within the other communities of the Durotrigan zone.

Fifteen kilometres west of Maiden Castle, the developed hillfort at Eggardon appears to
have been a prominent place within its locale. Similarly, the areas enclosed by the ramparts
of Rawlesbury (*colour plate 33*) and Nettlecombe Tout hillfort, 9km and 12km south-west of
Hod Hill, indicate that they would have been important for their local populations. These
three occupy strategic locations on the chalk escarpment overlooking the Marshwood and
Blackmore vales but little work has been done to understand the chronology and layout of
settlements within these hillforts or of the various small settlements occupying the chalk
downland between Eggardon and Rawlesbury. Similarly, near Woodbury hillfort in east
Dorset, a scatter of Iron Age coins and evidence from small-scale excavation indicate an

extensive settlement and community focus at Bagwood Copse. A programme of survey and excavation in this area of Winterbourne Kingston and Bere Regis began in 2009. Miles Russell of Bournemouth University is testing sites revealed by aerial photographs that suggest 'banjo' and necked settlement enclosures continued west of the Stour.

In Somerset the vast enclosure on Ham Hill contains many features and a range of artefacts comparable with those found within South Cadbury. Various excavations and a geophysical survey reveal the interior to be covered in occupation features, including a network of rectilinear enclosures. The northern arm of the hillfort may have been the place of last resort and this is where various skeletons were found in the nineteenth century, which indicates conflict between the British and Romans. Ham was a significant place but lack of fieldwork in its environs prevents a direct comparison with the settlement pattern around South Cadbury. In the Latest Iron Age, the suggested *oppidum* enclosure at Ilchester may have drawn elements of both populations towards the river, as part of the valley settlement trend that has been identified elsewhere.

Fieldwork in south Wiltshire has revealed blocks of land with different settlement characteristics and provides a good example for the evolution of different types of community.

The Warminster area appears strategically significant with its four hillforts clustered around the Wylye valley entrance into the chalkland. Most impressive of these are Battlesbury and Scratchbury. They are only 1km apart and appear to be paired enclosures similar to Hod/Hambledon and Badbury/High Wood.

North of Battlesbury, an extensive settlement has been excavated, with its earliest elements dated to *c*.1000 BC. It is one of the longest successively occupied locations anywhere within the Durotrigan zone. The Battlesbury Bowl evidence, together with observations made within Battlesbury itself, indicates that the population gradually moved south towards the site of the hillfort and became concentrated within the ramparts in the Late Iron Age. Scratchbury, to the east, has not been excavated but seems also to have been extensively occupied. Over 70 hut circles have been recorded there.

Whatever its relationship with Scratchbury, Battlesbury (*60*) is a developed hillfort comparable with Hod Hill, Maiden Castle and South Cadbury, containing Late Iron Age occupation evidence. There are contemporary occupation sites along the southern edge of Salisbury Plain and the upper Wylye valley but none of these farmstead sites are comparable in scale to the Warminster hillforts. Therefore this can be interpreted as a Hod/Hambledon type pattern with households, settlements and farmsteads surrounding large fortified settlements.

South of the Wylye, the Bury is only 2km south-west of Battlesbury and Scratchbury. This may prove to be a valley fort or *oppidum*, another example of the trend for status sites to move from hilltops to riverside locations in the first century AD. Geophysical survey within the Bury revealed that the interior of the 22ha univallate enclosure was once divided by rectilinear boundary ditches. However, although many Roman objects have been found on the site, no Iron Age artefacts have yet been reported.

At the east end of the Nadder-Wylye Ridge, the 'banjo' and multiple ditch systems of the Stockton, Hanging Langford, Hamshill Ditches and Ebsbury settlements are comparable with the features in Rushmoor Park and Gussage Hill on Cranborne Chase. The Nadder-Wylye Ridge earthworks are also associated with three mini-hillforts (Bilbury, Groveley Castle and Wick Ball Camp) constructed on spurs of land above the river valleys. These

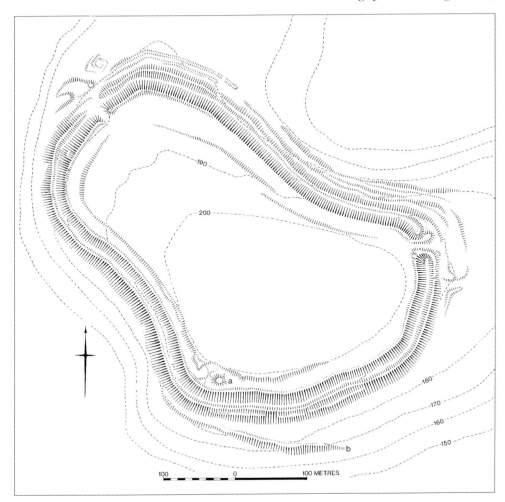

60 Earthwork plan of Battlesbury hillfort. (McOmish, Field & Brown 2002, 78) *Copyright English Heritage*

are likely to be contemporary outworks. This group of four major settlements, ranging in area from 16ha to 32ha, originated in the Late Iron Age and continued in use through the Roman period. Mark Corney emphasised the significance of these sites and suggested that they were interrelated. He compared them with eastern settlements like Blagdon Copse in Hampshire which contains a square funerary enclosure like that at Ebsbury. He thought that if the Nadder-Wylye Ridge sites were inter-related, the combined settlement group would be of sufficient scale to compare with a developed eastern *oppidum* such as *Camulodunum* (Colchester) or *Calleva Atrebatum* (Silchester).

Immediately to the south the settlement character changes again. The Vale of Wardour and the Ebble-Nadder Ridge seem empty of Late Iron Age settlements in comparison with the surrounding areas. There are earthworks of field systems and a series of cross-ridge dykes dividing the land, but the known settlements at Swallowcliffe and Fifehead Bavant are Early Iron Age and the dykes are also thought to date to this period. The island of settlement seems to be in and around the developed hillfort of Castle Ditches. The character of the area appears to be a Maiden Castle pattern of settlement concentrated at the hillfort.

In contrast, beyond the Ebble valley, the Oxdrove Ridge has extensive evidence of Late Iron Age settlement, the western part divided by large Late Iron Age cross-ridge dykes associated with contemporary occupation evidence. Perhaps the core settlement area was the Rushmore and Berwick group of linears and enclosures on the spur slopes surrounding the Tollard Royal valley on the northern edge of Cranborne Chase.

The east end of the Oxdrove and Ebble-Nadder ridges and the land north-east of Bokerley Dyke, near Salisbury, appears to lie outside the Durotrigan zone. This is suggested by different settlement forms, ceramic evidence and lack of coinage revealed during landscape surveys and excavations (e.g. Whitsbury Castle Ditches; Harnham Hill, Highfield, Yarnbury). Nevertheless, there was no barrier to trade: people used the Avon valley to take products like Kimmeridge shale and Gallo-Belgic pottery into Wiltshire and Hampshire from Hengistbury Head.

It is in south Wiltshire and north-east Dorset that community diversity is especially apparent, due it seems to influences from the east and north and the influx of new populations into the area.

To the west, hillforts remain an important element of the settlement pattern, to the east farmsteads and villages take various forms and hillforts were less significant.

Durotriges?

This summary of the evidence demonstrates that communities co-existed in close proximity with diverse forms of settlement. It is difficult to consider them as elements of a unified tribal group. These communities may all have been using the same sort of pottery by the end of the Iron Age but their belief systems and loyalties appear disunited. How might the ideas behind traditional pit burial at Hod Hill be reconciled with the new burial rites conceived in south Dorset?

Yet by the end of the Iron Age, these communities did lie within an area which used distinctive coinage and, therefore, were apparently linked together. Certainly, the distribution and concentration of these coins is hard to dismiss or explain away without some common economic and political structure (*61*).

In Chapter Two, it was noted how Roman historical sources indicate the process of smaller groups banding together and forming alliances in the Late Iron Age. The coin distribution maps provide evidence for this gradual process of alliance within the Dorset environs and this eventually led to the formation of the Durotrigan zone. It might be compared with the modern Euro zone, with its constituent communities protecting their personal interests but grudgingly acknowledging the value of remaining in the 'club'. The adoption of Poole Harbour pottery seems to have been a necessary part of membership. Whether all members joined freely or were coerced would be difficult to prove.

If forcible annexation took place, it is most likely to have happened in south Somerset in the last decades of pre-Roman Britain. The benefit of free access through south Somerset would have enabled an improved trade route for the Durotrigan communities

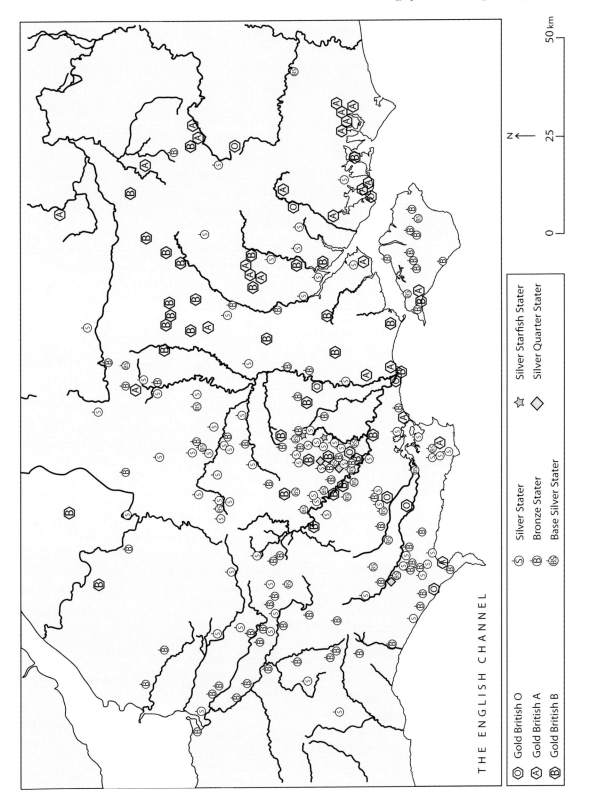

THE ENGLISH CHANNEL

Ⓞ Gold British O	Ⓢ Silver Stater	☆ Silver Starfish Stater
Ⓐ Gold British A	Ⓑ Bronze Stater	◇ Silver Quarter Stater
Ⓑ Gold British B	Ⓑ Base Silver Stater	

61 Distribution of British A, B, O and south-western series/Durotrigan coins.

from the ports of Hengistbury and Poole Harbour along the Brue-Parrett corridor to the Bristol Channel. South Somerset had strong ties with its western and northern neighbours, expressed in the decorative styles of its pottery and carvings. The use of these styles ends abruptly with the adoption of Durotrigan ceramics. Friction between differing communities is likely and it is also likely that the Durotrigan zone was not an entirely peaceful formation.

Decades before the Roman Conquest it has been seen that Romanisation had substantially changed the societies of the Dorset environs. Contact with traders from Rome, Gaul and east Britain had begun to transform them into market economies, seen most clearly in the Poole and Christchurch Harbour areas. Therefore, it cannot be claimed that the Durotrigan zone was insular, although the inland areas lack the range of commodities found on sites to the east.

The group name Durotriges may or may not be the name these pre-Roman people were united by. Ptolemy gives us the name and as his records of other British tribal and community names have been supported by historical and archaeological records, perhaps we should trust him. Some peoples in Britain are recorded before the conquest and their group names continue as Roman administrative districts (for example the Iceni whose *civitas* capital was *Venta Icenorum*). Therefore one might imply that the Durotriges existed as an entity before and after AD 43-44 although we lack the written evidence. Perhaps one day an inscription may be unearthed in Dorchester to prove this. Until there is more written evidence there will be uncertainty, and we cannot know whether the various communities in the Dorset environs considered themselves to be Durotrigan or part of some other group with its own legends, loyalties and identity.

THE FADING OF THE DUROTRIGES

The evidence suggests that the communities of the Durotrigan zone formed a vibrant and expanding trading block. They were independent, the political groups to the east and north cushioning them from the powerful and expanding Catuvellauni/Trinovantian nation.

The coin distribution demonstrates a north-south trade route linking the peoples of the Gallic coast, now part of Normandy, with the Dubunnic area of present day Somerset and Gloucestershire. A trail of Durotrigan coins demonstrates that ships left the Dorset coast and stopped in the Channel Islands on the way to Gaul. In return ships brought exotic commodities from Gaul to Hengistbury Head; to the Isle of Wight further east; and Poole Harbour to the west. Durotrigan-type coins predominate at coastal settlements here and along the coast to Weymouth, Portland and West Bay. The rivers Avon, Stour, Frome and Piddle were routeways along which goods were transported. During the period when Augustus, Tiberius and Caligula ruled the Roman world and Jesus was preaching in Judaea, Durotrigan coin distribution was spreading deeper into the West Country.

How did it all end? A Victorian romantic like Charles Warne or a Roman historian such as Cornelius Tacitus would enhance the drama. They would describe the fall of *Vectis*, the Roman army landing at Poole. The news carried to the power houses of Dorset. Chiefs would make patriotic speeches to inspire their nobles, their warriors and retainers. Men would leave their farms and settlements and gather at their principal places. After sacred ceremonies and dances, dressed and armed in distinctive style, the peoples of Maiden Castle, Hod, Hambledon and Gussage would converge on east Dorset: slingers, spearmen, horsemen and chariot teams. The combined Durotrigan host assembled at Badbury to halt the Roman soldiers at the Stour and cleanse them from the land.

It has already been noted that the evidence for conflict varies between areas. This is limited to a scatter of ballista bolts at Hod Hill and across Cranborne Chase. The burial of the war dead was carried out with dignity at Maiden Castle but, in contrast, the bodies found at Ham Hill and South Cadbury were thrown into ditches or left to rot where they fell. Roman forts at Hod, Waddon, Lake Farm, South Cadbury, Ham Hill, Ilchester and probably Dorchester were generally occupied until the mid-60s AD.

The subtle indoctrination of Roman culture into the Durotrigan communities is revealed in the archaeological record by the decrease in distinctive Iron Age traits. Continuity of settlement into the Roman period is generally found, although some disruption may have taken place in south Somerset during the late first and early second centuries (Tabor 2004b, 92).

The Latest Iron Age riverside settlements at Ilchester, Dorchester, Crab Farm, Iwerne valley and perhaps the Bury all continue to be occupied until the late fourth century. Sometimes settlements and farmsteads became small towns or high-status villas while others remained comparatively undeveloped.

Within Dorchester, the evidence from the excavation of numerous graves demonstrates that the Durotrigan burial rite continued well into the second century. Even after this, when extended burials became more common than contracted, black burnished jars rather than more exotic pottery normally accompanied the dead and cremation remained a rare form of burial in the area.

Iron Age storage pits also continued to be used into the second century. They were gradually phased out once Roman agricultural practices became accepted. At Woodcutts, a second-century corn-drying oven installed near backfilled storage pits is one example of Roman farming innovation and change.

Durotrigan/south-western series uninscribed coins continued in circulation into the second century (Haselgrove & Mays 2000, 248) and many were used by Roman soldiers, examples being found within the forts at Hod Hill and Waddon Hill. The hoard at Downton, Wiltshire, strongly suggests that some cast Durotrigan coins continued to be minted into the second century.

Durotrigan/Poole Harbour pottery developed into Black Burnished Ware. Its extensive distribution, particularly across western Britain (Allen & Fulford 1996, 223-281) demonstrates its success after its widespread adoption by the Roman army. The army continued to use BB1 into the fourth century and it formed the main coarse ware component of ceramic assemblages excavated from Britannia's northern frontier forts.

Although Romanisation changed the lifestyle of the Durotrigan communities, a sense of identity and aspects of their belief system probably continued. Iron Age sacred sites such at Badbury and Jordan Hill became Romano-Celtic temples and continued to be places of worship until the end of the fourth century.

Each of the Durotrigan communities probably remained distinctive and presumably maintained a degree of autonomy. They became the *pagi* or districts of the *civitas* and small towns developed at their principal places. One of these was at Ilchester in south Somerset, which may subsequently have been promoted to *civitas* status to become the *Durotrages Lindiniensis* of the Hadrian's Wall inscriptions. Others can be suggested where imperial taxation points and inns (*mansiones*) may have been established.

The large settlement at Crab Farm was probably *Vindocladia* of the *Antonine Itinerary*. Other locally significant settlements developed along the Iwerne valley below Hod Hill and beside the Wylye, below Battlesbury, halfway between Old Sarum (*Sorbiodunum*) and Bath (*Aquae Sulis*).

Boundaries between established groups may have been marked out as linear earthworks before and after the Roman Conquest. Combs Ditch, Winterborne Whitechurch may be one of these, crossing the high point of the downs, halfway between the settlements of Crab Farm and Bagwood Copse, Bere Regis.

In the fifth century, as security within the Roman province declined, Badbury Rings was reoccupied (Papworth 2004, 182-183). The old refuge was refortified and the Roman road from Old Sarum was cut at the boundary earthwork of Bokerley Dyke. It has recently been suggested that old feuds and frontiers were revived in the sub-Roman period, as the provinces of Britannia broke up (Laycock 2006, 10-15). However, the distribution of pagan Saxon burials in barrows north-east of Bokerley Dyke and east of the Avon (Winterborne Gunner, Salisbury; Bargates, Christchurch) indicates that the Saxons soon became the principal enemy.

It appears that for a while the Saxons were successfully kept from the core communities of the Durotrigan zone, although finds of fifth- and sixth-century metalwork between Hod Hill and Bokerley Dyke may suggest a Saxon enclave occupying Cranborne Chase.

At places like Ulwell in Purbeck, Tolpuddle Ball and Poundbury near Dorchester, cemeteries of east-west burials without grave goods have been radiocarbon dated to the fifth to seventh centuries (Hearne & Birbeck 1999, 226-231). This burial evidence suggests that by this time many people in Dorset had become Christians and that the area became independent for one or two centuries before being absorbed into the Saxon kingdom of Wessex (Eagles 1994, 13-32).

In the same way that the word Durotriges linked diverse communities, the emerging Saxon political powers brought together many other groups. This is best documented in Mercia where in AD 655 Penda formed an alliance of 30 groups to fight the Northumbrians. A document, known as the *Tribal Hidage*, names the peoples of the Mercian kingdom and the taxable land each controlled. Their areas ranged from 300 hides for the *Feppingas* to 7000 hides for the *Wreocensaeten*. Some of these groups, like the *Elmetsaeten*, were British in origin and possibly preserved elements of group identity extending back to the Iron Age (Fisher 1973, 108-109). A *Tribal Hidage* does not survive for Wessex but similar districts existed and hundreds of meeting places at ancient sites such as Badbury and Eggardon remained in use into the medieval period.

PRESENT AND FUTURE WORK

In the last few years I have re-examined past archaeological research, reviewed archaeological thinking, added significant new fieldwork evidence and the result has been a personal interpretation based on a meticulous collection of information. This has not been a special-ist work on pottery or coinage. It has concentrated principally on settlement patterns but used all available sources.

The research has created the impetus for some significant new fieldwork. This has included excavations within Badbury Rings/High Wood and extensive geophysical surveys of the Crab Farm, Bradford Down and Sweetbriar settlements surrounding Badbury. There have also been complete gradiometer surveys of the interiors of Badbury and Hod Hill and a new temple at Norden has been discovered and surveyed. This work has been supplemented by an up-to-date review of the Iron Age coins. This together with Ann Garvey's fabric analysis of the pottery from the Badbury environs and Pilsdon Pen has considerably enhanced under-standing by comparing her findings with other pottery assemblages from the Dorset area.

Previously, a confederacy of groups had been suggested for the region (e.g. Cunliffe 1991, 159), but these groups had not been described and analysed to any great extent. Each researcher in an area had concluded their work by fitting their results to a perceived whole. In this book I have suggested a process by which discrete communities gradually merged to form a coin-using alliance. Settlement diversity and different forms of control are appar-ent both in the number of principal places that existed in any area and whether they included or excluded satellite occupation. Regional reviews of this type were advocated in 'Understanding the British Iron Age an Agenda for Action' (Haselgrove *et al.* 2001, 24). My work has enabled a wider perspective that has resolved the conflict between central places and non-centralised societies (Cunliffe 1995, 91-94; Hill 2001, 101). Now it can be seen that both existed in relative degrees in various locations during the Iron Age. The recently out-lined concept of multi-functional hillforts, their importance waxing and waning through time (Payne, Corney & Cunliffe 2006, 151-162) has been confirmed in this study. General models for the southern British Iron Age are difficult to adhere to. Each area was idiosyn-cratic and included unique elements.

The region under study lay on the edge of the zone of movement from hillforts to valley settlements. Unlike the areas to the north and east, this process was clearly still taking place at the time of the Roman Conquest. Mine has been a historical approach, that views the Late Iron Age communities as people affected by the same general power struggles, migrations and cultural absorptions that have been documented for the historical period. Therefore I have used historical examples as potential explanations for observed trends.

Of course, further work will improve understanding. Fabric and typological analysis of significant assemblages of pottery from past excavations should be carried out, particu-larly for Marnhull and Hod Hill. More geophysical surveys are required on previously unsurveyed hillforts like Hambledon and Eggardon, also on settlements like the Bury and Bagwood Copse. Research continues around Hod Hill, and Dave Stewart's geophysical surveys and evaluation trenches at Iwerne are revealing the time-depth and density of occupation beside the river. Area ground probing radar surveys are now being piloted and this technique will significantly enhance existing geophysical data. Initial LiDAR surveys of the Kingston Lacy Estate and Hod Hill have shown the potential for this technique in defining ploughed down earthwork evidence and sites hidden by trees. Perhaps extensive DNA analysis of burials from across the region will better define the origins of populations, if funding for such research becomes available.

Further targeted excavation is also desirable at many places: the Nadder-Wylye Ridge settlement group and the Warminster group of hillforts are important but poorly understood. Trial trenches at Battlesbury, including the presumed burial ground at its west entrance, combined with comparative work at Scratchbury and the Bury would build a chronology that can be compared with that for Badbury/Crab Farm. The date of the Bury is not known and for this reason a section will be excavated across the rampart and ditch in 2010.

In 2009, Bournemouth University began their 'Durotriges Project' to look at Late Iron Age and early Roman settlement near Bere Regis and Winterborne Whitechurch. This will help understand the settlement pattern surrounding the Bagwood Copse/Woodbury focal area west of the Stour.

By expanding the database, improved comparisons can be made. Research has been hampered by gaps in the understanding of certain settlement patterns, particularly in west Dorset. Future survey work (perhaps using LiDAR) may locate new sites there.

Social change took place most rapidly from 100 BC–AD 100 and an insufficiently precise chronological framework prevents understanding of the process of social re-organisation in this period. The reliance on the existing coin and pottery typologies inhibits progress. They need to be refined by comparison with alternative dating techniques.

Radiocarbon dating is entering a new era. The results from the revised dating programme for Early Neolithic causewayed enclosures and long barrows have excited new optimism. More precise measurements based on numerous radiocarbon samples and using Bayesian statistics have reduced date ranges from centuries to decades, leading to the claim that prehistory can be written as history:

> The centrality of chronology is being reasserted. Archaeologists, especially prehistorians have tended to downplay the importance of chronology in recent years. They have been preoccupied with landscapes, ritual processes and cultural identities … the new dates allow archaeologists to view what is happening at the same time in different places, they learn that contemporary people were not all acting in the same way. We can think in terms of generations and individual life-spans, and we have more sensitive means with which to explore social memory. (Bayliss, Meadows & Whittle 2007)

Therefore we can hope for a future programme of radiocarbon dating of sites within the Durotrigan zone. This will enable a more precise chronological framework for the region. Perhaps comparative dates from the Maiden Castle cemetery and the Spetisbury, South Cadbury and Ham Hill massacre deposits may prove whether or not they were contemporary. Linking pottery types with Carbon-14 dates derived from articulated bone found in the same sealed grave and pit groups will also enable increasingly enhanced dating. From this, more definite assertions can be presented concerning the ways communities developed and merged in the Dorset area during the Late Iron Age. This will bring us closer to the men, women and children who inhabited the land, the people we wish to reach out to across the millennia and understand.

BIBLIOGRAPHY

Aitken, G. & N., 1990, 'Excavations at Whitcombe, 1965-1967', *Proceedings of the Dorset Natural History and Archaeological Society* 112, 57-94

Alcock, L., 1972, *'By South Cadbury is that Camelot' Excavations at Cadbury Castle 1966-1970*, London: Thames & Hudson

———, 1980, 'The Cadbury Castle sequence in the first millennium BC', *Bulletin Board of Celtic Studies* 28, 656-718

Allen, D.F., 1961, 'The Origins of British Coinage: a Reappraisal' in S.S. Frere (ed.) *Problems of the Iron Age in Southern Britain*, London: London Institute of Archaeology, 97-128

———, 1968, 'The Celtic Coins' in Richmond, I., *Hod Hill, Volume II*, London: Trustees of the British Museum, 43-57

Allen, J.R.L. & Fulford, M.G., 1996, 'The Distribution South-East Dorset Black Burnished Category I Pottery in South-West Britain', *Britannia* 27, 223-281

———, 'Distribution of Purbeck products in the 1st century AD', *Britannia* 35

Bailey, J., 1967, 'An Early Iron Age/Romano-British Site at Pins Knoll, Litton Cheney', *Proceedings of the Dorset Natural History and Archaeological Society* 89, 147-159

Barrett, J.C., Bradley, R. & Green, M., 1991, *Landscape, Monuments and Society. The Prehistory of Cranborne Chase*, Cambridge: Cambridge University Press

Barrett, J.C., Freeman, P.W.M. & Woodward, A., 2000, *Cadbury Castle, Somerset. The later prehistoric and early historic archaeology*, English Heritage Archaeological Report 20

Bellamy, P., Graham, A. & Richards, J., 1993, 'Dorchester First School', *Proceedings of the Dorset Natural History & Archaeological Society* 115, 152

Bennett, Rev. J.A., 1890, 'Camelot', *Proceedings of the Somerset Archaeological & Natural History Society* 36, 1-19

Bersu, G., 1940, 'Excavations at Little Woodbury, Wiltshire, Part 1', *Proceedings of the Prehistoric Society* 6, 30-111

Bowen, H.C., 1990, *The Archaeology of Bokerley Dyke*, London: HMSO

Boyd-Dawkins, 1900, 'The Exploration of Hod Hill near Blandford Dorset in 1897', *Archaeological Journal* 57, 52-68

Brailsford, J.W., 1949, Interim Report on the Preliminary Excavations at Hod Hill 1949, *Proceedings of the Dorset Natural History & Archaeological Society* 71, 41-50

———, 1957, 'The Durotrigan Culture', *Proceedings of the Dorset Natural History & Archaeological Society* 79, 118-121

Brown, L., 1991, 'Later Prehistoric Pottery' in N. Sharples *Maiden Castle excavations and Field Survey 1985-6*, English Heritage Archaeological Report 19, London, 185-205

———, 1997, 'Marketing and Commerce in Late Age Dorset: the Wareham/Poole Harbour pottery industry' in Gwilt, A., & Haselgrove, C., *Reconstructing Iron Age Societies*, Oxbow Monograph 71

Brown, L., Corney, M. & Woodward, P.J., 1995, 'An Iron Age and Romano-British Settlement on Oakley Down, Wimborne St Giles, Dorset', *Proceedings of the Dorset Natural History & Archaeological Society* 117, 67-79

Bulleid, A. & Gray, H.St.G., 1911, *The Glastonbury Lake Village Volume I*

————, 1917, *The Glastonbury Lake Village Volume II*

————, 1948, *The Meare Lake Village Volumes I-III*

————, 1953, *The Meare Lake Village*

Burnham, B.C. & Wacher, J., 1990, *The 'Small Towns' of Roman Britain*, London: Batsford

Bushe-Fox, J.P., 1915, *Excavations at Hengistbury Head, Hampshire in 1911-12*, Oxford Society of Antiquaries Res. Report 3

Calkin, J.B., 1948, 'The Isle of Purbeck in the Iron Age', *Proceedings of the Dorset Natural History & Archaeological Society* 70, 29-59

Chambers, S.A., 1978, *An Analysis of Iron Age Inhumation Burials in the Dorset Area and an Assessment of their Value as Indicators of Social Organisation*, Leeds University, Unpublished Certificate Dissertation

Coles, S. & Pine, J., 2009, 'Excavation of an Iron Age and Roman settlement and salt production site at Shapwick Road, Hamworthy, Poole, Dorset, 2005-6', *Proceedings of the Dorset Natural History & Archaeological Society* 130, 63-98

Collis, J., 1977, 'The proper study of mankind in pots' in John Collis (ed.) *The Iron Age in Britain: a review* 29-31, Sheffield: Sheffield University

————, 1977, *The Iron Age in Britain: a review*, Sheffield: Sheffield University

————, 1984, *Oppida, Earliest Towns North of the Alps*, Sheffield: Sheffield University

Colt-Hoare, R., 1821, *The Ancient History of Wiltshire*, Volume II pt II

————, 1827, 'Account of Antiquities found at Hamden Hill, with fragments of British Chariots', *Archaeologia* 21, 39-42

Corney, M., 1989, 'Multiple Ditch Systems and Late Iron Age Settlement in Central Wessex' in M. Bowden, D. Mackay & P. Topping (eds) *From Cornwall to Caithness, Some Aspects of British Field Archaeology*, BAR Series 209

Cox, P.W. & Hearne, C.M., 1991, *Redeemed from the Heath*, DNHAS Monograph 9

Crawford O.G.S. & Keiller, A., 1928, *Wessex from the Air*, Oxford: The Clarendon Press

Creighton, J., 2000, *Coins and Power in Late Iron Age Britain*, Cambridge: Cambridge University Press

Cunliffe, B.W., 1982, 'Iron Age Settlements and Pottery 650 BC – 60 AD' in M. Aston & I. Burrow (eds) *The Archaeology of Somerset*, Taunton: Somerset County Council

————, 1983, *Danebury: Anatomy of an Iron Age Hillfort*, London: Batsford

————, 'Iron Age Wessex: Continuity and Change' in B. Cunliffe & D. Miles, 1984, *Aspects of the Iron Age in central southern Britain*, Oxford University Committee for Archaeology Monograph 2, 12-45

————, 1987, *Hengistbury Head, Dorset, Volume 1: The Prehistoric and Roman Settlement 3500 BC-AD 500*, Oxford University Committee for Archaeology Monograph 13

————, 1991, *Iron Age Communities in Britain*, 3rd edn, London: Routledge

————, 1992, 'Pits, Preconceptions and Propitiation in the British Iron Age', *Oxford Journal of Archaeology* 11, 69-82

————, 1993, *Danebury*, London: Batsford

————, 1994, 'After Hillforts', *Oxford Journal of Archaeology* 13, 71-84

————, 1995, *Danebury an Iron Age hillfort in Hampshire, Volume 6 A hillfort community in perspective*, CBA Research Report 102

————, 2000, *The Danebury Environs Programme, the Prehistory of a Wessex Landscape, Volume 1 Introduction*, English Heritage and OUCA Monograph 48

————, 2005, *Iron Age Communities in Britain*, 4th edn, London: Routledge

Cunliffe, B.W. & de Jersey, P., 1997, *Armorica and Britain, Cross-Channel relationships in the late first millennium BC*, Studies in Celtic Coinage, Number 3, OUCA Monograph 45

Cunliffe, B. & Miles, D., 1984, *Aspects of the Iron Age in central southern Britain*, Oxford University Committee for Archaeology Monograph 2

Cunliffe, B.W. & Phillipson, D.W., 1968, 'Excavations at Eldon's Seat, Encombe, Dorset, England', *Proceedings of the Prehistoric Society* 34, 191-237

Davies, S.M., 2002, *Excavations at Alington Avenue, Fordington, Dorchester, Dorset, 1984-87*, Dorset Natural History & Archaeological Society Monograph 15

De Jersey, P., 2000, 'Durotrigan cast bronze' *Chris Rudd Celtic Coin List* 49

———, 2001, *Celtic Coinage in Britain*, Princes Risborough, Buckinghamshire: Shire

Evans, Sir J., 1864, *Coins of the Ancient Britons*, London: J. Russell Smith

Field, N.H., 1976, 'The Discovery of a Roman Fort near Badbury Rings, Dorset', *Britannia* 7, 280-283

———, 1982, 'The Iron Age and Romano-British Settlement on Bradford Down, Pamphill, Dorset', *Proceedings of the Dorset Natural History & Archaeological Society* 104, 71-92

———, 1992, *Dorset and the Second Legion*, Tiverton: Dorset Books

Fisher, D.J.V., 1973, *The Anglo-Saxon Age*, Harlow: Longman

Fitzpatrick, A.P. & Megaw, J.V.S., 1987, 'Further Finds from Le Catillon Hoard', *Proceedings of the Prehistoric Society* 53, 433-444

Fitzpatrick, A.P., 1996, 'A 1st-Century AD Burial from Portesham, Dorset', *Proceedings of the Dorset Natural History and Archaeological Society* 118, 51-70

Fowler, P.J., 1964, 'Cross-dykes on the Ebble-Nadder Ridge', *Wiltshire Archaeological and Natural History Society Magazine* 59, 46-57

Frere, S.S., 1978, *Britannia, A History of Roman Britain*, London: Routledge

Fulford, M., 2000, 'Synthesis, The Oppidum-Latest Iron Age and Earliest Roman' in M. Fulford & J. Timby, *Late Iron Age and Roman Silchester, Excavations on the site of the Forum-Basilica 1977, 1980-86*, Britannia Monograph Series 15, 545-581

———, 2006, 'Corvees and Civitates' in R.J.A. Wilson (ed.) *Romanitas, Essays in honour of Sheppard Frere on the occasion of his ninetieth birthday*, Oxford: Oxbow

Gale, F.E., 1979, 'The Ceramic Fabrics' in Dr G.J. Wainwright, *Gussage All Saints: An Iron Age Settlement in Dorset*, London: HMSO

Gale, J., 1995, 'Ringmoor, Turnworth, Dorset: Geophysical Investigation', Unpublished Bournemouth University Report

Gater, J., Leech, R.H. & Riley H., 1993, 'Later Prehistoric & Romano-British settlement sites in South Somerset: some recent work', *Proceedings of the Somerset Archaeological & Natural History Society* 137, 41-58

Gelling, P., 1977, 'Excavations at Pilsdon Pen, Dorset, 1964-71', *Proceedings of the Prehistoric Society* 43, 263-286

Graham, A.H., 2006, *Iron Age and Romano-British settlement, Barton Field, Tarrant Hinton*, Dorset Natural History and Archaeological Society Monograph 17

Green, M., 2000, *A Landscape Revealed 10,000 Years on a Chalkland Farm*, Stroud: Tempus

Gresham, C.A., 1939, 'Spetisbury Rings, Dorset', *Archaeological Journal* 96, 114-131

Grose, F., 1779, 'A description of ancient fortifications near Christchurch, Hampshire', *Archaeologia* 5, 237-240

Gunter, J., 2004, *The Wylye Valley and the Dobunni, The Search for an Iron Age Tribal Boundary*, Unpublished Dissertation, University of Bristol

Haggett, P., 1979, *Geography, a Modern Synthesis*, New York: Harper & Row

Haselgrove, C., 1994, 'Social Organisation in Iron Age Wessex' in A.P. Fitzpatrick & E.L. Morris (eds) *The Iron Age in Wessex Recent Work*, Salisbury: Trust for Wessex Archaeology

Haselgrove, C., Armit, I., Champion, T., Creighton, J., Gwilt, A., Hill, J.D., Hunter, F. & Woodward, A., 2001, *Understanding the British Iron Age: An Agenda for Action*, Trowbridge: Cromwell Press

Haselgrove, C. & Mays, M., 2000, 'Iron Age Coinage', in J.C. Barrett, *et al. Cadbury Castle, Somerset*, London: English Heritage

Hawkes, C.F.C., 1931, 'Hill forts', *Antiquity* 5, 60-97

Hearne, C.M. & Birbeck, V., 1999, *A35 Tolpuddle to Puddletown Bypass DBFO, Dorset, 1996-8*, Wessex Archaeology Report No 15

Hill, J.D., 1993, 'Can we recognise a different European past? A contrastive archaeology of later pre-historic settlements in southern England', *Journal of European Archaeology* 1, 57-75

———, 1995, 'Ritual and Rubbish in the Iron Age of Wessex', BAR 242

———, 2001, 'Hillforts and the Iron Age of Wessex' in T.C. Champion & J.R. Collis, *The Iron Age in Britain and Ireland: Recent Trends*, Sheffield: J.R. Collis

Hodder, I., 1977, 'How are we to study Distribution of Iron Age Material' in J. Collis (ed.) *The Iron Age in Britain: A Review*, Sheffield: University of Sheffield

Hutchins, J., 1774, *The History and Antiquities of the County of Dorset*, 1st edn, London: Printed by W. Bowyer and J. Nichols

Jones, S., 1997, *Archaeology and Ethnicity*, London: Routledge

Ladle, L., 2009, *Bestwall Excavations*, English Heritage Monograph

Laycock, S., 2006, 'Britannia, the threat within', *British Archaeology* 87

Leach, P., 1982, *Ilchester Volume 1, Excavations 1974-1975*, Western Archaeological Trust Monograph 3

———, 1993, *Ilchester Volume 2, Excavations and fieldwork to 1984*, Sheffield

Lester, M.J., 1990, Lambert's Castle, Marshwood, W. Dorset, *Proceedings of the Dorset Natural History & Archaeological Society* 112, 115

Liddell, D.M., 1935, 'Report on the excavations at Hembury Fort 1934-5', *Proceedings of the Devon Archaeological Exploration Society* 4, 135-170

Light, T. & Ellis, T., 2009, *Bucknowle, a Romano-British Villa and its antecedents: Excavations 1976-1991*, Dorset Natural History & Archaeological Society Monograph 18

Longworth I. & Haith, C., 1992, Henry Durden and his Collection, *Proceedings of the Dorset Natural History & Archaeological Society* 114, 151-160

Lucas, R.N., 1993, *The Romano-British villa at Halstock, Dorset, Excavations 1967-1985*, Dorset Natural History & Archaeological Society Monograph 13

Mack, R.P., 1953, *The Coinage of Ancient Britain*, London: Spink

Markey, M., Wilkes, E. & Darvill, T., 2002, 'Poole Harbour an Iron Age Port', *Current Archaeology* 181, 7-11

Mays, M., 2005, 'Draft Introduction, Durotrigan Coinage', Unpublished Manuscript

McKinley, J.I., 1999, 'Excavations at Ham Hill, Montacute, Somerset 1994 and 1998', *Proceedings of the Somerset Archaeological & Natural History Society* 142, 77-137

McOmish, D., Field, D. & Brown, G., 2002, *The Field Archaeology of the Salisbury Plain Training Area*, Swindon: English Heritage

Mepham, L., Cooke, N., Knight, S. & Leivers, M., 2006a, 'Badbury Rings, Shapwick, Dorset Finds Reports', Unpublished Report for the National Trust

Miles, H. & Miles, T.J., 1969, 'Settlement sites of the Late pre-Roman Iron Age in the Somerset Levels', *Proceedings of the Somerset Archaeological & Natural History Society* 113, 17-55

Papworth, M., 2000, 'Evaluation Excavation, Badbury Romano-Celtic Temple. Interim Report', *Proceedings of the Dorset Natural History & Archaeological Society* 122, 148-150

———, 2008, *Deconstructing the Durotriges: A Definition of Iron Age Communities Within the Dorset Environs*, BAR British Series 462, Hedges

———, 2004, 'Shapwick, Excavations at Badbury and Crab Farm, Interim Report', *Proceedings of the Dorset Natural History & Archaeological Society* 126, 181-186

Payne, A., Corney, M. & Cunliffe, B., 2006, *The Wessex Hillforts Survey*, London: English Heritage

Pitt Rivers, A., 1887, *Excavations in Cranborne Chase near Rushmore on the borders of Dorset and Wiltshire. Volume I. Excavations in the Romano-British village on Woodcutts Common and Romano-British antiquities in Rushmore Park*, London

———, 1888, *Excavations in Cranborne Chase near Rushmore on the borders of Dorset and Wiltshire 1880-1888. Volume II. Excavations in barrows near Rushmore. Excavations in Romano-British village, Rotherley. Excavations in Winkelbury Camp. Excavations in British Barrows and Anglo-Saxon cemetery, Winkelbury Hill*, London

Powlesland, I., 2004, *The Later Prehistoric Landscape of the Bristol Avon Region*, Unpublished
   Dissertation, Bristol University

Putnam, W.G., 1976, 'Dewlish Interim Report', *Proceedings of the Dorset Natural History &
   Archaeological Society* 98, 54-55

Rahtz, P., Corney, M., Davies, S., Woodward, A., Hartley, B., Mackreth, D. & Peacock, D., 1990,
   'Bower Chalke 1959: Excavations at Great Ditch Banks and Middle Chase Ditch', *Wiltshire
   Archaeological and Natural History Society Magazine* 83, 1-49

RCHM, 1952, Historical Monuments in the County of Dorset I West, London: HMSO

———, 1970a, Historical Monuments in the County of Dorset II South-East, London:
   HMSO

———, 1970b, Historical Monuments in the County of Dorset III Central, London: HMSO

———, 1972, Historical Monuments in the County of Dorset IV North, London: HMSO

———, 1975, Historical Monuments in the County of Dorset V East, London: HMSO

RCHME, 1988, Whitesheet Hill, Wiltshire, Unpublished Survey Report, NMR

———, 1995, Pilsdon Pen, Dorset, Unpublished Survey Report, NMR

———, 1996, Hambledon Hill, Dorset, Unpublished Survey Report, NMR

———, 1997, Ham Hill, Somerset, Unpublished Survey Report, NMR

———, 1998, Badbury Rings, Dorset, Unpublished Survey Report, NMR

Richardson, K.M., 1940, 'Excavations at Poundbury, Dorchester, Dorset, 1939', *Antiquaries Journal* 20,
   429-448

Richmond, I., 1968, *Hod Hill, Excavations Carried out between 1951 and 1958*, II, London: Trustees of
   the British Museum

Rivet, A.L.F., & Smith, C., 1979, *The Place Names of Roman Britain*, London: Book Club Associates

Roymans, N., 2005, *Ethnic Identity and Imperial Power: The Batavians in the Early Roman Empire*,
   Amsterdam: Amsterdam University

Salway, P., 1993, *A History of Roman Britain*, Oxford: Oxford University Press

Sauer, E., 2005, 'Alchester, In Search of Vespasian', *Current Archaeology* 196, 168-176

Sellwood, L., 1984, 'Tribal Boundaries Viewed from the Perspective of Numismatic Evidence' in
   B. Cunliffe & D. Miles (eds), *Aspects of the Iron Age in Central Southern Britain*, Oxford: Oxford
   University Committee for Archaeology

———, 1987, 'The non-Durotrigan Celtic coins' in B.W. Cunliffe, *Hengistbury Head, Dorset*,
   Volume 1: The Prehistoric and Roman Settlement 3500 BC-AD 500, Oxford University Committee for
   Archaeology Monograph 13, 138-140

Sharples, N., 1990a, 'Whitcombe Excavations, Discussion', in G.M. & G.N. Aitken, Excavations at
   Whitcombe, 1965-1967, *Proceedings of the Dorset Natural History & Archaeol Society* 112, 90-93

———, 1990b, 'Late Iron Age Society and Continental Trade in Dorset' in A. Duval, J-P. Le Behan
   and Y. Minez (eds) *Les Gaulois d'Amorique. Actes du XIIe Colloque AFEAF Quimper Mai 1988*,
   Revue Archeologique de l'Ouest Supplement 3, 299-304

———, 1991, *Maiden Castle excavations and Field Survey 1985-6*, English Heritage Archaeological
   Report 19, London: English Heritage

Smith, R.J.C., Healy, F., Allen, M.J., Morris, E.L., Barnes, I. & Woodward, P.J., 1997, *Excavations Along
   the Route of the Dorchester By-pass, Dorset, 1986-8*, Wessex Archaeology Report No 11

Sparey-Green, C., 1987, *Excavations at Poundbury Vol. I*, DNHAS Monograph 7

Stewart, D., 2006, *Assessing the Condition of Archaeological Remains: A Multi-Method Geophysical Study
   at Hod Hill, Dorset*, Bournemouth University, Unpublished Dissertation

Sunter, N. & Woodward, P.J., 1987, *Romano-British Industries in Purbeck*, DNHAS Monograph 6

Tabor, R., 2004, 'Cadbury Castle: Prehistoric Pottery Distribution in the Surrounding Landscape',
   Proceedings of the Somerset Archaeological and Natural History Society 147, 29-40

Van Arsdell, R.D., 1989, 'The Badbury Shapwick hoard and the date of the Maiden Castle coins
   from Mortimer Wheeler's 1934-37 excavations', *Oxford Journal of Archaeology*, 8, 347-351

Victoria County History of Wiltshire, Vol. I, 1957, Oxford: Oxford University Press for The Institute of Historical Research

Victoria County History of Wiltshire, Vol. II, 1973, Oxford: Oxford University Press for The Institute of Historical Research

Wainwright, G.J., 1968, The excavation of a Durotrigan farmstead near Tollard Royal in Cranborne Chase, southern England, *Proceedings of the Prehistoric Society* 34, 102-147

———, 1979, *Gussage All Saints: An Iron Age Settlement in Dorset*, London: HMSO

Warne, C., 1872, *Ancient Dorset the Celtic, Roman, Saxon and Danish Antiquities of the County*, Bournemouth: D. Sydenham

Webster, G., 1979, 'Final Report on the Excavations of the Roman Fort at Waddon Hill, Stoke Abbott', 1963-69, *Proceedings of the Dorset Natural History & Archaeological Society* 101, 51-90

Wellington, I., 2001, Iron Age Coinage on the Isle of Wight, *Oxford Journal of Archaeology* 20, 39-57

Wells, C., 1978, 'Excavations by the Late George Rybot, FSA, on Eggardon Hillfort 1963-66', *Proceedings of the Dorset Natural History & Archaeological Society* 100, 53-72

Wheeler, R.E.M., 1943, *Maiden Castle*, Society of Antiquaries Report 12, Oxford: Oxford University Press

Whimster, R., 1981, *Burial Practices in Iron Age Britain*, BAR British Series 90

White, D.A., 1970, 'Excavation of an Iron Age barrow near Handley, Dorset', *Antiquaries Journal* 70, 26-36

Whitley, M., 1943, 'Excavations at Chalbury Camp, Dorset', *Antiquaries Journal* 23, 98-121

Williams, A., 1950, 'Excavations at Allard's Quarry, Marnhull, Dorset', *Proceedings of the Dorset Natural History & Archaeological Society* 72, 20-75

Woodward, P.J., 2006, *The Excavation and Survey at Norden Farm, Corfe Castle 2005, exploring the context of a Durotrigan stater coin hoard and a 1st-century AD patera*, Dorset Natural History & Archaeological Society, Unpublished Report

Woodward, P.J., Davies, S.M. & Graham, A.H., 1993, *Excavations at the Old Methodist Chapel, Greyhound Yard, Dorchester, 1981-1984*, Dorset Natural History & Archaeological Society Monograph 12

Documents

Caesar, Julius, *The Conquest of Gaul*, Translated by S.A. Handford 1951, Harmondsworth: Penguin

Suetonius Tranquillus, Gaius, *The Twelve Caesars*, Translated by Robert Graves 1957, Harmondsworth: Penguin

Tacitus, Cornelius, *The Annals of Imperial Rome*, Translated by Michael Grant 1956, Harmondsworth: Penguin

Tacitus, Cornelius, *The Agricola and the Germania*, Translated by H. Mattingly 1948, Harmondsworth: Penguin

INDEX

Bold entries denote pages particularly about this topic

Italic entries denote an illustration of this site on this page

'P' followed by a number indicates the number of the colour plate featuring this site